Jack Harper

Cavalier in Buckskin

THE OKLAHOMA WESTERN BIOGRAPHIES
RICHARD W. ETULAIN, GENERAL EDITOR

Cavalier in Buckskin

GEORGE ARMSTRONG CUSTER AND THE WESTERN MILITARY FRONTIER

By Robert M. Utley

UNIVERSITY OF OKLAHOMA PRESS : NORMAN AND LONDON

By Robert M. Utley

Custer and the Great Controversy: Origin and Development of a Legend (Los Angeles, 1962, 1980)

The Last Days of the Sioux Nation (New Haven, Conn., 1963)

(Ed.) *Battlefield and Classroom: Four Decades with the American Indian, 1867–1904* (New Haven, Conn., 1964; Lincoln, Nebr., 1987)

Frontiersmen in Blue: The United States Army and the Indian, 1848–1865 (New York, 1967; Lincoln, Nebr., 1981)

Frontier Regulars: The United States Army and the Indian, 1866–1891 (New York, 1973; Bloomington, Ind., 1977; Lincoln, Nebr., 1984)

(with Wilcomb Washburn) *The American Heritage History of the Indian Wars* (New York, 1977)

(Ed.) *Life in Custer's Cavalry: Diaries and Letters of Albert and Jennie Barnitz, 1867–68* (New Haven, Conn., 1977; Lincoln, Nebr., 1987)

The Indian Frontier of the American West, 1846–1890 (Albuquerque, 1984)

If These Walls Could Speak: Historic Forts of Texas (Austin, Texas, 1985)

Four Fighters of Lincoln County (Albuquerque, 1986)

High Noon in Lincoln: Violence on the Western Frontier (Albuquerque, 1987)

Cavalier in Buckskin: George Armstrong Custer and the Western Military Frontier (Norman, 1988)

Library of Congress Cataloging-in-Publication Data

Utley, Robert Marshall, 1929–
    Cavalier in buckskin : George Armstrong Custer and the western military frontier / by Robert M. Utley. — 1st ed.
        p.   cm. — (The Oklahoma western biographies : v. 1)
    Bibliography: p. 213
    Includes index.
    ISBN 0–8061–2150–5 (alk. paper)
    1. Custer, George Armstrong, 1839–1876.   2. Indians of North America—Wars—1866–1895.   3. West   (U.S.)—History—1848–1950.
    4. Generals—United States—Biography.   5. United States. Army—Biography.   I. Title.   II. Series.
E467.1.C99U85   1988
973.8′2′0924—dc19   88–5426

Cavalier in Buckskin: George Armstrong Custer and the Western Military Frontier is Volume 1 in *The Oklahoma Western Biographies*.

The paper in this book meets the guidelines for permanence and durability of the Committee on Production Guidelines for Book Longevity of the Council on Library Resources, Inc. ∞

Copyright © 1988 by the University of Oklahoma Press, Norman, Publishing Division of the University. All rights reserved. Manufactured in the U.S.A. First edition, 1988; second printing, 1989.

For John Alexander Carroll

Contents

Illustrations

Maps

Series Editor's Preface

FROM its dramatic opening to its provocative conclusion, Robert Utley's vividly written biography of George Armstrong Custer admirably fulfills the goals of The Oklahoma Western Biographies. Drawing upon his lifetime study of the frontier military and his more recent stress on Indian affairs, Utley places Custer at the center of his brightly limned canvas while concurrently painting in the soldier's times in broad and bold strokes. A master at narration and description, Utley carefully balances his stirring scenes of action with probing character portrayals of Custer and his supporting cast.

Although often flashing the dark mirrors of Custer's arrogance, petulance, and probable infidelities, Utley also unabashedly praises Custer's apt leadership, many of his military tactics, and his irresistible charisma. Though finding much about Custer to praise in this revisionist account, Utley does not overlook his subject's erratic behavior. Custer often wore orders like a crown of thorns, hoping to rid himself of such irritants as soon as his superiors disappeared over the horizon. Eschewing the simplistic, damning portraits of Custer appearing in several media of American popular culture in the 1960s and 1970s, Utley delineates instead a complex hero, a flawed, brilliant man driven by his monumental ambitions.

Equally noteworthy is Utley's impressive grasp of Custer's times. He movingly depicts the military and political forces that defined Custer's mid-nineteenth-century world, noting guidelines and barriers that Custer often bruised and sometimes eluded in his willful struggle to find himself. Yet Custer, as Utley provocatively demonstrates, was not a man above or outside his times; he shared its conspicuous consumption, its brazen selfishness, and its willingness to blink at broken promises and disobeyed orders in the rush toward achievement and notoriety.

Utley's biography of Custer is a superb blend of man and milieu.

Not only a stirring story of a remarkable westerner but also a splendidly told narrative of the frontier, this volume provides an auspicious beginning for The Oklahoma Western Biographies.

RICHARD W. ETULAIN

University of New Mexico

Preface

DO we really *need* another biography of George Armstrong Custer? With this question, many reviewers will introduce their evaluations of my book, for *need* is a governing criterion in academia. More than a quarter of a century ago, I opened a review of another biography of Custer, by Jay Monaghan, with that question (and answered it in the affirmative).

Since the advent of Monaghan's *Custer* in 1959, a steady stream of publications has added vastly to an already mountainous bibliography of Custer literature. No biography of the scope of Monaghan's, however, has appeared.

Whether or not a biographical hiatus of nearly three decades establishes need, I did not write this book to fill a gap in the historiography of General Custer. My motives were threefold:

First, although the world is unlikely to reach a consensus on what manner of man Custer was, I sought something to coerce me into deciding what I thought. I have lived with him intimately since the age of eleven, when Errol Flynn introduced me through the medium of *They Died with Their Boots On*. I spent six collegiate summers, 1947–52, standing on Custer Hill talking to park visitors come to view the scene of the famous Last Stand. My interest in Indians and soldiers, expressed in several books, has kept me in more or less close touch ever since. Even so, over a span of years now approaching fifty, I never succeeded in penetrating the enigma of George Armstrong Custer, in either his mortal or his immortal incarnation. This book was intended to supply a discipline that would force conclusions.

Second, the University of Oklahoma Press wanted to launch a new series featuring brief biographies of people significant in the history of the American West. Any such series that omitted Custer could hardly pretend to be comprehensive.

Third, the publisher also wanted the series to reach into larger themes personified by the person treated. Custer offered an ideal mechanism for presenting a range of topics associated with the military-Indian frontier and thus, set in broader context, for softening the judgment of critics worried about need. Readers engrossed in the Custer saga instead of the themes exemplified should endure the digressions in the certainty that the story will soon get back to the person.

These needs—mine and the press's (and the series editor's)—intersected, and this book is the result. I now have a better conception of George Armstrong Custer, but I confess to failing to penetrate the enigma. No one ever has, and I am convinced that no one ever will.

Seven people read the entire manuscript in draft and contributed enormously helpful comment.

Deserving special recognition and thanks is Professor Paul A. Hutton, of the University of New Mexico. His comment, both written and oral (we are neighbors), led to important changes. Because of his thoughtful arguments, I added new material and altered or refined some of my interpretations. Also, he let me borrow books and other material from his ample library of Custeriana.

The series editor, Professor Richard Etulain, of the University of New Mexico, does not know much about Custer but knows what the book ought to contain. I have profited from his advice.

Four others know a great deal about Custer. Their reviews have added dimensions that would not have occurred to me and that saved me from errors that would have been pounced upon by the legion of Custer specialists. These experts merit my profound gratitude: Professor Brian Dippie, of the University of Victoria (British Columbia); Professor Gregory J. W. Urwin, of the University of Central Arkansas; Brian C. Pohanka, of Time-Life Books; and John M. Carroll, of Bryan, Texas. Carroll also let me use his microfilm copy of the Marguerite Merington Papers in the New York Public Library, a cornerstone of this book, and helped in many other ways that upheld his reputation for knowledge and generosity.

The seventh reader, and as usual my hardest critic, was Melody Webb, of the National Park Service, who also happens to be my wife. Her reviews forced painful revisions and led to major improvements.

Thanks are also due others who helped. Chief Historian Edwin C. Bearss, National Park Service, reviewed my Civil War chapter. James S. Hutchins, Smithsonian Institution, kept up a steady flow of invaluable material resulting from his own similar researches. Robert Aldrich, of Bryan, Texas, assembled some highly revealing evidence bearing on the Little Bighorn, which he made available and which has been incorporated into my text. Douglas Youngkin, of Salt Lake

City, lent me his microfilm copies of the Elizabeth B. Custer Collection at Custer Battlefield National Monument, which saved me the expense of buying my own. At Custer Battlefield, Park Historian Neil C. Mangum carried on the tradition of personal and official helpfulness that extends forty years back to "Historical Aide" Robert M. Utley.

ROBERT M. UTLEY

Santa Fe, New Mexico

Cavalier in Buckskin

CHAPTER I

Immortality

MASSACRED.

GEN. CUSTER AND 261 MEN THE VICTIMS.

NO OFFICER OR MAN OF 5 COMPANIES LEFT TO TELL THE TALE.

3 DAYS OF DESPERATE FIGHTING BY MAJ. RENO AND THE REMAINDER OF THE SEVENTH.

SQUAWS MUTILATE AND ROB THE DEAD.

VICTIMS CAPTURED ALIVE TORTURED IN MOST FIENDISH MANNER.

WHAT WILL CONGRESS DO ABOUT IT?

SHALL THIS BE THE BEGINNING OF THE END?

THE *Tribune Extra* hit the dusty streets of Bismarck, Dakota Territory, on the morning of July 6, 1876, its strident headlines fixing the tone for newspapers all over the United States.

The nation's senior generals read the headlines in the Philadelphia papers. William Tecumseh Sherman and Philip H. Sheridan, attending the festivities in Independence Square marking the centennial of American independence, had remained to tour the great exposition celebrating one hundred years of national progress.

Reporters sought out the generals to ask about the headlines. Sheridan pointed out that the report bore all the marks of a fanciful tale by an imaginative frontier scout. Sherman refused to take the

3

dispatch seriously either. In the absence of any confirmation from
official sources, he said, the press item had to be discounted as mere
rumor. As he spoke, an aide handed him a telegram: "Dispatches
from General Terry . . . confirm the newspaper reports of a fight on
the 25th of June, on the Little Horn, and of General Custer's death."

Custer dead? To the generals as well as all who read the papers that
morning, the story seemed preposterous. For more than a decade
George Armstrong Custer had basked in public adulation as a national hero. In the Civil War he had won headlines as the "Boy General." With flowing blonde locks and gaudy uniform, he had led a
full division of Sheridan's cavalry at age twenty-four and had fought
his way from one resounding triumph to another. Since Appomattox, with fringed buckskins replacing blue and gold, and as lieutenant colonel of the Seventh U.S. Cavalry, he had kept his name bright
with Indian victories and hunting exploits on the western plains. By
1876 the public saw him as the very embodiment of the Indian-fighting army, civilization's advance guard opening the way for hardy pioneers who would subdue the western wilderness and, as divinely en-
joined, make it blossom with the fruits of honest toil. Even to hard-
eyed realists like Sherman and Sheridan, the vaunted Custer could
hardly fall victim to a calamity such as the newspapers reported.

But the unthinkable was true after all. For forty-eight hours the
telegraph key in the Northern Pacific depot at Bismarck never stopped
clicking as the fateful details sped eastward to pack newspaper columns for days on end. Custer and his regiment, about six hundred
strong, had come upon an Indian village that numbered about eight
thousand people, with perhaps two thousand fighting men. He had
divided his command and attacked. Major Marcus A. Reno and three
companies had been repulsed and had joined with Captain Frederick
W. Benteen and three more companies, together with the supply
train and still another company, in hilltop positions. For two days
they had held out against besieging warriors. When help finally arrived, driving the Indians off, scouts had found the bodies of Custer
and the men of five companies, 210 officers and enlisted soldiers, scattered along a ridge four miles down the Little Bighorn River from
Reno's hill. No man of that force survived.

Such were the bare details, but they were promptly buried under
an avalanche of emotional prose as editors hurried to sensationalize
one of the biggest news stories of the time. In the florid prose of the

day, correspondents penned vivid accounts drawn from fertile imagination. Typical was one in the *New York Herald*:

> In that mad charge up the narrow ravine, with the rocks above raining down lead upon the fated three hundred, with fire spouting from every bush ahead, with the wild, swarming horsemen circling along the heights like shrieking vultures waiting for the moment to sweep down and finish the bloody tale, every form, from private to general, rises to heroic size, and the scene fixes itself indelibly upon the mind. "The Seventh fought like tigers," says the dispatch; yea, they died as grandly as Homer's demigods. In the supreme moment of carnage, as death's relentless sweep gathered in the entire command, all distinctions of name and rank were blended, but the family that "died at the head of their column" [Custer, two brothers, a nephew, and a brother-in-law] will lead the throng when history recalls their deed. . . . Success was beyond their grasp, so they died—to a man.

The press also plunged into a bitter controversy over the character and actions of the star player of the drama. On the very eve of his last campaign, Custer had gained notoriety by charging the presidential administration of Ulysses S. Grant with fraud and corruption on the frontier. With the 1876 presidential-election contest heating up, editorial writers chose sides according to their paper's political affiliation. Democratic journals portrayed the dead hero as the tragic victim of Grant's Indian policy, while Republican papers assailed him as a foolhardy glory hunter.

"Who Slew Custer?" asked the *New York Herald*. "The celebrated peace policy of General Grant," it answered, "which feeds, clothes and takes care of their noncombatant force while the men are killing our troops—that is what killed Custer. . . . That nest of thieves, the Indian Bureau, with its thieving agents and favorites as Indian traders, and its mock humanity and pretence of piety—that is what killed Custer."

Not so, editorialized the *Chicago Tribune*; Custer caused his own death. He "preferred to make a reckless dash and take the consequences, in the hope of making a personal victory and adding to the glory of another charge, rather than wait for a sufficiently powerful force to make the fight successful and share the glory with others."

The disagreements among editorial writers mirrored disagreements within the military fraternity. Among his fellow officers, the young luminary had always inspired mixed opinions. Many disliked him personally, envied his success and eminence, and regarded him as a creature of press-agentry, altogether lacking in military merit. Others idolized him, or simply admired his record as a soldier.

The nation's most venerated soldier led in the attack. "I regard Custer's Massacre as a sacrifice of troops," declared President Grant, "brought on by Custer himself, that was wholly unnecessary— wholly unnecessary."

Others picked up the theme. Unnamed officers in Washington as well as at General Sheridan's headquarters in Chicago accused Custer of disobeying orders and rushing blindly into an ambush, all because of "that foolish pride which so often results in the defeat of men." Samuel D. Sturgis, Custer's immediate superior as colonel of the Seventh Cavalry, told reporters that his subordinate "was a brave man, but also a very selfish man. He was insanely ambitious of glory;" he was "tyrannical and had no regard for the soldiers under him;" and on the Little Bighorn, he "made his attack recklessly, earlier by thirty-six hours than he should have done, and with men tired out from forced marches." Even Sherman and Sheridan conceded that Custer was "rashly imprudent to attack such a large number of Indians."

Few officers on active duty charged to Custer's defense, although many, notably the aggressive Colonel Nelson A. Miles, backed him wholeheartedly, and even Sherman and Sheridan later softened their indictment. Strangely, Custer's most vigorous support came from former Confederate foes. One was General Joseph E. Johnston. Another, General John McCausland, said that he would have done just what Custer did. "The only way to fight with cavalry is with a dash—to charge. I don't blame him." A third, General Thomas L. Rosser, a West Point comrade, absolved his old friend and Civil War opponent of recklessness and laid the blame entirely on Major Reno, who "took to the hills, and abandoned Custer and his gallant comrades to their fate."

Within weeks after the news of the Little Bighorn electrified the nation, the groundwork had been laid for one of the most universal and enduring legends of all time. The mystery of what happened on the Custer battlefield, combined with the dazzling and controversial persona of George Armstrong Custer, kindled a fascination in the public mind destined to grow out of all proportion to the true significance of the man and the event.

On the popular front the newspapers created an enormous body

of imaginative falsehood that subsequent writers drew on uncritically. Custer's first biographer bears major responsibility. Frederick
Whittaker, a sometime dime novelist and Civil War veteran who
idolized Custer, rushed his thick, turgid tome into print within six
months after the Little Bighorn. Crammed with misinformation
from the press, it served as a principal source for a generation of
scribblers of adventure books, tabloids, and penny dreadfuls, many
of whom flagrantly plagiarized it.

This sample, typical of much that pretended to history, is from
J. W. Buel's *Heroes of the Plains* (1881):

> Men had sunk down beside their gallant leader until there was but
> a handful left, only a dozen, bleeding from many wounds, and hot
> carbines in their stiffening hands. The day is almost done, when, look!
> heaven now defend him, the charm of his life is broken, for Custer
> has fallen; a bullet cleaves a pathway through his side, and as he falters
> another strikes his noble breast. Like a strong oak stricken by the
> lightning's bolt, shivering the mighty trunk and bending the writhing
> branches down close to the earth, so fell Custer; but like the reacting
> branches, he rises partly up again and striking out like a fatally
> wounded giant lays three more Indians dead and breaks his mighty
> sword on the musket of the fourth; then, with useless blade and
> empty pistol falls back the victim of a dozen wounds. He is the last
> to succumb to death, and dies, too, with the glory of accomplished
> duty in his conscience and the benediction of a grateful country on
> his head.

By the close of the nineteenth century so much demonstrable un-
truth of this sort had been crammed into the collective American
memory as to be forever beyond eradication. (No one knows when
he died, or how he died, or even where he died. He bore two
wounds, not a dozen. Neither he nor anyone else carried a sword.)

On the professional front the debates in military circles over the
commander and his decisions lent the subject respectability while
adding zest and broad appeal to its mythological life. The army officially disposed of the dispute in 1879, when a military court of inquiry took testimony and gave Major Reno an insipid exoneration
of any fault in the disaster. But that only stoked the controversies
over who deserved the blame. Did Custer dash heedlessly to his
doom in quest of glory? Did he disobey the orders of his superior?
Did he rashly divide a command that should have been kept intact? Did he launch his assault blindly, without proper reconnaissance? Among not only professional soldiers but an army of stu-

dents as well, these arguments have raged endlessly generation after generation.

Ever present in the background of the controversies was the shadow of Elizabeth Custer. The tragic figure in black, widowed at thirty-four, prompted silence in many who might have spoken in criticism. On her own, furthermore, she shaped the public's memory—and thus posterity's conception—of her dead husband. She worked closely with Frederick Whittaker to ensure that the image projected by his *Life of Custer* coincided with her own. She wrote three books herself—*Boots and Saddles* (1885), *Following the Guidon* (1890), and *Tenting on the Plains* (1893). All were intimate portrayals of a saintly husband and an idyllic marriage, and they made their legions of readers see him as she wanted him seen.

Libbie Custer devoted the rest of her life to protecting and defending the memory of her "Autie." And if there was a "conspiracy of silence" to defer attacks on him until she died, it was a futile conspiracy, for she outlived all the conspirators. She died on April 6, 1933, two days short of her ninety-first birthday, and almost fifty-seven years after the July day when the steamboat Far West nosed into the Fort Lincoln landing with Major Reno's wounded from the battlefield of the Little Bighorn.

Not only prose, but poetry, art, and drama glorified the Boy General. Poets began framing verse on the very day of the first dispatch. On July 7, 1876, no less an interpreter of the American scene than Walt Whitman penned a paean to "Thou of the sunny, flowing hair," and both John Greenleaf Whittier and Henry Wadsworth Longfellow ultimately made their contribution. In verse after verse, Longfellow's "The Revenge of Rain-in-the-Face" recounted the saga of the Little Bighorn and immortalized one of its most persistent myths:

> But the foemen fled in the night
> And Rain-in-the-Face, in his flight,
>   Uplifted high in the air
> As a ghastly trophy, bore
>   The brave heart, that beat no more
> of the White Chief with the yellow hair.

Almost a century after the Little Bighorn, one authority had identified no less than 150 poetic renditions of Custer's death on the bleak Montana ridge. Most were by unknown hacks, but even more than the Whitmans, Whittiers, and Longfellows, they captured the essence of the Custer legend. First the newspapers, then Whittaker,

had told how, as the battle neared its end, a Crow Indian scout had
offered to lead Custer to safety:

> A second's silence. Custer dropped his head,
> His lips slow moving as when prayers are said—
> Two words he breathed—"God and Elizabeth,"
> Then shook his long locks in the face of death,
> And with a final gesture turned away
> To join the fated few who stood at bay.
> Ah! deeds like that the Christ in man reveal
> Let Fame descend her throne at Custer's shrine to kneel.

Painters and illustrators lost no more time than the poets in embracing the subject, as the newspapers and magazines of 1876 amply
attest, and decade after decade the mountain of artwork portraying
Custer and the Little Bighorn has risen ever higher. Nearly two
thousand depictions have been identified, ranging from giant, me-
ticulously detailed canvases through magazine illustrations to the
"pop art" of modern advertising.

By all odds, the most famous is the Adams-Becker painting. No
faces in American history have inspired greater boozy contemplation
than those of the men who peer out from this work. Cassilly Adams
painted the original in 1886—a huge, stilted, undramatic composi-
tion intended as a traveling exhibition. But it remained for Otto
Becker, recreating the canvas for lithograph by the Anheuser-Busch
Brewing Company, to beget the version that adorned the saloon
walls of America for a generation. Ultimately, more than a million
copies rolled off the presses, prompting one authority to speculate
that it had been viewed by more low brows and fewer art critics than
any other picture in American history.

The dramatic arts also quickly turned to Custer and the Last
Stand. The typical theater stage was scarcely large enough to encom-
pass so magnificent a subject, but some thespian troupes tried. It
remained to the great tent-sheltered Wild West shows of Adam Forepaugh and Buffalo Bill Cody, however, to do the drama justice.
Forepaugh regularly reenacted "Custer's Last Rally" as part of his
production, while Cody staged it as the grand climax of his show.

These and other Wild West circuses, of course, merely prefigured
the greater splendor of the motion pictures. The very first of the
silent film makers found Custer irresistible. Between 1909 and 1913
no less than five features, including one directed by D. W. Griffith,
focused on Custer and the Little Bighorn. Others appeared in the

1920s, especially as the fiftieth anniversary, in 1926, fired fresh public interest.

The twentieth century loosed new floods of prose. An unending procession of novels, including several respectable juveniles, featured stock characters riding with the Boy General. A new crop of historians took up the old controversies as the professional soldiers of the Indian-fighting years died off. Custer did not escape the school of fashionably cynical debunkers that formed coincident with the Great Depression. In *Glory Hunter*, published in 1934, Frederic F. Van de Water pictured a Custer in every way the opposite of Whittaker's gallant cavalier: tyrannical, brutal, detestable, vain, ambitious, selfish, arrogant, reckless, and incompetent.

The anti-hero image put down deep roots in American prose, but did not entirely crowd out the hero image. For many, Custer continued to be the shining knight of old. Frederick Whittaker would have applauded Warner Brothers' 1941 spectacle *They Died with Their Boots On*, in which Errol Flynn swashbuckled his way from Bull Run to the Little Bighorn, along the way fighting Rebels, Indians, dim-witted superiors, and corrupt politicians. Olivia de Havilland's Libbie furnished the love angle. The picture perpetuated almost every cliché in the Custer repertory, but a nation just entering World War II found it a stirring celebration of America's military heritage.

In the twentieth century, Custer not only endured as legend but also came to life as symbol. Because it was instantly recognizable by almost everyone, the single word, "Custer," became synonymous with whichever character traits one wished to assign him—from the suicidal rashness of Van de Water to the selfless courage of Whittaker. Bridging all personality extremes, Custer was a synonym for the lost cause, the forlorn hope, the total disaster looming momentarily in whatever context one applied it. This symbolism took the form of admonitory rhetoric, editorial commentary, political cartoons, and the one-liners of comedians. Nearly every political crisis brought forth a rash of cartoons depicting a beleaguered public figure, bristling with arrows and surrounded by fallen troops, standing alone atop the last-stand hill.

In the decades following World War II, a darker and deeper symbolism also surfaced—Custer as emblem of America's misdeeds against the Indians. "Custer Died for Your Sins," Vine Deloria declared in the title of his 1968 best seller, which signaled the beginning of the American Indian protest movement. "Custer Died for Your

Sins," proclaimed the bumper stickers, picking up the theme. Almost overnight, George Armstrong Custer became the symbol for all the iniquities perpetrated by whites on Indians—and some that were not.

Custer could symbolize the nation's guilt complex because his name carried two essential ingredients of a usable symbol: it was almost universally recognized, and it evoked the appropriate historical connotations. Moreover, the Van de Water characterization had become common enough that, with a bit of embroidery, Custer could play the truly heavy villain. The films of the 1960s, which began to look at Indians as human beings rather than mere impersonal foils for white pioneers, also increasingly portrayed Custer as a bloodthirsty Indian killer, leading his troopers on murderous rampages that wiped out whole villages and cut down men, women, and children indiscriminately. For such a butcher, the posters announcing that "Custer had it coming" simply stated the obvious.

Butcher Custer reached an apogee in Arthur Penn's 1970 film version of Thomas Berger's novel, *Little Big Man*. Here Custer did double duty—as a metaphor for American barbarism in the Indian wars and for identical American barbarism in Vietnam. The lunatic Custer, raging about the Little Bighorn battlefield with insane laughter and incoherent shouts as the Indians closed in, personalized the madness of both conflicts. *Little Big Man* cried out against Vietnam while crying out for atonement to the American Indians.

In 1976, Custer again helped to advance the cause of Indian reform, when celebrants gathered at the Custer battlefield to mark the centennial of the Little Bighorn. Just as the army band struck up "Garry Owen," Custer's battle song, Indian drums sounded and up the road marched Russell Means, leader of the American Indian Movement (AIM), with two hundred followers. As a signal of distress, they dragged on the pavement an American flag, upside down. To dramatize the plight of the Indians, Means threatened to disrupt the ceremony and even torch the museum containing Custer memorabilia. A parley produced a truce, but the speeches proceeded in front of a nervous audience ringed by Indian activists in red berets with folded arms and menacing visages. Custer, as symbol of all that was reprehensible in America's treatment of the Indians, had been enlisted in the crusade for Indian rights. As Means knew, an Indian protest at Custer battlefield on the centennial of the battle could not fail to attract national attention, and he was right.

Popular fascination with General Custer and the Battle of the

Little Bighorn showed no sign of weakening. In the 1980s it took on new life as breathless press dispatches reported two summers of archaeological investigations on the Custer battlefield. Evan Connell's *Son of the Morning Star*, a vast, rambling potpourri of Custeriana, hit the best-seller list and promptly headed for television. Books, magazine articles, motion pictures, and television continued to dramatize the man's life and probe the mysteries of his death. The Little Big Horn Associates, a national organization dedicated to Custer and the Last Stand, counted more than eight hundred members and drew hundreds to annual conventions.

Clearly, the Custer of legend and symbol is a different person from the Custer of reality. For each generation of Americans since 1876, the mythic Custer tapped deep and revealing intellectual and emotional currents. He was what they wanted him to be, and what they made him told more about the creators than the created. In turn, this towering Custer of folklore endowed the Custer of history with a significance far beyond what he attained in his lifetime. It makes an examination of who he was and what he did more worthwhile than if he were simply another Civil War general turned Indian fighter. What he did is readily discoverable. Who he was is vastly more elusive.

George Armstrong Custer's admiring public saw him as the personification of the Indian-fighting army. As a leader of blue-clad troopers on the frontier, his name shone more brightly and constantly than all others, some of possibly greater achievement and skill. In many ways he merited the public's vision of him. Because both posterity and his contemporaries ranked him as the premier Indian fighter of all time, he affords an ideal medium for viewing and understanding the institution of which he was so conspicuous a part—the frontier army of the American West.

CHAPTER 2

Boy General

THE George Armstrong Custer who perished at the Little Bighorn was a complex man, enigmatic and full of contradictions. For the final decade of his life, the frontier years of 1866–76, he projected traits that made one set of contemporaries idolize him and another detest him. Hardly anyone regarded him with indifference. The mythic Custer has similarly sundered posterity. Paradoxically, the adolescent, the cadet, and finally the Boy General hid within no such puzzle. For his first twenty-five years he projected a readily understood makeup on the raw materials of history and left an imprint on his times not difficult to reconstruct.

He traced origins to an Ohio farm and a Michigan hamlet. Born on December 5, 1839, in New Rumley, Ohio, George Armstrong Custer was the offspring of a union between a widower and a widow, both of whom brought children into the marriage. Family and friends called him Armstrong, or "Autie," his own childish rendition of Armstrong. Other children followed: Nevin, Thomas, Boston, and Margaret. Emanuel Custer saved enough money as a village blacksmith to buy a farm near New Rumley. Maria Custer toiled as the frail, selfless, beloved mother.

For young Armstrong, however, his half sister had as much or more influence. Fourteen years his senior, Lydia Ann Kirkpatrick helped rear her mother's new family and grew lovingly close to the boy. She served both as surrogate mother and as friend and confidante. She dispensed authority if not discipline—no one disciplined Armstrong. And she shared with sympathetic and wise counsel his adventures, his misadventures, and his private thoughts.

After Ann married David Reed, who operated a drayage firm in Monroe, Michigan, Armstrong occasionally visited her in the little town on the western shore of Lake Erie. At age fourteen he went to live in the Reed household. In Monroe he attended Stebbins

Academy. During the summer he returned to the family farm in Ohio to help with the crops.

A high-spirited, rough-and-tumble family shaped young Autie's nature. A man of firm convictions firmly expressed, Emanuel Custer espoused a militant brand of Jacksonian Democratic politics and a militant brand of frontier Methodism. Though Nevin was sickly, Autie and his other brothers grew up brimming with boyish exuberance. Full of energy, good humor, and laughter, they engaged in strenuous athletics and even more strenuous horseplay. They inflicted the most ingenious and harrowing pranks on one another and on their father, who gave as good as he took. Hard play and the hard work of the farm endowed the youth with a powerful physique and extraordinary endurance. He never seemed to tire or to need much sleep.

Autie's inclinations nourished his physique more than his intellect. At Stebbins Academy he had a hard time concentrating on subjects that did not interest him, and his academic record was marginal at best. In 1855, however, he returned home to continue his education at McNeely Normal School, in Hopedale, Ohio, near Cadiz, and in the spring of 1856 he qualified to teach grammar school.

A "big-hearted, whole-souled fellow," recalled one of his friends of this period, when Armstrong presided over one-room country schools. With comrades of like vigor he loved to ride horseback, lead his hounds in hunts for coons and foxes, and get into "most of the tricks carried out in the slow old town."

Armstrong did not allow country romps to interfere with his amorous interests. Both in Michigan and in Ohio he pursued the opposite sex with an avidity more open than approved by convention. Boldness seemed to bring its reward, however, and the belles of Monroe and Cadiz alike responded with fervor to the handsome, laughing boy with the tawny curls and muscular frame. Before his twentieth birthday either Mollie, Lizzie, Mary, and one not named had been to bed with him, or he was adept at committing inventive fantasies to paper. Whichever, he penned some explicit language at variance with contemporary notions of propriety.

At the same time that he received his teaching certificate, Armstrong wrote to his congressman asking about appointment to the United States Military Academy at West Point, New York. His motivation rested on more pragmatic grounds than a burning ambition to be a soldier. West Point would earn him twenty-eight dollars a month for five years, he wrote sister Ann, and an education as well. John McNutt, he added, a previous appointee to the academy from Cadiz, "is now worth $200,000 which he made in the army." How Armstrong thought that such a sum could be gained honestly he did not explain, but the letter shows his lifelong preoccupation with money to have been well rooted by early age.

Nor did he explain how he, son of an outspoken Democrat, thought that he could win appointment from a Republican congressman. But already, at seventeen, a boundless optimism drove Armstrong to ignore seemingly insuperable obstacles, and as often as not persistence or luck justified the optimism. Representative John A. Bingham rewarded the optimism with the coveted appointment, to take effect in June 1857. John Wirt, New Rumley's leading merchant and a close friend of the Custers even though an abolitionist Republican, probably interceded in his behalf.

Cadet Custer achieved considerable distinction at West Point, though hardly of the approved sort. The host of trivial regulations did not rank high in his scheme of priorities, and he accumulated demerits at an alarming rate. One hundred "skins" in six months earned dismissal; repeatedly, Custer came within less than 10 of the limit. His four-year total stood at 726.

Nor did Armstrong flourish in academics. He still had trouble applying himself to subjects that did not interest him. The books he checked out of the library featured dashing cavaliers, flashing swords, and beautiful women.

Significantly, the frolicsome cadet did well in strenuous outdoor instruction. He excelled at horsemanship, riding bareback effortlessly, eclipsing his classmates in jumps and hurdles, and expertly slashing dummies with a saber. In temperament as well as riding skills, he clearly belonged in the cavalry.

Significantly, also, he did not flunk out. Whenever low marks threatened his stay, he dug into his books and staved off disaster. Whenever his skins neared the maximum, he went for months at a time without a single infraction.

On at least one occasion Custer resorted to extreme measures to avoid dismissal. In January 1861, the academic board found him and thirty-two other cadets deficient. This meant reexamination and, failing that, dismissal. Custer set forth to obtain a copy of the questions that would be asked. He broke into the instructor's room, found the book in which they were listed, and proceeded to copy them. Foot-

steps sounded in the hall. In panic he tore the page from the book
and fled. The instructor, of course, discovered the evidence of tam-
pering and altered the questions.

Recounting this adventure in a letter to a cousin, Cadet Tully
McCrea observed of his friend Custer:

> He is one of the best-hearted and cleverest men that I ever knew. The
> great difficulty is that he is too clever for his own good. He is always
> connected with all the mischief that is going on, and never studies any
> more than he can possibly help. He has narrowly escaped several times
> before, but unluckily did not take the warning, and now it is too late,
> and he will always have cause to repent his folly.

McCrea assessed his friend with sharp insight but was wrong on
two counts. It was not too late, and he never repented. Paradoxically,
of the thirty-three deficient cadets, only Custer passed the reexamination and remained at West Point.

The episode revealed not only the lengths to which Custer would
go to win but also the incredible good luck that had blessed him
from childhood. He would be similarly lucky for the rest of his life.
Time and again fortune smiled, either to extricate him from a scrape
or to see him through a difficult enterprise in which the odds were
all against him. "Custer's Luck" became his hallmark, a phenomenon
for incredulous wonder by friends and observers, an article of faith
in his self-appraisal. He came genuinely to believe himself fated to
win regardless of the risks.

Only when dismissal loomed did Custer allow education to interfere with fun. After his first year no cadet surpassed Custer in hazing
underclassmen, or "animals." He and his friends delighted in surprising a plebe sentinel, bowling him backward into a wheelbarrow,
and speeding to dump him into Hangman's Hollow. One plebe's first
"interview" with Custer shattered his sleep and, as he described it in
third person, brought him awake "just in time to look full into the
laughing face of Custer who had firm hold of the ends of [the
plebe's] blankets, and sent him whirling down the company ground,
and left him to scramble back to his quarters as best he could."

"Fanny," his classmates called him, and those who did not love
him at least found constant amusement in his antics. He organized
and led many an all-night excursion to Benny Havens's, the already
legendary off-post drinking establishment. Here the cadets tipped
their glasses, sang, and listened to Benny's reminiscences before stealing back to their barracks in time for reveille. Although he did not

use tobacco—"a filthy, if not unhealthy, practice"—he enjoyed a social glass as much as any cadet, and even more, almost obsessively, he loved to wager on the turn of a card.

When the sectional crisis burst on the nation in 1861, Armstrong Custer never wavered. Despite his Democratic politics, and even as his southern friends departed, he pronounced resolutely for the Union. Upon entering West Point, he had taken an oath of allegiance, and he regarded it as binding.

At graduation ceremonies on June 24, 1861, George Armstrong Custer received his diploma. He ascended the podium thirty-fourth in a line of thirty-four. The precious diploma, so narrowly gained, won him another piece of parchment as well, a commission as second lieutenant in the Second Regiment of United States Cavalry.

His military career almost ended even before he shed the cadet gray. A fist fight erupted between a "yearling"—a second-year cadet— and a plebe unsubmissive to hazing (the yearling was William Ludlow, whose career would intersect Custer's on the frontier). As officer of the guard, Custer should have ended the altercation. Instead, in a typically impulsive gesture, he commanded the gathering crowd to stand back and let there be a fair fight. At this critical moment the officer of the day, Lieutenant William B. Hazen, chanced onto the scene and had Custer placed in arrest. Court-martialed, he emerged with a reprimand instead of the dismissal that might have been his fate in normal times. Once again "Custer's Luck" had saved him.

With the rest of the regular Second Cavalry, Second Lieutenant Custer spent most of July 21, 1861, impatiently waiting for orders that never came. In the rolling Virginia countryside around Manassas, he watched the Rebels flank and rout the Union infantry and joined in the rain-drenched night retreat back to the Potomac.

The cavalry's idleness at First Bull Run reflected the state of military thought at the outset of the war. The Confederates learned quickly, but not for two years did Union generals see any benefit in employing cavalry as a separate arm. As a result the horsemen were parceled out to infantry generals, who could think of no better use for them than as couriers, pickets, scouts, and glittering personal escorts. "Whoever saw a dead cavalryman?" the foot soldiers shouted derisively and truthfully. In the cavalry Lieutenant Custer could not look forward to much fighting. His regiment, renumbered the Fifth Cavalry, wound up in the defenses of Washington.

Sick leave in Monroe saw the young officer through part of the winter of 1861–62. There he made the most of his shoulder straps and brass buttons to court a bevy of female admirers, most particularly Fanny Fifield. He also caroused with old friends and other officers on leave.

And he reached a momentous personal decision. A protracted revel left him almost powerless to make his way home and led to a moving dialogue with his sister Ann. From that emotional exchange Armstrong Custer emerged with a solemn resolve never again to imbibe an alcoholic beverage. And he never did.

Luck obliged the fledgling lieutenant by liberating him from the cavalry during the two years of its oblivion, for officers trained at West Point were in great demand for staff duty. For a time during the summer of 1861 he had served as aide to Brigadier General Philip Kearny, an aloof, one-armed, coldly competent martinet who taught him much about military discipline. In the spring of 1862, as Major General George B. McClellan launched the Peninsula Campaign toward Richmond's back door, Custer joined the staff of Brigadier General William F. ("Baldy") Smith, commander of an infantry division. In turn, that assignment brought the young officer to the attention of McClellan himself, who invited him to join his staff as an aide-de-camp with the rank of captain.

The newly minted captain served his chief faithfully and worshipfully. With most of the Army of the Potomac, he idolized McClellan, according him an affection and loyalty that survived all of the setbacks "Little Mac" suffered, and that almost derailed his own career. The Peninsula Campaign, with its missed opportunities so clearly attributable to McClellan's caution, failed to quench Armstrong's enthusiasm for his leader's genius, and the costly but indecisive victory at Antietam, Maryland, in September 1862, only strengthened his esteem.

Two characteristics marked Custer's career as a staff officer. First, he knew what the general needed to know, knew where to get it, and knew how to report it precisely and concisely. In battle he kept his head, observed calmly and accurately, and remembered what he had seen. Second, Custer ranged the area of operations widely and indefatigably, not always with the approval or even the knowledge of his chief. Combat usually found him at the point of heaviest fighting, and often in the midst of it himself. Time and again he discarded his staff role to plunge into battle, charging with or even leading troops, rallying faltering lines, or stiffening defenses against an enemy assault.

No estimate of Custer as a staff officer surpasses that penned by General McClellan himself: "In these days Custer was simply a reckless, gallant boy, undeterred by fatigue, unconscious of fear; but his head was always clear in danger and he always brought me clear and intelligible reports of what he saw when under the heaviest fire. I became much attached to him."

But McClellan did not survive. When the "slows" that had first surfaced on the Peninsula reappeared after Antietam, the imperious commander was replaced by Major General Ambrose E. Burnside. Custer and other staff hotheads blustered about headquarters with wild threats to mutiny and march on Washington. But early in November 1862, when General McClellan went home to New Jersey, Captain Custer, still an officer of his staff, went quietly home to Michigan.

Custer spent nearly all of the winter of 1862–63 in Monroe, awaiting orders. While the Army of the Potomac wallowed in the mud of the Rappahannock Valley and surged in wave after bloody wave against Robert E. Lee's impregnable defenses at Fredericksburg, Captain Custer enjoyed the bounty of David Reed's table, the joys of speeding over the snow-packed landscape in a sleigh full of laughing damsels, and the unaccustomed respect of a town proud to claim a member of General McClellan's staff.

But the highlight of the winter occurred late in November when, during a party at Boyd's Seminary, he was formally presented to Elizabeth Bacon. Daughter of Judge Daniel S. Bacon, one of Monroe's leading citizens, Libbie was two years younger than Armstrong. Monroe's young men competed for her attentions, for her slim figure, beautiful face, luxuriant chestnut hair, and stylish wardrobe made her an ornament in any gathering. In addition, she was intelligent, educated, gay, and full of zest for life. Smitten, Armstrong paid her tenacious court—though without neglecting other women, notably Fanny Fifield.

Libbie responded only tepidly. For one thing, she had chanced to witness his public display on "that awful day" a year earlier when he had staggered up the street in front of her home. For another thing, Libbie disapproved of Armstrong's wide-ranging feminine attentions. And to settle the matter, Judge Bacon did not condone his only daughter's intimacy with a product of a lower social order, especially one who was also a soldier.

Still, Captain Custer made a handsome, sparkling escort. She went out with him often. And gradually she began to experience emotions that she debated in her diary whether to label love. Shortly after returning to duty, Armstrong betrayed his own ambivalence in a letter to Ann: "There are not more than a dozen girls in Monroe that I like better than Libbie, and that is the truth."

After helping General McClellan write his final report, Custer returned to the Army of the Potomac late in April 1863. His patron's staff having been disbanded, Captain Custer, U.S. Volunteers, reverted to First Lieutenant Custer, Fifth Regular Cavalry.

He came back to the cavalry at an auspicious moment. Burnside's disaster at Fredericksburg had sent him the way of McClellan, and Major General Joseph Hooker had taken over the Army of the Potomac. Like Burnside, Hooker's strengths did not lie on the battlefield, as Chancellorsville dramatized early in May. But he did introduce organizational and administrative reforms that gave the cavalry new life and purpose. He also named an ambitious new commander, Brigadier General Alfred Pleasonton. Although the two division commanders, John Buford and David McM. Gregg, were highly competent, the corps still needed bold, aggressive officers in its top ranks.

Detailed to Pleasonton's staff, Lieutenant Custer swiftly demonstrated himself a bold, aggressive officer. At first reluctant because of his fierce loyalty to McClellan, he gradually developed a high regard for his new chief.

Pleasonton liked Custer, too. As with Generals McClellan and Smith, the young officer had a talent for gathering and reporting important intelligence. He also had a pronounced gift for combat leadership that Pleasonton admired and encouraged. In the cavalry actions of June 1863 that exposed Lee's northward move into Pennsylvania, Custer demonstrated a mastery both of utterly fearless individual combat and of the far more exacting craft of animating and directing soldiers in battle.

Quickly unit commanders perceived the confidence that the commanding general placed in his young aide, and they accorded him a deference that encouraged his already strong disposition to slip from a staff into a command role. As his orderly recalled, "If Lt. Custer observed that it was important to make a movement or charge he would tell the commander to do it, and the commander would have to do it, would not dare question, because he knew Lt. Custer was

working under Genl. Pleasonton who would confirm every one of
his instructions and movements."

On June 22, Pleasonton received his second star, which allowed
Custer to sew captain's straps back on his uniform. He had enough
appreciation of his own potential, however, to want more. Many
of his West Point comrades had already gained field rank. Judson
Kilpatrick, for example, had graduated only a month before Custer;
now he was a full colonel commanding one of Pleasonton's brigades.
A wild youth, vain, reckless, and unstable, Kilpatrick earned the so-
briquet "Kilcavalry." But he would fight, which was what Pleasonton
wanted in his commanders.

In his quest for higher rank, Custer had compiled an impressive
packet of endorsements from generals and other notables supporting
his petition to command one of the new Michigan cavalry regiments,
either the Fifth or the Seventh. But Governor Austin Blair gave these
prized colonelcies to others. Custer's politics were wrong, and in
addition he was increasingly known as a "McClellan man"—a ruin-
ous label as McClellan grew vocally prominent in Democratic circles
critical of the Lincoln administration and even of the war itself.

Pleasonton had a trio of young officers, all captains, who enjoyed
his patronage and who had demonstrated skill and audacity on the
battlefield. Besides Custer, another was Wesley Merritt, a tall, slim,
beardless youth who had graduated from the Point a year ahead of
Custer. The third was Elon J. Farnsworth, two years older than
Custer, who had made a name for himself as adjutant of the Eighth
Illinois Cavalry. In these officers Pleasonton saw potential combat
leaders, and he sent in papers for their promotion. Mischievously, he
said nothing about his action.

In the waning days of June 1863, Lee's Army of Northern Virginia
crossed the Potomac and embarked on its fateful thrust into Pennsylvania. Through choking dust and stifling heat, the Army of the
Potomac hurried to intercept the Confederates, Pleasonton's cavalrymen screening the front and flanks. On June 28, with battle imminent, the army suffered through still another change in the top command. Paying the penalty for his crushing defeat at Chancellorsville, General Hooker handed over the leadership to Major General
George Gordon Meade.

On this same June 28, an envelope reached Pleasonton's headquarters in Frederick, Maryland, that stunned Captain Custer. It was ad-

dressed to Brigadier General George A. Custer, U.S. Volunteers. He could scarcely believe the document inside: orders jumping him four grades, from captain to brigadier. In one great leap he had become, at twenty-three, the youngest general in the Union army.

Pleasonton had indulged in no wild impulse. He had not singled out Custer alone. Colonels Kilpatrick and Alfred Duffié had received promotions earlier in June, and Captains Merritt and Farnsworth got their stars at the same time as Custer. All were men in their early to middle twenties who had displayed qualifications for high command. Custer and Merritt vindicated Pleasonton's judgment, Kilpatrick and Duffié less so. Farnsworth never got the chance. He died at Gettysburg, the victim of Kilpatrick's impulsiveness.

Pleasonton intended to use three of his new generals to energize a green two-brigade division that had just reported to him from the Washington defenses. The able Buford and Gregg led the First and Second divisions. Pleasonton gave the new division, numbered the Third, to Kilpatrick and its two brigades to Farnsworth and Custer.

Custer learned that he would command the Second Brigade of the Third Division. It was an assignment rich in irony, for this brigade consisted of the First, Fifth, Sixth, and Seventh regiments of Michigan Cavalry. The new brigadier had tried and failed to get the colonelcy of the Fifth or Seventh. Now he commanded the entire Michigan Cavalry Brigade.

Less than a week later General Custer made his debut at the Battle of Gettysburg. For two days the Army of Northern Virginia fought fiercely, and at appalling cost to both sides, to dislodge the Army of the Potomac from its strong positions in and around the town of Gettysburg. On the third day, in a last desperate attempt to breach Meade's defenses, Lee prepared to fling 12,500 infantrymen, under Major General George E. Pickett, against the Union center on Cemetery Ridge.

As Pickett prepared his epic charge, the Confederate cavalry corps moved into positions on a low hump three miles in the rear of the Union center. These were the feared and fabled gray horsemen of the dashing "Jeb" Stuart—Major General James Ewell Brown Stuart. For nearly two years Stuart's "Invincibles" had consistently outfought their adversaries in the Yankee cavalry.

Under General Gregg, three Union brigades faced Stuart, two of his own and Custer's Michiganders from Kilpatrick's division. Like the larger action to the west, the cavalry battle east of Gettysburg opened with an artillery duel, followed by an attack by dismounted Confederate skirmishers. Advancing to a rail fence, Custer's Fifth Michigan shattered one lunge after another with its Spencer repeaters but had to fall back, closely pressed, when ammunition ran low.

Seeing the Fifth about to be overrun, Gregg ordered the Seventh Michigan to charge. As the horsemen trotted to the front, sabers drawn, Custer galloped to the head of the column and shouted, "Come on, you Wolverines!" With a wild cheer, the regiment broke into a charge and drove the southerners back in confusion. Ingloriously, however, the Seventh crashed into a stone wall, and the charge ended abruptly. Back and forth across the wall, sometimes hand to hand, the two sides struggled until the Michiganders breached the wall. Twice they charged beyond and were thrown back. As they readied the third assault, a Confederate force hit their flank. Prudently, Custer led the regiment back to the cover of artillery.

Stuart seized this critical moment to launch an attack by eight mounted regiments. Sabers drawn, flags snapping, the southern horsemen advanced in aligned ranks. Artillery shot and shell blew gaps in the formation, but they closed and kept coming. Gregg had but one regiment left intact, the veteran First Michigan. Again Custer dashed to the head, and in column of squadrons the unit charged. As the two forces neared, neither swerved. Just before they collided, a burst of canister shredded the front Confederate ranks. As they faltered, again Custer shouted, "Come on, you Wolverines!" With a cheer, the Michiganders piled into the foe. "So sudden and violent was the collision," wrote an observer, "that many of the horses were turned end over end and crushed their riders beneath them. The clashing of sabers, the firing of pistols, the demands for surrender, and cries of the combatants, filled the air." From both flanks other blue troopers pitched into the melee. The gray mass briefly stood firm and then collapsed under the momentum of the assault.

For the first time the federal cavalry had vanquished the dauntless Jeb Stuart. He fell back, if not defeated, at least prevented from going where he had intended. His repulse coincided with Pickett's repulse three miles to the west. What might have happened had Stuart overrun Gregg and got into the Union rear just as Pickett reached his objective is one of the Civil War's most intriguing unknowns.

Although the steady, capable Gregg deserved much credit, the clear victor of the cavalry fight east of Gettysburg was a twenty-three-year-old youth who had been a general less than a week. On July 3, 1863, George Armstrong Custer came of age. In one spectacular burst he emerged a general in fact as well as name. Nor was Gettysburg a splashy anomaly. In the Union cavalry's harassment of Lee's retreat from Pennsylvania and in the subsequent maneuvers of the two armies in Virginia, Custer displayed superior leadership time and again.

Not only his conduct impressed the Wolverines. In appearance, manner, and garb, he cut a distinctive figure. Reddish-gold hair fell in curls almost to his shoulders. A brushy mustache hid a dimpled, receding chin. His fair complexion burned easily in the sun, giving his high cheeks and aquiline nose a perpetually flushed aspect and setting off bright blue eyes. The quick, jerky movement of his sinewy frame, together with speech rushing forth in high-pitched bursts bordering on a stutter, betrayed an unceasing and hyperkinetic restlessness.

In bizarre costume Custer had no peer in the Union army. The broad collar of a blue sailor's shirt fell over a black velveteen jacket ornamented with two rows of brass buttons and gold braid spangling the sleeves from cuff to elbow. Top boots with jangling spurs contained trousers of the same material seamed in twin gold stripes. A silver star perched on each shoulder and the low crown of his broad-brimmed hat. A scarlet necktie fell from his collar. A heavy straight sword, trophy of an early exploit, hung from his belt.

More than simple vanity motivated this eccentricity. He had a sure sense of what made effective military leadership and what gave a unit identity and esprit. He intended to be as conspicuous as possible, especially in combat, both to his own men and to the enemy. He devised a personal flag, a red-and-blue swallow-tailed pennant with crossed white sabers. Borne by an orderly, it followed him everywhere. So did a contingent of musicians. Forming a brigade band, Custer mounted the brass players to ride with him in battle. "At Yankee Doodle every man's hand went to his saber," recalled an officer. "It was always the signal for a charge."

Expressing the Wolverines' estimate of their commander, red ties blossomed throughout the brigade. They had a general who knew how to lead, led them to one success after another, shared their dangers, and made them feel good about themselves and their organization. In turn they earned admiration throughout the army as the best brigade in the cavalry corps.

The brigade commander also attracted wide attention, both in and out of the army. Newspaper reporters instantly saw him as superb copy—a modern Murat—and headlines extolled the deeds of the dashing youth they labeled the "Boy General."

In September 1863, after a grazing shot ripped Custer's boot and injured his leg, Pleasonton awarded him a fifteen-day leave. It proved momentous. Parading around Monroe in his brigadier's uniform, he discovered himself still smitten by Libbie Bacon. Fannie Fifield receded into obscurity. On September 28, at a masquerade ball at the Humphrey House, Autie and Libbie sat on a sofa as Libbie indirectly made a portentous announcement. Previously she had said that she would marry him if she loved him and if her father consented. Now she promised to marry him if her father consented.

Custer's leave did not afford the time to resolve that "if"—a big one, it turned out. With the brigade band belting out "Hail to the Chief," he reached his Virginia headquarters on October 8. Three days later, in a desperate battle with Stuart near Brandy Station, he triumphed once more. Now even those contemptuous of his flamboyance or jealous of his swift rise began to yield grudging admiration. "No soldier who saw him that day at Brandy Station," recalled an officer, "ever questioned his right to wear a star, or all the gold lace he felt inclined to wear. He at once became a favorite in the Army of the Potomac."

As the blue and gray armies went into winter quarters, Custer turned all his persuasive powers on Judge Bacon and his daughter. Although a general's star conferred much greater acceptability in Monroe, the judge still found the prospect of surrendering Libbie difficult to·confront. On her deathbed Libbie's mother had charged him with the proper care of their only daughter, he wrote to Armstrong on October 22, and he might have to ponder the matter for "weeks or even months."

Another obstacle was Libbie herself. She would need at least a year to prepare her mind and her trousseau, she protested. In truth her mind did need preparation, for Autie had some traits that she looked upon as failings. Although he had foresworn liquor and tobacco, he remained improvident. "I could keep a family with the money I spend needlessly," he confessed to his sister, "but I am going to make a change some of these days." Another, not unrelated, was gambling. He had resolved to quit wagering money, he assured Libbie on November 22, in the first of many such vows.

With that resolution, he disclosed, he had "bad adieu to every vice except one." That was profanity, and he was not ready to give that up. It proved too useful in combat. She had heard, Libbie wrote to him on December 29, that "Genl. Kilpatrick used an oath with every sentence he uttered, and that General Custer was not much better." "God cure you of it," she concluded.

Another concern distressed Libbie. Religion meant a great deal to her, and Sunday church services played an essential role in her life. Custer had early decided that, while not an atheist, he would embrace no particular faith nor trouble himself with spiritual matters. Libbie made the best of it, "thankful that I am marrying a man who, though not professing religion, is not an unbeliever."

Custer handled both the judge and Libbie as if Jeb Stuart had carelessly exposed a flank: charge. All defenses crumbled under the force of the attack. Finally the father consented to the marriage, and the daughter conceded that she did not need a full year to prepare for the event.

The ceremony took place on February 9, 1864. Custer and his staff, resplendent in blue and gold, and Libbie with her bridesmaids, equally radiant in white, dazzled the crowd that filled the pews and packed the aisles and vestibule of the First Presbyterian Church of Monroe. It was a storybook wedding, and it launched (at least to outward appearances) a storybook marriage.

After a whirlwind honeymoon the couple arrived at the headquarters of the Michigan Brigade on February 17. Settling in the farmhouse that served as headquarters, Libbie began a tradition that persisted throughout their marriage. Wherever he went, she went too, if at all possible. Aided by Eliza Brown, a seventeen-year-old runaway slave who had "jined up with the Ginnel" in the autumn, Libbie kept house in plantation mansions, farmhouses, tents, and even wagons—wherever headquarters came to rest. When she could not be with him, she retreated to a boarding house in Washington, D.C., and anxiously awaited his summons.

When separated, they wrote long letters to each other every day. Libbie's told of her adventures with the capital's notables, who fawned over her and, made bold by free-flowing spirits, took liberties that tested the ingenuity of her defenses. Autie's described military life and occasionally touched on his own exploits. Both went on interminably with professions of admiration and adoration. The few letters that survived testify conclusively to an extraordinarily profound love that each felt for the other, and they hint at a passion that expressed itself in an intense and creatively varied sexual life.

In spring 1864 a pivotal command shakeup decisively influenced Custer's destiny. Ulysses S. Grant came east to assume command of all the Union armies, with the grade of lieutenant general. Without dislodging Meade, Grant positioned himself with the Army of the Potomac and became in fact its commander. Despite his record of upgrading the cavalry, Pleasonton fell casualty to the change, as did Kilpatrick, whose wild antics had increasingly earned Custer's disdain. Both were shipped off to western theaters.

The new cavalry chief was Major General Philip H. Sheridan. A scrappy, profane Irishman, West Point 1854, and thirty-three years old, Sheridan looked anything but military. Abraham Lincoln described him as "a brown, chunky little chap, with a long body, short legs, not enough neck to hang him, and such long arms that if his ankles itch he can skratch them without stooping." But he brought with him from the West a superb record as a combat leader, bold, energetic, audacious, and unswerving in the pursuit of victory. Men gave their final measure for the stubby, bullet-headed little fighter with the flashing eyes.

Although stunned by the abrupt exile of Pleasonton, Custer quickly judged Sheridan "an able and good commander." General Grant, however, gained no such approval. Not only had he unhorsed Pleasonton, he had brought other western cronies with him who had to be placed. Custer thought he should have the division command vacated by Kilpatrick, but Grant gave it to James H. Wilson, an engineer without command experience and Custer's junior as a brigadier. "Your time will come I have no doubt of it," consoled Michigan Congressman Francis W. Kellogg. "No true man like you can be killed by such gross favoritism on the part of the Chief of the Army."

Custer's time would indeed come, first because he continued to rack up one triumph after another with the Michigan Brigade, and second because his performance earned him Sheridan's approval and esteem. By midsummer 1864, Sheridan had won over Custer, supplanting McClellan and Pleasonton as his idol and gaining his lasting loyalty and devotion.

More important, Custer had won over Sheridan. Both Custer and

Merritt emerged as the cavalry chief's favorites—or "pets," as the uncharitable saw it. Lacking Custer's dash and flamboyance, Merritt probably impressed Sheridan as the more reliable. Always he ranked Custer, but always Custer outshone him, in Sheridan's eyes and in the nation's. For the rest of his life Custer's career drew crucial propellant from the patronage of "Little Phil" Sheridan.

As Custer proved himself to Sheridan, so Sheridan proved himself to Grant. With Grant's support he broke free of the conservative Meade and established once and for all the cavalry's utility as an independent arm. As the Army of the Potomac sidestepped Lee and, in the Wilderness campaign, gradually worked its bloody way southward, Sheridan led the cavalry corps in a successful raid to the very edge of Richmond. There, at the Battle of Yellow Tavern, one of Custer's Wolverines brought down Jeb Stuart himself. Wade Hampton, a better general than Stuart, took his place, but the southern horse never again measured up to the Union horse.

More than Stuart's death, that shift in relative capabilities reflected the leadership of Sheridan, and he swiftly received his reward. As Grant settled into siege positions around Petersburg, south of Richmond, Lee sought to relieve the pressure by the classic diversion that had worked so well in 1862: threaten Washington from the Shenandoah Valley. Like Stonewall Jackson before him, Lieutenant General Jubal A. Early thrust down the valley, swept through Maryland, and panicked Washington by appearing in front of the northern defenses of the capital. Forced to weaken his Petersburg lines in order to drive off "Old Jube," Grant resolved to end that Confederate strategy for all time. In August 1864, he gave Sheridan an army of forty thousand infantry and cavalry and sent him to make certain that the South never again used the Shenandoah Valley as an invasion corridor.

The valley afforded a fine new stage on which Custer might demonstrate his generalship and add new laurels to his fame. On September 19, Sheridan attacked Early in strong positions around Winchester. All day the battle raged, with Sheridan and his infantry battering the Confederate center east of town while most of the cavalry pounded the left north of town. As Early began to weaken his flank to firm up his center, Custer gathered some five hundred of his combat-scattered men and charged. The saber-swinging Wolverines rolled over an entire brigade of infantry, scooped up seven hundred prisoners, including fifty-two officers, and captured two artillery caissons and seven battle flags. The Confederate defenses collapsed, and Early's army fled south to new positions on Fisher's Hill. There, on September 22, Sheridan won another victory, driving the foe still farther up the valley.

Winchester crowned Custer's record with the Michigan Brigade, for now he received the reward that he had thought his due five months earlier—a division of his own. A shakeup the previous spring, when General Wilson took over the Third Cavalry Division, had moved Custer and the Michiganders to the First Division, under Merritt. Late in September, Grant sent Wilson back to the West. It was a big promotion rather than an exile, and Wilson performed superbly. No one in Sheridan's army regretted his departure, however, especially when Custer moved up to lead the Third Division.

The Third Division happily welcomed its new commander with a splash of red neckties, while the downcast Wolverines circulated petitions urging the transfer of the Michigan Brigade back to the Third Division. As an Ohio trooper explained, "while Wilson had command of the 3d Division . . . scarcely a member of it would willingly acknowledge his connection with it, but now it was very different. Every member felt proud to be known as one of Custer's division."

The division's first action under the new chief was Tom's Brook, on October 9. After Fisher's Hill and a further advance as far south as Harrisonburg, Sheridan marched back down the valley, applying a scorched-earth strategy intended to leave it untenable for military use. Confederate cavalry snapped at his heels. In addition to the dispirited horse of Winchester and Fisher's Hill, the Confederate cavalry now included the newly arrived Laurel Brigade of Brigadier General Thomas L. Rosser, Custer's old friend and West Point comrade. Sheridan ordered his cavalry to turn and whip the Rebels or get whipped. Advancing on a two-division front, Merritt and Custer overwhelmed Rosser and in a storybook saber charge chased him and the rest of Early's cavalry twenty miles up the valley. The Battle of Tom's Brook became known as the Woodstock Races.

In the lower valley the army went into camp along Cedar Creek while Sheridan entrained for the capital to discuss future strategy. That trip almost cost him his army.

Before daybreak on October 19, as a thick fog hung low on the valley, Jubal Early threw five Confederate infantry divisions against the Union left. The surprise assault overran the defenses and sent

half-clad federals streaming northward in panic flight. From the right
flank Merritt and Custer shoved their divisions into the breach and
slowed the attack, but they had little hope of averting catastrophe.

At this critical moment Sheridan himself, astride a lathered horse,
raced dramatically onto the field. All along the road from Winchester
and on the battlefield itself his animated presence and rousing curses
turned the retreating mass around and prodded it into a wildly cheer-
ing counterattack. Contending battle lines took shape, and all day
the two sides struggled. On the right flank Custer's division beat off
attempts by Rosser's southern cavalry to get in the Union rear. Late
in the day a Confederate brigade feinted north in an effort to turn
the Union right. A gap opened in the gray line. Sheridan spotted it
and raced over to Custer, who had seen it too and had already
formed for a charge. In a repeat of Winchester Custer smashed into
the Confederate left with such force that the entire line disintegrated
and the enemy fled up the valley.

That night an exhilarated Custer stormed up to Sheridan's headquarters. In a notable lapse of military decorum, he seized the commanding general, lifted him off the ground, and danced around the
campfire. "By God, Phil!" he shouted, "We've cleaned them out of
their guns and got ours back!"

The next day Custer was off by rail to Washington commanding a
squad of thirteen troopers, each carrying a Confederate battle flag
that he had captured. At the War Department, as Libbie watched
proudly, each soldier presented his flag to Secretary of War Edwin M.
Stanton. Responding, Stanton declared that good generals and good
soldiers worked together and announced that he had made their
commander a major general. Shaking Custer's hand, the secretary
concluded, "General, a gallant officer always makes gallant soldiers."

The promotion was by brevet (largely an honorary distinction),
and one also went to Custer's rival, Wesley Merritt. But it allowed
them both, as division commanders, to wear two stars on their
shoulder straps and arrange their uniform buttons in rows of three
instead of two.

Although Cedar Creek, on top of Winchester and Fisher's Hill, all
but ruined Early's Confederate army, it still posed enough of a threat
to tie Sheridan to the Shenandoah Valley all winter. While most of
his infantry and artillery returned to the siege lines at Petersburg, the
cavalry kept constantly in motion, watching Early, sparring with the
aggressive Rosser, and continuing to lay waste the valley. Far worse

than Confederates, rain, sleet, snow, mud, and freezing temperatures made the winter an agonizing ordeal for the cavalry.

Few ordeals disheartened the irrepressible Custer. Libbie spent the winter at his headquarters, a spacious farmhouse near Winchester. In November, moreover, a new aide-de-camp smartly saluted and reported for duty: Second Lieutenant Thomas Ward Custer. Nineteen years old, brother Tom had compiled an outstanding combat record as an infantryman in the western armies. Armstrong had got him commissioned in a Michigan cavalry regiment and then assigned to the Third Division staff. In battle Tom was even more the wild daredevil than his brother, and he made a fine officer. Tom's assignment marked the beginning of Armstrong Custer's career as one of the most accomplished nepotists in an army full of assiduous nepotists. His success at packing his military "family" with friends and relatives continued to the last day of his life.

Fittingly, the Shenandoah Valley campaign ended with General Custer and the Third Division in the forefront. Eager to join Grant for what turned out to be the final campaign of the war, in late February 1865 Sheridan advanced up the soggy valley intent on disposing of Early once and for all. On March 2, in the lead, Custer discovered what was left of the Confederate forces entrenched in strong defenses in front of Waynesboro, with the Blue Ridge at their back. A reconnaissance disclosed a gap between Early's left flank and the South River. Without waiting for the following units to come up, Custer attacked. Three regiments slipped through this gap into Early's rear, while two brigades stormed up the muddy slope against the Confederate center—"Custer's gleaming sabre and scarlet cravat being conspicuous among the foremost," as an officer remembered.

The two-pronged assault destroyed Early's little army. Sixteen hundred prisoners, two hundred supply wagons, fourteen cannons, and seventeen battle flags fell to the exultant Third Division. In front of a formation of seventeen mud-spattered troopers, each bearing a Confederate banner, Custer happily reported his victory to Sheridan.

An elated Sheridan knew that now the Shenandoah Valley could be safely left behind. Early's army no longer existed, and anyway the valley could no longer support it or any other army. Sheridan had devastated it so thoroughly that, as he boasted, a crow flying overhead would have to carry provisions.

Back with Grant in front of Petersburg, Sheridan resumed command of the Cavalry Corps of the Army of the Potomac. On the left of Grant's siege line the cavalry set forth at the end of March 1865 to get around Lee's right and tear up the railroads from the west that kept him supplied. At the hard-fought battles of Dinwiddie Court House and Five Forks, March 31 and April 1, Custer and his division plunged into the thick of the fray and acquitted themselves handsomely. These two battles broke the winterlong stalemate at Petersburg. Under cover of night on April 2, Lee slipped out of his defenses and headed west. Grant gave chase, thus launching the Appomattox Campaign, in which Custer burnished his record with still more triumphs.

The mission of Sheridan's cavalry, as Lee's army limped westward in a desperate attempt to break free, was to slow the retreat until Grant's overpowering infantry and artillery could come up and finish the job. Impoverished in weapons, ammunition, rations, and clothing, a mere shadow of its once mighty strength, the Army of Northern Virginia had plenty of fight left in it. The veteran infantrymen could still wreak havoc on the cavalry that swarmed on their flanks and rear. In savage fighting, the foot soldiers held back the Union horse while Lee continued his retreat.

They paid a fearful price, and Custer led in exacting it. At Sayler's Creek on April 6, a third of the Confederate army, seven generals and nine thousand men, surrendered, many of them to the Third Division. Custer gave food and shelter to a party of southern officers and sat far into the night talking with one of them, Major General Joseph B. Kershaw. Next morning Kershaw watched sadly as Custer's escort for the day formed in front of his tent: thirty-one troopers, each bearing a Confederate flag seized the day before.

Also at Sayler's Creek, Tom Custer demonstrated his prowess. Leaping southern breastworks, he seized a Confederate flag, only to be shot full in the face at point-blank range. Even so, he killed the color bearer and rode back to the Union lines with the banner floating in the breeze. Three days earlier, with similar bravery, he had captured another flag at Namozine Church. For these two actions Tom attained the rare distinction of pinning two Medals of Honor to his tunic.

Late on April 8, Custer learned that three railroad trains, loaded with ammunition and rations, awaited Lee at Appomattox Station. Spurring forward in the dusk, he seized this vital treasure just as Lee's advance appeared to contest the capture with bursting artillery rounds. While some troopers who had once been engineers fired the

locomotives and pulled the trains out of range, Custer led the Second
Ohio Cavalry in a charge on the Confederate guns. As darkness set
in, he captured twenty-four cannons and pulled back to Appomattox
Station for the night.

Bolstered by the First Division, Custer now lay squarely across
Lee's line of march. The next morning federal infantry came up, and
by daybreak of April 9, Lee was boxed. On a wooded hillside, as the
Third Division formed for yet another charge, a lone gray horseman
approached bearing a soiled white towel affixed to a pole. He presented himself to General Custer and declared that General Lee
wished to meet with General Grant.

Fittingly, this emblem of war's end came to the young general
who, by age twenty-five, had written a record of military exploits
that few soldiers exhibit in a lifetime. General Sheridan recognized
the achievement. Sheridan stood by as Grant and Lee met in Wilmer
McLean's parlor at Appomattox Court House. Afterward Sheridan
paid McLean twenty dollars for a historic reminder of that momentous conference. Next day he penned a note to Libbie Custer: "I
respectfully present to you the small writing table on which the conditions for the surrender of the Army of Northern Virginia were
written by Lt. General Grant—and permit me to say, Madam, that
there is scarcely an individual in our service who has contributed
more to bring about this desirable result than your gallant husband."

The surrender table acknowledged and symbolized one of the
Civil War's most extraordinary careers. From Gettysburg to Appomattox George Armstrong Custer wrote a virtually faultless record
of battlefield success, made the more remarkable by his sudden rise
and his extreme youth. His generalship combined audacity, courage,
leadership, judgment, composure, and an uncanny instinct for the
critical moment and the action it demanded. He pressed the enemy
closely and doggedly, charged at the right moment, held fast at the
right moment, fell back at the right moment, deployed his units with
skill, and applied personal leadership where and when most needed.

Individually, he fought with a fury and tenacity astonishing to all
who witnessed his feats of daring. That he emerged from the war
with so few scars he and others attributed to "Custer's Luck." He
did seem to lead a charmed life, especially since his gaudy uniform
and personal flag made him conspicuous in battle. But more logi-
cally, as one of his officers observed, the general made a poor target
because he was a moving target. "He never was still, he was always

on the move," recalled the officer. "I believe he owed his marvelous preservation to that." Aside from his own love of battle, Custer knew that such exploits enhanced his leadership and inspired his men.

Representative of many estimates was one made the more credible because penned by a loyal member of Wesley Merritt's staff:

> He was certainly the model of a light cavalry officer, quick in observation, clear in judgment, and resolute and determined in execution. Brave as a lion himself, he seemed never for a moment to imagine that any subordinate, down to the meanest private soldier in his command, would hesitate to follow him even to the death, and indeed he had reason to be firm in this belief. It was said that he was ambitious and grasping; but as far as I could see . . . his ambition seemed to be more to surprise and startle both friend and foe with the brilliancy of his deeds, than anything else, and his claims for special honor were always for his Division rather than for his personal account.

No experts more shrewdly gauge a general than his own subordinates. Affecting braided jackets and red ties like their chief, Custer's officers idolized him. Said one:

> He was remarkable for his keenness and accuracy in observation, for his swift divination of the military significance of every element of a situation, for his ability to make an instant and sound decision, and then, for the instant, exhaustless energy with which he everlastingly drove home his attack. And the swiftness and relentless power of his stroke were great elements in the correctness of his decisions as well as in the success of his operations.

And a regimental commander: "He was brave as a lion, fought as few men fought. . . . Fighting was his business; and he knew that by that means alone could peace be conquered. He was brave, alert, untiring, a hero in battle, relentless in the pursuit of a beaten enemy, stubborn and full of resources on the retreat."

Even more authoritative were the enlisted men who fought under him. A private told his wife that General Custer "commanded in person and I saw him plunge his saber into the belly of a rebel who was trying to kill him. You can guess how bravely soldiers fight for such a general." And a second: "The rebs say they dasent shoot a cannon for if they do general Custer is shure to go for it and take it away from them."

As these portraits suggest, General Custer in 1865 was the "born soldier," but little else. For the wartime years, his early twenties, Custer's life was a blur of brilliant military feats, of flashing swords, blazing guns, whipping flags, and pounding hooves amid swirling dust and smoke and the din of battle. Behind this one dimension of military proficiency, little depth of character had taken shape. Marriage had plumbed depths of passion and emotion but remained in its first blossom. War had stirred spiritual ruminations and even produced an open declaration for Christ, but the commitment weakened with the advent of peace. In 1865 the essential man beneath the glittering stars remained to be developed—or revealed.

The glitter, however, was authentic. In April 1865 the Army of the Potomac and the American public at large saw Custer as second only to Sheridan as a cavalry general. Wesley Merritt may have been as good, but he was never as conspicuous; to Merritt's lifelong resentment, Custer always won more glory. At war's end only a handful of generals—Grant, Sherman, Sheridan—commanded greater public acclaim or, except for the inevitable jealousies that any star attracts, greater respect within the army.

Almost at once, however, the Civil War Custer gave way to the frontier Custer, and a decade later the frontier Custer gave way to the mythic Custer. Those last two Custers tarnished the name and dimmed the superlative record of the first. Had Confederate shrapnel struck him dead at Appomattox Station on April 8, 1865, he would be remembered as the great cavalry general that he was, second in the Union army only to Sheridan. But in exchange for solid stature as a Civil War hero, known chiefly to the fraternity of Civil War students, he would have forfeited immortality as a folk hero of worldwide renown.

The Civil War Custer enjoyed one final triumph. On May 23, 1865, the Army of the Potomac paraded down Pennsylvania Avenue and passed in front of the White House. Custer led his beloved Third Division, ablaze with the scarlet neckties that proclaimed their identity. Shortly before the division reached the bunting-draped reviewing stand, a little girl threw a garland of flowers at the general. His horse bolted and carried him, hatless and with tawny curls and scarlet tie streaming in the wind, galloping past the president and other dignitaries taking the salute. Reining in the horse, he returned to head the division in its ceremonial farewell.

The world has always wondered whether the mount beneath that matchless horseman really did bolt.

CHAPTER 3

Regular Army

"OH, could you but have seen some of the charges that were made!" General Custer wrote to a Monroe friend in the autumn of 1863. "While thinking of them I cannot but exclaim 'Glorious War!' "

He loved war. It nourished and energized him. It triggered those complex mechanisms of intellect and instinct that made his tactical decisions nearly flawless. It afforded the environment in which a youth so endowed could gain the obedience and adulation of several thousand followers and inspire them to fight and die for him. In combat as in no other milieu, Custer flourished. It was the catalyst that drove a young man hardly past the threshold of manhood to measure up to the stars that adorned his shoulder straps.

The return of peace found him an adult in achievement, renown, and responsibility but still a boy in years. For George Armstrong Custer, peace would prove a far more formidable challenge than war. Peace would deprive him of the one activity in which he excelled. Peace would also free the boy who had been held in check for two years by the awesome demands of "Glorious War"—not just the exuberant, fun-loving boy but the immature, foolish boy as well. For the decade remaining to him, the boy and the man would struggle for dominance, producing the contradictions of personality and behavior that marked his frontier years.

The first test came scarcely a month after the Grand Review in Washington. General Sheridan had been sent to New Orleans to assemble an army to occupy Texas, ostensibly to round up Confederate forces that had not surrendered but chiefly to threaten the French puppet in Mexico, Emperor Maximilian. Sheridan called for both Custer and Merritt. Custer's assignment was to organize a cavalry division at Alexandria, Louisiana, and move it to Texas. By late June 1865, with Libbie and Eliza, he had settled into a plantation house in the sultry bottoms of the Red River.

Volunteer regiments from the Midwest made up Custer's division.

They were full of veterans who had fought bravely in the western campaigns during the war and thus differed little from the Red Ties who had followed their Boy General so worshipfully from Gettysburg to Appomattox. But the war was over, and these men wanted to go home, not to Texas. They arrived in Alexandria in a foul humor, insubordinate, even mutinous, deserting by the score, and foraging liberally on the local population.

As an officer Custer had never experienced resistance to his will. It baffled and infuriated him, and it deeply frustrated him because he could not turn to the one technique that had always worked—combat leadership. He responded with harsh discipline and cruel, even unlawful, punishment. Depredations on citizens, for example, earned offenders twenty-five lashes and shaved heads. Deserters and mutineers could expect worse, even the firing squad.

A test of wills developed at once. Custer convened a court-martial to try a private of an Indiana regiment for desertion and a sergeant of a Wisconsin regiment, Leonard Lancaster, for mutiny. Lancaster, a man of high principle with a fine war record, had been a leader in circulating and presenting a petition asking an unpopular regimental commander to resign and go home. Technically this was mutiny, and the general intended to make an example of the culprit. For both offenders the court decreed death by firing squad.

The prospective execution of the popular Lancaster nearly set off a genuine mutiny. Rumors of assassination if Custer tried to carry out the sentence hardened his resolve to establish unquestioned mastery. In a scene heavy with menace, he lined up the entire division to witness the executions and silently dared would-be assassins to carry out their threats. None tried. With the two victims blindfolded and seated on their own coffins, the firing squad took position. Custer allowed the commands of "Ready" and "Aim" to be given; then before "Fire," he had Lancaster led aside. At "Fire," only the deserter died.

Whether this melodrama exhibited compassion or cruelty depended on one's point of view—especially since Lancaster suffered a dishonorable discharge and a term of imprisonment in Florida's Dry Tortugas. It did not, however, create a disciplined, obedient division. Custer's ruthless measures, which Sheridan endorsed, failed altogether. Both in Louisiana and Texas the soldiers and their general warred constantly.

For the first time Custer commanded men who did not revere him

and who in fact loathed him. The estimate of one captured the
abrupt change: "He was only twenty-five years of age, and had the
usual egotism and self-importance of a young man. He was a regular
army officer, and had bred in him the tyranny of the regular army.
He did not distinguish between a regular soldier and a volunteer. He
did not stop to consider that the latter were citizens, and not soldiers
by profession. . . . He had no sympathy in common with the private
soldiers, but regarded them simply as machines, created for the spe
cial purpose of obeying his imperial will." No trooper of the Michigan Cavalry Brigade or the Third Cavalry Division would have written that.

In August the division embarked on the long hot march into
Texas. There the command went into camp near Hempstead and
then, in November, took station at Austin, the state capital. The
threat of war over Mexico subsided, and the troops settled into routine occupation duties, which did not improve the temper of men
kept in the service while others went home.

Except for the nagging problems of discipline, Custer enjoyed
Texas. He had Libbie by his side, Tom reported for duty on his staff,
and he even got his father, Emanuel, appointed a forage agent for
his division. He found the planter class congenial in values and out-
look, as he had been drawn similarly to southern cadets at West
Point. In Texas he developed a passion for fast horses and packs of
hunting dogs. Surrounded by wife, friends, and family, he found
escape from the trials of disgruntled soldiery in riding, racing, hunting, and sightseeing.

The Texas interlude ended early in 1866, as the disbanding of the
volunteer army finally reached Custer. Effective February 1, he was
mustered out of the volunteer service. Immediately after Appomattox he had been promoted to full major general of volunteers. In
December 1865 Sheridan strongly urged that he receive a brevet of
major general in the regular army, which would help if he decided to
stay in the military. But for now, Major General Custer, U.S. Volunteers, reverted to Captain Custer, Fifth U.S. Cavalry.

He did not know what to do, and he used an extended leave to
explore career possibilities in the East. New York City, with its glitter
and luxury, captivated the Ohio farm boy. By night he and army
friends such as Pleasonton and Merritt dined sumptuously, went to
the theater or opera, and were honored guests at extravagant parties
staged by the rich. They bantered with streetwalkers—"Nymphes du

Pave"—and were titillated by the low-cut gowns of society ladies. Seated on a sofa beside a baroness, Armstrong marveled in a letter to Libbie, "I have not seen such sights since I was weaned." But he assured her, too, that "at no time did I forget you."

By day Custer met with the financial barons of Wall Street, who lionized him as a war hero and left him convinced that his fame could be translated into wealth. Railroads and mining both tempted him. "For you and you alone I long to become wealthy," he wrote Libbie, "not for the wealth alone but for the power it brings. I am willing to make any honorable sacrifice."

Another possibility materialized. The minister to the United States of the Mexican government of Benito Juárez offered Custer sixteen thousand dollars a year, twice his major general's pay, to serve as adjutant general of Juárez's army in the struggle with Maximilian. Drawn by visions of another glorious war, Custer applied for a year's leave of absence from the U.S. Army. General Grant and Secretary Stanton endorsed the application, but Secretary of State William H. Seward, fearful of offending France, blocked approval.

The sudden death of Judge Bacon on May 18, 1866, cut short the New York visit. Back in Monroe, however, still other prospects beckoned the undecided general. A political innocent, he allowed himself to be lured into the vicious controversies racking the nation over treatment of the conquered South, and he even toyed with the notion of running for Congress.

Custer did poorly at stating his views, which in any event tended to shift with prevailing political winds. In the last year of the war, especially as he fought for Senate confirmation of his general's appointment, his words made him sound like a Radical Republican bent on vengeance against the beaten South. Now, with the ascendancy of Andrew Johnson, he spoke for moderation.

Moderation more nearly represented his true opinions. He did not favor crushing the South. Ever since West Point, even during the war, he had found southerners personally agreeable. He believed in elevating blacks but not at the expense of whites. He decried recruitment of blacks into the military, judging shovels and hoes as more fitting for them than muskets. And as for black suffrage, a key plank in the Radical platform, "I should as soon think of elevating an indian Chief to the popedom of Rome."

In September 1866 Custer joined President Andrew Johnson in his "swing around the circle," a desperate effort to win popular support

for his policy toward the South. The trip aligned Custer conspicuously with the president's cause. Custer vehemently denied newspaper charges that in return Johnson had promised him a regular army
colonelcy. That may have been true, but obscured the fact that only
weeks earlier he had written directly to the president asking for such
a commission (though specifically not in a black unit).

As the presidential train made its swing, not even Custer's stature
as a war hero shielded him from the savage attacks of the Radicals,
who twisted his words, branded him a copperhead, and treated him
to the same raucous insults they heaped on the chief executive. Custer was glad enough to leave the presidential party before the trip
ended.

Bruised in the political arena, Autie and Libbie decided to stay in
the army. He had not learned a lasting lesson about politics, nor had
he given up on the business or financial world. But for now the army
seemed the best prospect. In July, Congress had enlarged the regular
army, which opened possibilities more appealing than the lowly station of company commander to which his captaincy relegated him.
Sheridan had recommended him for the full colonelcy that he had
sought directly from the president, but the War Department offered
an appointment as lieutenant colonel of one of the new regiments,
the Seventh Cavalry. Custer accepted.

In the Army Act of July 28, 1866, Congress fashioned the postwar
regular army to perform three missions: Reconstruction of the
South, protection of the western frontier, and defense of the sea-
coasts. For these missions the act authorized a regular army of
roughly fifty-four thousand—a strength three times that of the pre-
war army.

Staff and line made up the army. The staff departments, concentrated in Washington, D.C., and the various headquarters of divisions and departments, gave administrative, technical, and logistical
support to the line, the fighting arm. In the line the Army Act ex-
panded the old regular army from six to ten cavalry regiments and
nineteen to forty-five infantry regiments while keeping the artillery,
concerned chiefly with coastal defense, at five regiments. To the disgust of Custer and many others opposed to any hint of racial
equality, two cavalry and four infantry regiments were to consist of
black soldiers and white officers.

In the years after the Civil War the political furor over Reconstruction came close to spawning two armies—the forces occupying the South, beholden largely to Congress; and the army on the frontier and in the coastal fortifications, serving the Executive. Except for one short interlude, Custer's service was with the frontier army. In this institution, with traditions, character, and doctrine differing in many ways from units posted to the South and the coasts, he made a new name for himself, one destined to overshadow his image as Boy General.

Officers who wished to remain in the army competed fiercely for preferment, summoning the help of military friends as well as political supporters. For regulars such as Custer, opportunities for higher rank existed mainly in the new regiments, even though the law reserved part of the new vacancies for volunteer officers who had served with distinction in the war but had never been in the regulars. The law provided for only seventeen general officers of the line, and that number would shortly shrink even more. With his youth and comparative lack of seniority in the regulars, Custer could count himself fortunate in gaining a lieutenant colonelcy, an appointment he owed to his patron, Sheridan. Far from being demoted, as is often portrayed, Custer was actually promoted, from captain to lieutenant colonel.

The rivalry for rank also centered on brevets, for in theory they proclaimed battlefield gallantry. The liberality with which War Department boards showered brevets on staff and line alike diluted this distinction, but they still certified wartime service. They also had practical benefits because officers could be assigned to duty by the president in their brevet grade, and brevet rank automatically took precedence in certain circumstances. Furthermore, officers could wear the uniform and be addressed according to brevet rank. This wrought monumental confusion because most regimental commanders were generals by brevet and most company commanders were majors or colonels by brevet. At length Congress decreed that officers wear only the uniform and insignia of their regular rank.

Again Custer was fortunate. After another forceful plea from Sheridan in May 1866, he received a brevet of major general in the regular army.

For the postwar regulars frontier defense was not a new mission. Frontier needs had prompted the creation of the regular army in 1784 and, except for two foreign wars and one civil war, had fixed its principal mission and employment ever since. Campaigning against

Indians, protecting pioneer settlers, exploring new territory, and constructing internal improvements, the regulars had kept pace with the advancing frontier all the way from the Appalachians to the edge of the Great Plains. After the Mexican War transformed the United States into a continental nation, the regulars ventured onto the Plains and into the mountains and deserts of the Far West. They guarded the overland emigration, gave security to burgeoning mining camps, and contended with Indian tribes that resisted the westward advance of the white people.

The close of the Civil War opened a new chapter in the westward movement and thus in the army's frontier mission. Peace released unprecedented national energies, which set off an explosive development of the frontier West as well as an explosive industrial expansion in the East. In two decades a surge of migration sent four million people into the West, spanned the continent with railroads, sank mountain shafts that yielded mineral riches, overspread the grasslands with cattle herds, sprinkled towns and farms all over the region, and fulfilled the oratorical clichés about the nation's manifest destiny.

The army's task was to deal with the Indians who stood in the way of this irresistible movement. Some 270,000 Indians in more than 125 distinct groups inhabited the Trans-Mississippi West. Many of these had already been decimated and neutralized or conquered and herded onto reservations supervised by the Bureau of Indian Affairs in the Department of the Interior. In 1866 only a few tribes retained the power and the will to fight. On the Great Plains they were the Sioux, Cheyenne, Arapaho, Kiowa, and Comanche. In the Rocky Mountains they were the Nez Perce, Ute, and Bannock. In the Pacific Northwest they were the Paiute and Modoc. In the Southwest they were Apache. Not exceeding 100,000 people, these "hostile" Indians engaged the United States in the final struggle for the American West.

The army brought to the task no new strategy. In fact, there had never been any formal strategy for fighting Indians, and there never would be. The generals looked on Indian warfare as a momentary distraction from their principal concern—preparing for the next foreign war. A network of forts had extended across the West, less as a result of deliberate planning than as erratic responses to the demands of pioneer communities for security and local markets. In the years after the Civil War, more than a hundred such posts, mostly little one- and two-company stations hastily thrown together from whatever building materials the vicinity afforded, made up the western defense system and provided a framework for operations against Indians. Always undermanned, the forts gave nearby settlers reassurance, if not always protection, and they furnished troops and logistical services when commanders judged offensive movements to be necessary.

As his station Brevet Major General and Lieutenant Colonel Custer drew Fort Riley, Kansas. The War Department had designated Riley as the headquarters of the new Seventh Cavalry. Here, beginning in September 1866, the Seventh would be organized and prepared for frontier duty.

Fort Riley and its sister posts in Kansas, some even then in the course of construction, watched over the farming settlements creeping onto the prairies west of the Missouri River, gave protection to the Santa Fe Trail and the more recent Smoky Hill Trail to Denver, and guarded construction workers on the new railroad pushing up the Smoky Hill River. Labeled the Union Pacific, Eastern Division, it would soon organize as the Kansas Pacific.

The Kansas forts fell within the Department of the Missouri, a geographical command embracing Missouri, Kansas, Colorado, and New Mexico. Major General Winfield Scott Hancock commanded from headquarters at Fort Leavenworth, Kansas. In turn, the Department of the Missouri was one of three departments making up the Military Division of the Missouri, commanded from headquarters in Saint Louis by William Tecumseh Sherman, the army's lieutenant general now that Grant had been given four stars. In the affection of Americans, Sherman stood second only to Grant, venerated for the capture of Atlanta and the fabled March to the Sea. With grizzled red beard and piercing eyes, the blunt, irascible, and thoroughly honest Sherman would stamp his distinctive mark on the postwar regular army.

The troops in Kansas faced some of the most formidable Indians in North America. The Southern Cheyennes and Arapahoes ranged the High Plains between the Platte and Arkansas rivers all the way to the Front Range of the Rocky Mountains. A few bands of their friends and allies, the Oglala and Brule Sioux, hunted along the Platte and the Republican and sometimes could be found as far south as the Arkansas. Along the Arkansas and southward into Indian Ter-

ritory lived the Kiowas, Comanches, and Plains Apaches. All were
proud peoples, superb at warfare, who followed the great herds of
buffalo that blackened these virgin grasslands. All had resisted white
inroads in the past. All had occasionally fought the bluecoats. And
all felt especially restless now that the white people had quit fighting
each other and were moving westward in such threatening numbers.

Mid-October 1866 found the Custers at their new station. After a
gala holiday in Saint Louis they rode the cars to end of track and
there loaded aboard army ambulances for the remaining ten miles to
Fort Riley. The party consisted of the general and Libbie, a young
Monroe friend of Libbie's, the ubiquitous Eliza, a "worthless colored
boy" acquired in Texas, three blooded horses, and a pack of deer
hounds presented by planter friends in Texas. Tom would show up
a month later, bearing a regular army commission as first lieutenant
in his brother's regiment.

Like all other mounted regiments, the Seventh consisted of twelve
companies, each with a paper strength of one hundred privates, cor-
porals, and sergeants but with actual strength usually much less.
Each company rated a captain, a first lieutenant, and a second lieutenant, nearly always reduced to two or even one by details to detached service. The field grades were a colonel, a lieutenant colonel,
and three majors. In theory each major commanded a battalion of
four companies, although this rarely happened in practice.

Contrary to the popular image, Custer did not organize and train
the Seventh Cavalry. Early in November he went back to Washington, D.C., to appear before the examining board for his new commission and did not return until just before Christmas. Meantime,
officers of the Second Cavalry based at Riley had formed the recruits
into companies. Major John W. Davidson, of the Second, served as
the Seventh's commander until the new colonel reported for duty
on November 25. He was Brevet Major General Andrew Jackson
Smith, a blunt but kindly old dragoon who had graduated from West
Point in 1838, fought Indians on the frontier for a quarter of a century, and commanded a cavalry division in the western armies during
the Civil War.

By the time Smith assumed command of the regiment, only three
companies remained at Riley. The rest, in charge of their new officers, had marched westward to garrison other forts on the Smoky
Hill and Santa Fe trails.

Thus the Seventh's experience mirrored that of other regiments,

old and new, mounted and foot, stationed on the frontier. Only
rarely did they come together as regiments but rather were distrib-
uted in contingents of one, two, and three companies at scattered
forts, sometimes even in different departments. The company, not
the regiment, functioned as the basic tactical unit, and its training,
morale, and effectiveness reflected the leadership of company officers
more than regimental officers. At Forts Hays, Harker, Wallace,
Dodge, Lyon, and Morgan (the last two in Colorado), as well as at
Fort Riley, the Seventh's companies took shape under their captains
and lieutenants.

Insofar as any field-grade officer had more influence than the line
officers, the distinction belonged to the senior major, Alfred Gibbs,
West Point 1846, a brevet major general. Intemperance, old wounds,
and hard service had broken his health but not his stubborn dedication to military trivia. Troops under his command who failed to look
smart and perform evolutions flawlessly risked the retribution of an
accomplished parade-ground tyrant. The regimental band of the Seventh owed its splendid proficiency to the nourishing care of Major
Gibbs.

Custer's intimate association with the Seventh began on February
26, 1867, when Colonel Smith relinquished command to his lieutenant colonel in order to head the District of the Upper Arkansas.
Henceforth, in the perception of the regiment, the army, and the
public at large, the Seventh would be Custer's regiment. Other officers would command, even for long periods, but until the climactic
day on the Little Bighorn a decade later, the Seventh belonged to
George Armstrong Custer.

The Seventh Cavalry of 1867 fell far short of being a crack regiment, as did the other regiments as well. Except for Smith and
Gibbs, the officers lacked frontier and Indian experience. Most came
out of the volunteer service and had much to learn about the regulars. Most drank heavily, some so heavily as frequently to unfit them
for duty. One, Major Wickliffe Cooper, shot and killed himself in a
fit of delirium tremens during the summer campaign of 1867.

The enlisted men also drank to excess, making whiskey the curse
of this and every regiment. The recruits came from diverse ethnic,
economic, and educational origins. Many had wartime experience,
but as a whole they contrasted unfavorably with the bright, motivated youth of the Civil War years. Oppressed by hard service and
harsh discipline, drawn by tales of gold in the Rocky Mountains,

they deserted by the score. By the beginning of 1867, out of 963 recruits 80 had deserted.

The officers also exhibited diverse backgrounds. The oldest was Captain William Thompson, fifty-four, a former Iowa congressman who had commanded one of Custer's mutinous regiments in Texas. The youngest captain, not only in the regiment but the regular army, was twenty-two-year-old Louis M. Hamilton, grandson of Alexander Hamilton and an able officer. Captain Edward Myers, a German immigrant, and Lieutenant Myles Moylan had come up from the ranks. Lieutenants Henry Jackson and Henry J. Nowlan had served in the British army, while the daredevil Irishman, Captain Myles W. Keogh, had fought in the Papal Zouaves in Italy. Lieutenant William W. Cooke hailed from a wealthy family in Canada, Lieutenant Edward G. Mathey from France. Lieutenant Donald McIntosh was a half-blood of Scotch and Indian parentage. Captain Robert M. West boasted a brevet of brigadier general in the volunteers, young and capable Major Joel Elliott no brevet at all.

The Seventh, then, as Libbie Custer recognized, was "a medley of incongruous elements," and they fell to bickering as soon as they began to come together. Ill feeling arose between volunteers, West Pointers, and appointees direct from civil life; between "rankers" and officers who felt that shoulder straps did not convert a former enlisted man into a gentleman; and between the commanding officer's "loyalists" and those who did not like him.

Custer's youth, success, and pride in his record excited jealousy or simply disgust in many. The officer who most deeply and abidingly detested Custer was Captain Frederick W. Benteen, a cranky but able troop leader who had been brevetted colonel for bravery in the western armies during the war. Captain West joined Benteen in opposing Custer. By contrast, the Custer clique respected and even venerated their leader. Among them were brother Tom, Moylan (who owed his commission to Custer), Captain George W. Yates (an old Monroe friend who had served with him on Pleasonton's staff), Lieutenant Thomas B. Weir (veteran of Custer's staff in Texas), Lieutenant Algernon E. Smith ("Fresh" Smith, in contrast to "Salt" Smith, an old sailor), and others.

"To bring that motley crowd into military subjection," Libbie recalled, posed a hard task for her husband. He knew the solution. Libbie must "neither look for fidelity nor friendship in its best sense," he counseled her, "until the whole of them had been in a fight together; that it was on the battle-field, when all faced death together, where the truest affection was formed among soldiers." So it had been in the Civil War. It was not to be in the Seventh; far from healing, the rifts grew ever wider with the passing years.

Custer's introduction to the Great Plains and their native inhabitants came promptly. If the heavy travel across Kansas and the rapid progress of railroad construction made the Indians restless, the Indians also made the military authorities restless. On the northern Plains, in December 1866, Red Cloud's Sioux had wiped out Captain William J. Fetterman and eighty men near Fort Phil Kearny. Although the Cheyennes, Arapahoes, Kiowas, and Comanches of the central Plains had not been at war for more than a year, Generals Sherman and Hancock thought they might be inclined to follow Red Cloud's example once the spring grass sprouted. Actually, with the classic ambiguity that characterized so many confrontations between whites and Indians, virtually all the chiefs wanted peace, while their unruly young warriors toyed with visions of raids against white travelers and settlers.

A show of force, Sherman and Hancock decided, might cow the Indians or provoke them into a fight that would teach them a lasting lesson. Late in March 1867, gathering a force of fourteen hundred infantry, cavalry, and artillery from a half-dozen of his forts, Hancock moved down the Santa Fe Trail to the Arkansas River. Custer headed the mounted component, eight companies of the Seventh Cavalry. It was the first time so much of the regiment had assembled, and on the march from Fort Harker to Fort Larned they practiced mounted evolutions, complete with echoing bugle calls, flashing sabers, and snapping guidons.

Dealing with the Southern Cheyenne and Sioux bands camped on Pawnee Fork above Fort Larned proved more difficult. Smith, Gibbs, and Indian Agent Edward W. Wynkoop told Hancock that the Indians were more frightened than belligerent. The Cheyennes had vivid memories of Sand Creek, two and a half years earlier, when Colonel John M. Chivington and Colorado militia had nearly obliterated the village of Black Kettle, leading peace chief of the Cheyennes. The chiefs who met with Hancock at Fort Larned on April 12 trusted him no more than they did Chivington or any other soldier

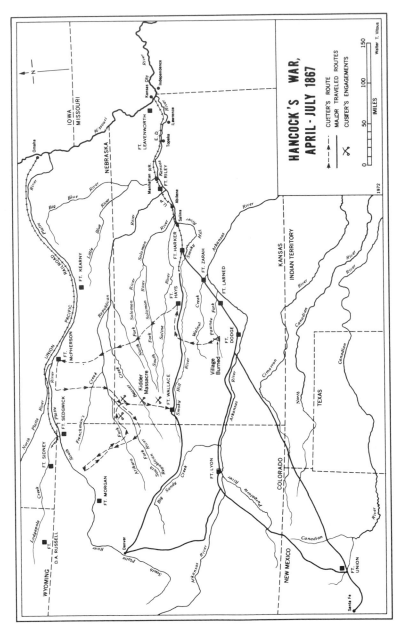

Hancock's War, April–July 1876

chief, and they failed to reassure him of their peaceful intentions. The general therefore announced that he would march up to their village for further talks.

Predictably, the Indians disliked this idea. Large groups of mounted warriors demonstrated on the column's front and flanks, and on April 14 a phalanx of colorfully bedecked Indians drew up across the line of march. A parley averted a clash, but the soldiers continued to advance. Camping near the village of some 250 tipis, Hancock ordered the chiefs to come in for another talk the next morning. During the night, however, a scout alerted him that the Indians were slipping away. He had Custer throw a cordon of cavalry around the encampment, but the lodges were deserted.

The flight of the Indians, which even Custer ascribed to fear, convinced Hancock of their treacherous disposition. "This looks like the commencement of war," he concluded, and dispatched Custer with the cavalry in pursuit. Scattering into small parties, the fugitives left no trail large enough to follow (one of many lessons the fledgling Indian fighter learned about his new business on this campaign).

After a rapid march northward, Custer reached the Smoky Hill Road. He found it a shambles—stage stations burned, stock run off, and citizens butchered. When a courier brought word of these outrages to Hancock, he decided to burn the abandoned Indian village. Agent Wynkoop and Colonel Smith protested, pointing out that fear of another Sand Creek had set off the stampede and that these particular Indians may not have committed the depredations on the Smoky Hill. Guilty or not, Hancock decided, "I am satisfied that the Indian village was a nest of conspirators," and he had it put to the torch. In one judgment he was right: the events of April 12–15, 1867, did indeed mark the commencement of war.

For Custer they marked the beginning of a summer of mounting frustration. The Sioux and Cheyennes—whole families, not just warriors—had easily given him the slip. On the march he had taken off on his own in pursuit of a buffalo—a foolish act in the midst of Indian country—then in the chase had accidentally put a bullet in the brain of Libbie's favorite horse, Custis Lee, and found himself dumped unceremoniously in the midst of rolling plains, alone, lost, and confronting an enraged buffalo bull. Only his fabled luck got him out of that embarrassing scrape: the buffalo lost interest, and his command found him.

Putting in at Fort Hays before continuing the search for the quarry, he found himself suddenly immobilized. Forage thought to have been stockpiled had been delayed by high water. Week after soggy week the command lay in camp near Fort Hays, drenched by cold rains and floundering in sticky mud, waiting for forage and the spring grass. A constant stream of despairing letters came from Libbie, fidgeting in miserable loneliness at Fort Riley. Desertions soared; in six weeks ninety men went over the hill.

In Custer these reverses brought the petulant boy to the surface. He grew "depressed," "of somber mien," remembered his friend, *Harpers Weekly* artist Theodore Davis, who "never saw him so moody." Officers found him an overbearing martinet. "He is the most complete example of a petty tyrant that I have ever seen," wrote Captain Albert Barnitz, once a loyal follower, to his wife. "You would be filled with utter amazement, if I were to give you a few instances of his cruelty to the men, and discourtesy to the officers." When six men slipped into Fort Hays without permission to buy tinned delicacies at the post sutler's store, Custer had their heads shaved so as to bare half the skull and then paraded them through camp for all to see—this, Barnitz wrote in his journal, "to their own great humiliation, and the exceeding mortification, disgrace, and disgust of all right-minded officers and men in camp."

Custer's malaise magnified obstacles that he would normally have brushed aside. Although prodded by Hancock and Smith, not until the end of May did he judge his command ready to take the field.

By this time Indian depredations had shifted largely from the Smoky Hill to the Platte, in Nebraska. The Platte Road was the principal route to California and Colorado and the line of the Union Pacific Railroad, then building west from Omaha. Although Nebraska fell within the Department of the Platte, Custer was to lead six companies of the Seventh northward to Fort McPherson and from there sweep the belt of plains between the Republican and Platte rivers free of Indians.

Near Fort McPherson, Custer conferred with Pawnee Killer, chief of the Sioux band whose lodges, together with those of the Cheyennes, Hancock had burned near Fort Larned. Pawnee Killer professed peace, and Custer took him at his word. Actually, Pawnee Killer's Sioux, rather than the Cheyennes, had been responsible for the havoc wrought on the Smoky Hill Road that had prompted Hancock to fire the deserted village.

General Sherman thought Custer too trusting, and he told him so when the two met at Fort McPherson on June 17. He also gave Custer instructions: scout south to the forks of the Republican; put in for supplies and further orders at Fort Sedgwick, on the South Platte in Colorado; and then scour the headwaters of the Republican.

Sherman also made some vague remarks about Libbie joining her husband, implicitly by coming to Fort McPherson. This reinforced what had been uppermost in Custer's mind ever since leaving Fort Riley in March. Libbie had shared his tent near Fort Hays for two weeks in May, and now he eagerly sought another chance for her to join him. Assuming that he would be near the Platte all summer and fall, he wrote to her to come as soon as she could. Sherman had thought she would travel through Omaha by rail. Custer had other ideas. "If you can get a chance to come to Wallace," he said, referring to the Smoky Hill post in far western Kansas, "I will send a squadron there to meet you."

Detaching a squadron (two companies) in mid-campaign for this purpose seems not to have struck Custer as unusual. Indeed, whether consciously or not, his every major decision for the rest of the operation had more to do with Libbie than with Sherman, Indians, his mission, or the welfare of his command.

He did not put in at Sedgwick for supplies. Instead he sent a small detachment under Major Elliott to see if there were fresh orders, while dispatching a wagon train and two companies south to Fort Wallace for supplies—and Libbie. He explained that the route to Wallace was easier for wagons. Wallace, however, still distant from end of track, had difficulty provisioning its own garrison, while Sedgwick enjoyed direct access to the Union Pacific Railroad.

On June 24, while the command waited on the Republican, a raiding party tried to stampede the cavalry's horses. Custer signaled a parley, and again he and Pawnee Killer had a talk. After it broke off inconclusively, a small Indian decoy party worked a favorite stratagem, lured a company in pursuit, and led it into an ambush. Only the quick thinking and able leadership of Captain Hamilton averted casualties. Returning from Fort Wallace, meantime, the supply train and escort had to fight their way through swarming Sioux and Cheyenne warriors. They reached the command's camp on the Republican on June 27. To Custer's vast relief, Libbie had not been at Wallace and thus had not ridden the wagon train into the middle of an Indian war.

Major Elliott and his eleven-man party came into camp the next day. They had traveled rapidly and escaped detection. He brought no new orders. Had Custer sent to Sedgwick rather than Wallace for supplies, however, he would have received the new orders that reached Sedgwick the day after Elliott left. The post commander entrusted their delivery to Lieutenant Lyman S. Kidder and a ten-man detail of the Second Cavalry. Kidder did not enjoy Elliott's good fortune. Intercepted by Pawnee Killer, he and all his men fell in a running battle. Later Custer discovered their stripped and mutilated bodies tracing the course of the fight.

Operating under his original orders, Custer combed the headwaters of the Republican. Despite the orders, his movement so far west is hard to understand. Sherman clearly intended him to try to find and fight the Indians who had been striking at the travel routes. Clearly, Sioux and Cheyenne raiders were around the forks of the Republican and on the Smoky Hill in the vicinity of Fort Wallace. Also, convincing evidence placed the villages of these war parties on Beaver Creek, roughly midway between the Smoky Hill and the forks of the Republican. Yet Custer marched westward across waterless, sun-baked plains to the South Platte, deep in Colorado.

Not only did this march break down both men and horses, it brought the command close enough to the travel routes to raise, once more, the specter of desertion. While near Fort McPherson, thirty-two men had decamped, and on July 6–7, on the South Platte, thirty-four slipped off in twos and threes. Furious at one party brazenly riding away in full view of the command, Custer ordered Major Elliott with two officers and a handful of soldiers to give chase and "bring none in alive." They brought six in alive, although three bore gunshot wounds, one of whom later died. Custer loudly denied these men medical attention and then quietly ordered the surgeon to care for them.

On July 13 the column limped into camp near Fort Wallace. Neither horses nor men could take the field again until rested, refitted, and resupplied. Custer had several reasons for leaving the command at Wallace and going east to Harker or Riley: to seek new orders, to oversee the dispatch of supplies, to round up fresh horses (though not, as later alleged, to obtain rations, for Wallace had a month's supply; and not to forward medicine to combat the cholera epidemic, for it had not yet struck Wallace). However thin the excuses, no one would have censured him for boarding a stagecoach and heading east.

But the coaches ran on a highly uncertain schedule. Instead, Custer assembled four officers and seventy-two men and on July 15 embarked on a forced march of 150 miles in some 55 hours of almost unbroken travel. Heat and thirst exhausted the men and took their toll on the horses. "They do say that he just squandered that cavalry along the road!" wrote Captain Barnitz from Wallace. At one point Custer noted the absence of his spare mare and her attendant, and he sent a sergeant and six men back in search. Indians waylaid the detail and shot down two of the troopers. Custer refused to take time to look for them. The infantry guard at Downer's mail station later went out and found them, one dead and one wounded. Near Fort Hays twenty of the escort deserted, but the officers climbed in their ambulances and pushed on to Fort Harker, arriving about two hours after midnight on July 19. After a hurried conversation with the sleep-befogged district commander, Colonel A. J. Smith, Custer boarded the morning train for Fort Riley. At last he had joined Libbie and could personally conduct her to Fort Wallace.

But next day a clearheaded Smith heard the story of Custer's dash across Kansas. He promptly ordered his young subordinate placed in arrest and, with General Hancock's backing, preferred charges against him. Custer stood accused of absence without leave from his command and the catchall "conduct to the prejudice of good order and military discipline," the latter for overworking horses and using them and other government equipment for private business, and for his failure to look after the two men shot near Downer's Station. An angry Captain West brought another charge against Custer for ordering deserters shot without trial and refusing them medical attention.

Custer had knowingly challenged the system and lost, as Libbie acknowledged in a letter to a Michigan friend: "When he ran the risk of a court-martial in leaving Wallace he did it expecting the consequences . . . and we are quite determined not to live apart again, even if he leaves the army otherwise so delightful to us."

Despite this confession Custer fought the charges vigorously. For a month, beginning in mid-September 1867, the court sat at Fort Leavenworth and took testimony. The verdict, announced on October 11, was guilty on all counts, though with no criminality attached. The sentence was suspension from rank and command and forfeiture of pay for one year. On November 18, General Sherman announced

General Grant's approval of the findings, at the same time remarking on the leniency of the court in view of the gravity of the charges.

Thus ingloriously did Custer's first Indian campaign come to an end. Throughout he had acted uncharacteristically, at least as judged by his Civil War record. He let bad weather and supply failings intimidate him. He let Pawnee Killer dupe him and persisted in regarding this chief as friendly despite persuasive evidence to the contrary, including attacks on his command. He did not press the enemy tribesmen with his old aggressiveness, did not even try very hard to find them, and in fact marched away from where all signs indicated they were located. He treated both officers and men with an arrogance and cruelty that aggravated the bad feelings in the officer corps, alienated the enlisted complement, and worsened morale already depressed by campaign hardships. And finally, he so openly and callously subordinated the mission and the safety and welfare of the command to his determination to unite with his wife that he deepened the wounds already opening in the regiment.

Custer had always been adept at self-delusion, at reshaping facts and observations to produce pleasing results. This trait manifested itself in a fairly harmless tendency to exaggeration, "not from any willful disregard for the truth," observed a friendly fellow officer, "but because he saw things as bigger than they really were. He did not distort the truth; he magnified it." Thus his eyes counted more Confederates or Indians or buffalo than there actually were. His hunting conquests involved longer and more accurate shots and larger kills than strict accuracy condoned. His marches covered more miles in fewer hours than the official itinerist recorded. A plains sunset surpassed the colors of Bierstadt or Church, the western badlands the grandeur of Yosemite Valley.

But this tendency, subconscious though it may have been, could also be put to the service of self-glorification or self-justification, even at the expense of others. In a series of letters written for publication immediately after the campaign of 1867, he tortured facts and manipulated chronology so as to vindicate himself and blame Hancock for the summer's failure and his own disgrace. Later he had second thoughts, and in his memoirs he shifted the onus from Hancock to the Indian Bureau. Not entirely without reason, however, did Captain Benteen refer to Custer's memoirs as *My Lie on the Plains*.

What wrought so stark a change in personality and behavior?

What caused the peevish, mean, haughty, selfish, unreasonable boy to rise and seize control from the mature major general?

Much of the answer must lie in the stresses induced by the new world into which Custer had been abruptly thrust. It transported him from the heroics of glorious war to the lonely boredom of a quiet border outpost, from the acclaim of the nation to the anonymity of distant and unnoticed idleness. It removed him from command of several thousand men who adored him and reacted instantly and unquestioningly to his every order and desire, and it gave him command of several hundred men who followed him without enthusiasm and included many who loathed him, disparaged him, and undermined his leadership whenever they could. Most Civil War veterans who remained in the army experienced the same shock in more or less measure. All too many took refuge in the bottle.

Both personally and professionally, Custer's new world imposed new and hard terms not easily mastered. Militarily, the country itself levied requirements that had to be respected. The rolling, treeless plains, the great distances and rudimentary transportation, the sparse population, the widely scattered sources of water, and the extremes of weather both summer and winter created a military environment radically different from the Virginia countryside in which Custer had learned to soldier.

Demanding even greater military respect were the Indians, who tested their adversaries in ways undreamed by Jeb Stuart's horsemen. Their mode of warfare, their adaptation to the land, indeed their very culture had to be learned through experience tempered by humility. Veterans such as Colonel Smith and Major Gibbs had learned, but newcomers such as Custer and most of his officers found Indian warfare perplexing and at last defeating.

Defeated by the Indians, by the land, by the weather, by his own officers and men, by his superiors, and ultimately by himself, Custer may well have been plunged by the setbacks and frustrations of 1867 into what a later generation would call an identity crisis. With the glory days behind and the future unclear but apparently unpromising, he had to sort out and come to grips with who he was and who he wanted to be. The civilian world still looked enticing, especially in offering the possibility of wealth and the certainty of a married life untroubled by long separations.

Yet the military still pulled at him, and at Libbie, too. If he was to remain a soldier, come to terms with his new world, gain control of the juvenile who had taken charge of him, he needed the one thing that had served him in the past—victory on the battlefield, some frontier version of Winchester or Cedar Creek. With a year's suspension from duty looming, that did not seem an imminent prospect.

CHAPTER 4

Total War

Headquarters, Department of the Missouri,
In the Field, Fort Hays, Kansas,
September 24, 1868.

To General G. A. Custer, Monroe, Michigan
Generals Sherman, Sully and myself, and nearly all the officers of your regiment, have asked for you, and I hope the application will be successful. Can you come at once? Eleven companies of your regiment will move about the 1st of October against the hostile Indians. . . .

P. H. Sheridan,
Major General Commanding

CUSTER could have wished no more resounding vindication. Two months short of the end of his suspension he had been asked by high and low alike to return to the Seventh Cavalry and lead it against Indians.

Nor had the court-martial been a hard blow. The Custers and their friends saw it as a persecution contrived by General Hancock to divert attention from the failure of his spring and summer operations. Reinforcing that interpretation, General Sheridan himself thought his friend badly treated and said so. Moreover, Sheridan's firm Reconstruction measures in New Orleans had led President Johnson to relieve him and, much to Custer's pleasure, assign him to replace Hancock in command of the Department of the Missouri. Sheridan intended to take a long leave, and he advertised his feelings about the court-martial by inviting the Custers to occupy his quarters at Fort Leavenworth all winter. Gratefully, they accepted. After a gay social season, during which Custer also began writing his Civil War memoirs, they returned to Monroe for an idle summer. Here, in the autumn of 1868, the invigorating telegram found them restlessly awaiting the end of their banishment.

Custer returned to duty at a critical time, not only in his own career but in the unfolding relationship between the U.S. government and the western Indians. In the year of Custer's absence the pendulum of government policy had swung wildly between two extremes, from pugnacity to appeasement and back to the truculent militarism that prompted his recall from enforced furlough.

The oscillations in policy reflected divisions in public sentiment. Easterners tended to favor conciliation. Peace and humanitarian groups, and their friends in the Indian Bureau, called for kindness, generosity, and tolerance toward the Indians. Treat them fairly and justly, the argument ran, and they would respond reasonably and submissively. Most westerners ridiculed this as absurd idealism and demanded subjection and control by military force. Many even championed extermination of all Indians, or all who resisted the Great Father's dictates.

The army sided with the West in favoring military solutions but believed in tempering them with the humanity sought by the East. No officer of importance sanctioned extermination. Although some of General Sherman's militant rhetoric made him sound like an exterminationist, he never advocated the obliteration of a whole people. The proper approach, as most military authorities saw it, was to assign the army sole responsibility for Indians; it could then act the stern but kindly father, dispensing harsh punishment or benevolent supervision as necessary. For more than a decade Congress debated the transfer of the Indian Bureau from the Interior to the War Department, but no bill ever passed.

On one goal the two sides agreed. They believed that all Indians should be cleared from the plains between the Platte and Arkansas rivers and given new homes to the north and south. This belt of territory had become the principal funnel of the postwar westward movement, with railroads advancing up the Platte and Smoky Hill, heavy wagon traffic flowing on the Santa Fe Trail up the Arkansas, and farming settlements creeping up these and other streams draining the High Plains. The militarists and pacifists differed on means, but the army, because of the well-publicized effects of Hancock's clumsy campaign, found it expedient to go along with a major peace offensive aimed at the common objective.

In July 1867, therefore, Congress created a peace commission to negotiate with the Plains Indians and persuade them to withdraw to reservations north of Nebraska and south of Kansas. In mid-

October, in the pleasant wooded valley of Medicine Lodge Creek in southern Kansas, the commissioners met with chiefs of the Kiowas, Comanches, Cheyennes, and Arapahoes and talked them into signing treaties and taking their people south into Indian Territory.

The Medicine Lodge council illustrated the sham of such talks and the obstacles inherent in negotiations between the two races. Each looked at the other from a cultural framework of vastly different attitudes, assumptions, values, and political, social, and spiritual organization. Even with scouts or interpreters who had feet planted firmly in both worlds, the chances for genuine communication and understanding were meager. Captain Albert Barnitz, commanding one of the Seventh Cavalry companies guarding the commission, captured the essence of the proceedings in his diary. The Cheyennes, he wrote, "*have no idea that* they are giving up . . . the country which they claim as their own, the country north of the Arkansas. The treaty all amounts to nothing, and we will certainly have another war sooner or later."

Together with the Fort Laramie treaties with the Sioux and other tribes of the northern Plains, the Medicine Lodge treaties represented a high point of the peace movement. But Barnitz was right. The Cheyennes had no idea they had surrendered their traditional buffalo ranges. They spent the winter south of the Arkansas, but in July 1868 they came to Fort Larned to draw rations and other presents promised in the treaty. As reproof for a raid on a Kaw Indian village, the Indian agent withheld some firearms that had been promised. In foul humor, a war party set off to raid the Pawnees, but instead fell on the white settlements on the Solomon and Saline rivers. In a two-day sweep they robbed and burned cabins, ran off stock, killed fifteen men, and ravished five women.

The war forecast by Barnitz had erupted, shattering the peace movement and restoring the army to influence. For the rest of the summer Cheyenne raiders rampaged across Kansas. Sheridan's troopers of the Seventh and Tenth Cavalry conducted a precarious holding operation.

The general commissioned his aide, Major George A. Forsyth, to enlist a special company of seasoned frontiersmen to guard the railroad up the Smoky Hill. On September 17, on the Arikara Fork of the Republican, Cheyennes and Sioux (the latter under Custer's nemesis, Pawnee Killer) attacked the scouts. For a week, entrenched on an island in the dry stream bed, Forsyth and his men endured a siege punctuated by massed mounted charges. Finally, black "buffalo soldiers" of the Tenth Cavalry came to the rescue. The Battle of Beecher's Island dramatized the intensity of the conflict.

Also in September, to relieve pressure on the Kansas settlements, Sheridan sent a column against the Cheyennes south of the Arkansas. As commander of the District of the Upper Arkansas, Brevet Brigadier General Alfred Sully, lieutenant colonel of the Third Infantry, commanded. Major Elliott and eight companies of the Seventh Cavalry formed the mounted arm of the expedition. Sully had done good work against Indians in Dakota four years earlier, but now he grew timid, setting the pace in an ambulance. After only a week's march he turned back. "Oh, these sand hills are interminable," he explained.

Less than a week later, reflecting widespread disgust with Sully's lethargy, Sheridan's telegram sped over the wires to Monroe, Michigan.

Sheridan needed someone of Custer's vigor and tenacity to carry out bold new measures that he and Sherman had settled upon. Both generals had pioneered in the application of "total war," in ruthlessly subjecting an entire enemy population, not just the fighting men, to the horrors of war. In the Shenandoah Valley and the March to the Sea across Georgia, each had deliberately set out to spread such poverty and despair as to destroy both the ability and the will to fight. Now they planned the same treatment for the Indians—to search them out in their winter camps; kill or drive them from their lodges; destroy their ponies, food, and shelter; and hound them mercilessly across a frigid landscape until they gave up. If women and children fell victim to such methods, it was regrettable, but justified because it resolved the issue quickly and decisively and thus more humanely.

Total war meant winter campaigning, for rarely could the Indians be caught in the summer. In winter they were at their most vulnerable. Food ran short, ponies grew weak, war ardor cooled, and they holed up in their lodges along some distant stream for weeks or months at a time. If they could be found, they could sometimes be surprised and dealt a decisive blow.

Yet winter campaigning involved grave dangers for the campaigners. The sudden, fierce storms and plunging temperatures of the Plains could paralyze supply operations, annihilate mule and horse herds, and strike down men by starvation and exposure. When the savvy old mountain man Jim Bridger heard of Sheridan's plan, he hurried out from Saint Louis to warn against it.

But both generals were determined to take the risk. "These Indians require to be soundly whipped," declared Sherman, "and the ringleaders in the present trouble hung, their ponies killed, and such destruction of their property as will make them very poor." This had been successfully tried in the past, even in winter, but it remained to Sherman and Sheridan to raise it to the level of deliberate, sustained doctrine. "Go ahead in your own way," Sherman ordered his subordinate, "and I will back you with my whole authority. If it results in the utter annihilation of these Indians, it is but the result of what they have been warned again and again."

Early on October 4, in a buoyant mood, the lieutenant colonel of the Seventh Cavalry stepped off a special railroad car at Ellsworth, Kansas, and was escorted by a staff officer to General Sheridan's breakfast table at nearby Fort Hays. Custer met with a warm welcome, he wrote Libbie, and Sheridan declared that "now he could smoke a cigar in peace once more as Custer had never failed him."

Sheridan outlined his plan. It involved not only total war and a winter campaign but another strategy that would come to mark his approach to Indian fighting—converging columns. The winter camps of most of the Indians, he believed, lay to the south, on the Canadian and Washita rivers in Indian Territory. Against this area he intended to launch three expeditions: one, under Major Eugene A. Carr, southeast from Fort Lyon, Colorado; a second, under Major Andrew W. Evans, eastward from Fort Bascom, New Mexico. These would act as "beaters in" for the third and strongest, marching southward from Fort Dodge, on the Arkansas.

Technically, the last would be led by General Sully, as commander of the District of the Upper Arkansas. But Sheridan meant to be present himself, and he clearly meant for Custer to be the key field commander. "Custer," Sheridan said, "I rely in every thing upon you and shall send you on this expedition without giving you any orders leaving you to act entirely upon your judgment."

The Seventh Cavalry lay in camp on Cavalry Creek, forty-two miles south of Dodge, when Custer rode in on October 11. As Captain Barnitz wrote to his wife, "General Custer arrived (with his hair cut short, and a perfect menagerie of Scotch fox hounds!) . . . and on the very evening of his arrival sent out three columns in search of Indian encampments!" His electric energy roused the command, and nearly everyone welcomed him warmly. Even Captain West, his bitterest enemy of the year before, made peace overtures. Custer ac-

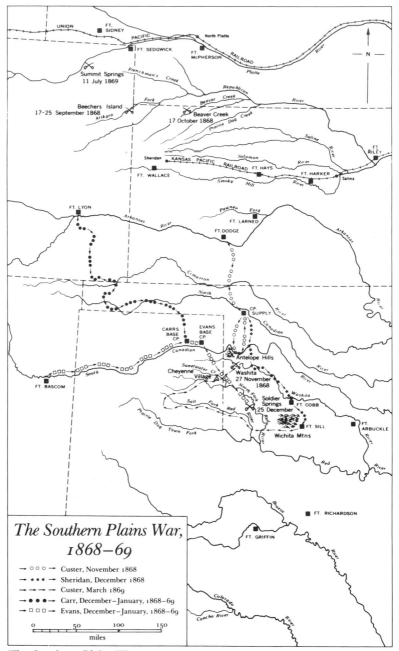

The Southern Plains War, 1868–69

cepted them with formal correctness but refused to shake West's hand in friendship.

Delays plagued the campaign. For one thing, rations and other supplies did not get to Fort Dodge when scheduled. Awaiting them, the Seventh Cavalry had to return to the Arkansas and camp near Dodge for almost a month. For another, a regiment of volunteer cavalry, the Nineteenth Kansas, had been accepted into federal service; under the state's governor, Samuel J. Crawford, it had to be mustered, organized, and marched to join the expedition. On November 12, however, with the Kansans still absent, Sully and Custer led eleven companies of the Seventh Cavalry, five companies of infantry, and a long wagon train across the Arkansas and pointed south. A week later the column reached the North Canadian River and at once began building a stockaded supply base, named Camp Supply, to be manned by the infantry while the cavalry took the offensive.

Two such different temperaments as Custer and Sully were bound to clash. The day before reaching the site of Camp Supply, the column cut the fresh trail of an Indian war party of about seventy-five men, riding northward. They could only have come from the very villages the expedition sought, and Custer wanted to take the back trail at once and attack. Sully refused. He would not sanction an offensive move until the Kansas regiment had arrived to bolster the command.

Sully prevailed because Sully commanded. Although a lieutenant colonel like Custer, he served as district commander in his brevet grade of brigadier general. But as Custer quickly perceived, Camp Supply lay beyond the boundaries of Sully's district. Moreover, when the Kansans arrived, Colonel Crawford would rank them both. Army regulations provided that when volunteers and regulars served together, brevet rank took precedence. As a brevet major general, Custer pointed out, he would rank both Sully and Crawford, and on that grounds he claimed seniority.

With his staff General Sheridan rode in on November 21. Applauding Custer's aggressive spirit, he resolved the dispute over rank by sending Sully back to Fort Harker to command his district.

Now Custer would have his chance at the back trail. Two days later, November 23, the troopers emerged from their tents in the predawn darkness to confront a raging blizzard that had already dumped a foot of snow on the ground. Custer was delighted. If only the snow remained for a week, he promised Sheridan, he would snare the enemy. The companies formed, the band played "The Girl I Left Behind Me," and the Seventh Cavalry vanished into the swirling snow.

To the south, in the Washita River Valley, some six thousand Cheyennes, Arapahoes, Kiowas, and Comanches had laid out their winter camps. Farthest upstream on the west were fifty-one lodges of Black Kettle's band. Long the foremost peace chief of the Cheyennes, he had suffered fearfully at Sand Creek in 1864. Even so, his dedication to peace had not wavered.

Not all of the chief's followers shared his sentiments. The young men, in particular, favored war, and some had helped make the trail northward that had excited Custer. Like all the other bands camped on the Washita, Black Kettle's could not be characterized according to the white people's simplistic labels of "peaceful" or "hostile." These Indians were neither, and they were both. Some wanted peace, others war, and the latter defied their chiefs to raid the Kansas settlements.

Down the Washita from these camps, at the old military post of Fort Cobb, General Sherman had set up an agency to oversee such Indians as wanted to settle on their new reservations and abide by the Medicine Lodge treaties. This responsibility had fallen to Sherman rather than the Indian Bureau because Congress, distrusting the civilian authorities, had decreed that the funds appropriated to carry out the treaties be spent under his supervision. To Colonel William B. Hazen fell the difficult task of deciding which Indians should be judged peaceful and which hostile. Custer knew Hazen as the officer who, eight years earlier, had placed him in arrest for failing to break up a fistfight at West Point.

On November 20, the day before Sheridan reached Camp Supply, Black Kettle came to Fort Cobb to convince Hazen of his peaceable character. In this he succeeded, but he had to admit that he could not control his young men. "Some will not listen," he said, and "I have not been able to keep them all at home." Fearing to offer sanctuary he could not guarantee, exactly the situation that had led to Sand Creek, Hazen advised Black Kettle to make his peace with the "great war chief" on the Arkansas, General Sheridan.

As Black Kettle headed home, the Seventh Cavalry floundered through deep snow. The back trail that Custer had intended to follow lay hidden beneath the snow, but on November 26, at the crossing of the Canadian near the landmark Antelope Hills, he sent Major

Elliott and three companies upstream in search of another trail. Within twelve miles Elliott found one. Made after the storm by a hundred warriors, it could not be more than two days old. Pointing south, it had to lead to the objective.

This word, carried to Custer by a courier, set off a whirlwind of activity. Sending orders back to Elliott to follow the trail, Custer hurriedly prepared the rest of the regiment for battle. In less than half an hour the command set forth on a forced march through snow now melting under a bright sun and balling heavily on the horses' feet. Most of the wagon train, with a token guard, followed at a leisurely pace. Under Lieutenant James M. Bell, regimental quarter-master, seven wagons loaded with ammunition toiled in the rear to keep up as the companies pushed forward. At sunset they cut the Indian trail, and at 9:00 P.M. they overtook Elliott in the Washita Valley. For four more hours the regiment crept cautiously down the valley as the temperature plummeted and a hard crust froze on top of the snow. Men and animals suffered acutely from exhaustion, cold, and hunger. After midnight, on a ridge overlooking the valley, the Osage trailer Little Beaver whispered to Custer, "Heap Injuns down there."

Below, in a timbered river bend on the south side of the Washita, lay Black Kettle's village. Only the day before he had returned from Fort Cobb, and only hours before he had held a council with other leaders of his band. He told them about his meeting with Colonel Hazen and of the need to make peace with the white war chief Sher-idan. One of the elders related that, earlier in the day, a Kiowa war party had come in with a report of a soldier trail to the north aimed at the Washita. Others discounted the story, arguing that the snow and cold would keep the soldiers in their tents. The meeting broke up with a decision to move the village next day to a new location downstream, where other Indians were camped, and to send emis-saries to find General Sheridan and inform him of the Cheyennes' wish to make peace.

The Cheyennes had hardly turned to their sleeping robes, how-ever, when Custer assembled his officers and sketched his plan of attack. "General," asked old Captain Thompson when he had fin-ished, "suppose we find more Indians there than we can handle?" Custer answered gruffly: "Huh, all I am afraid of is we won't find half enough. There are not Indians enough in the country to whip the Seventh Cavalry."

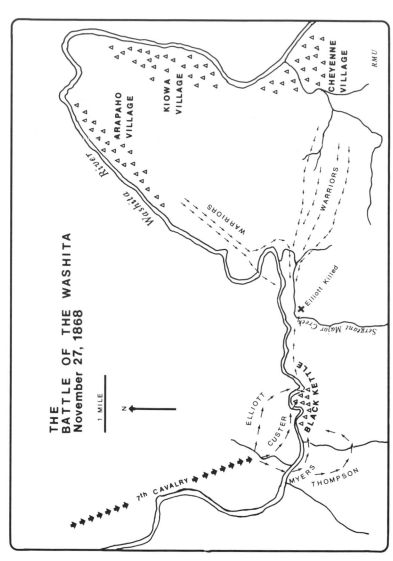

The Battle of the Washita, November 27, 1868

By dawn, November 27, the Seventh Cavalry had been stealthily deployed in four components with orders for a simultaneous attack: Major Elliott and three companies from the northeast; Captain Thompson and two companies from the south; Captain Myers and two companies down the valley from the west; and Custer himself, with four companies, Lieutenant Cooke's company of picked sharp-shooters, the band, and the scouts, from the north.

At first light a single rifle shot rang out in the village. Buglers blasted the staccato notes of "Charge," and the band struck up "Garry Owen." The instruments froze almost at once, but from this moment forward the rollicking Irish drinking tune would be the regimental battle song of the Seventh Cavalry.

The companies under Custer and Elliott forded the Washita and stormed into the village. "I rode right beside Custer just ahead of the command," recalled Chief of Scouts Ben Clark. "He would allow no one to get ahead of him. His horse cleared the stream at one jump and up the bank we went and into the village." Custer fired his pistol at one Indian and bowled over another with his mount and then, with Clark, took station on a low hill at the south edge of the camp to direct the battle.

Surprised in their sleeping robes, half-clad Indians poured from their tipis and ran in all directions. Shouting cavalrymen blasted the fleeing forms with six-shooters, slashed them with sabers, or ran them down with galloping horses. Delayed, Thompson and Myers at last attacked from the south and west. Thompson's approach failed to reach far enough to the east, leaving a large gap between him and Elliott. Many Indians escaped through this opening. Others raced to the riverbank and, standing in icy water, fired over the bank at the soldiers. Still others gathered in ravines and clumps of trees to put up a ragged defense. Mounted together on a pony, Black Kettle and his wife reached the river, only to be struck by bullets and dropped into the water, both dead.

So sudden and overwhelming was the attack of eight hundred horsemen from four directions that Custer had possession of the village within ten minutes. Individual encounters crackled across the battlefield as troopers tried to wipe out pockets of warriors and warily circled tipis that still sheltered people.

From the command-post knoll Ben Clark spotted a large group of women and children running up the slopes to the south, Myers's men giving chase and firing into them. Clark asked Custer if he wanted those people killed. "No," replied Custer. "Ride out there and give the officer commanding my compliments and ask him to stop it. Take them to the village and put them in a big tipi and station a guard over them." Clark followed orders, thus giving the troops the first of their prisoners.

Fleeing in confusion, the Indians inflicted few casualties on their assailants—four hit mortally and hardly more than a dozen wounded. One of the former, however, was the able and well-liked Captain Hamilton, pierced through the heart by a bullet in the first moments of the charge. Also, troopers carried in Captain Barnitz, shot in a personal duel with a warrior. Barnitz killed his opponent but took a bullet in the abdomen that everyone believed to be fatal. Astonishingly, it had missed all the vital organs. Barnitz recovered but had to retire on medical disability.

In the first rush Lieutenant Edward S. Godfrey had led a platoon of West's company around the south side of the village and had begun scooping up knots of grazing ponies. Gradually a growing herd was assembled on the slopes south of the valley. Continuing this mission, Godfrey and his men crossed to the north bank of the river and drifted farther down the valley. His veteran sergeants warned him against getting too far away from the command. Halting the platoon, the lieutenant climbed a low elevation to scan the valley to the east. "Peering over the ridge," he remembered, "I was amazed to find that as far as I could see down the well wooded, tortuous valley there were tepees—tepees. Not only could I see tepees, but mounted warriors scurrying in our direction." Fighting a rearguard action back to the village, Godfrey reported his discovery to a startled Custer.

Godfrey also informed Custer that while downstream he had heard heavy firing across the river. Major Elliott and a detachment had been seen to ride off in that direction, in pursuit of fleeing Indians. Godfrey suggested that Elliott might be under attack. "I hardly think so," replied Custer, "as Captain Myers had been fighting down there all morning and probably would have reported it."

In fact, Elliott was under attack. Sighting a group of Indians escaping to the east, through the uncovered sector between Elliott and Thompson, the major had called for volunteers to pursue. The regiment's sergeant major and eighteen men assembled. "Here goes for a brevet or a coffin," Elliott shouted to a fellow officer, and he galloped off at the head of the contingent. East of the village Elliott and his men ran into a large force of mounted warriors. Another appeared in their rear. Surrounded, he dismounted his followers and had them lie in the tall grass. One by one they were hit as the Indians fired bullets and arrows from higher positions. A final rush ended the unequal fight and left the major and all his men dead.

The warriors who wiped out Elliott were not runaways from Black Kettle's band but Cheyennes and Arapahoes from the villages downstream. By the hundreds they donned their war paint and galloped to the sound of the firing. After slaying Elliott and his men, these fighters, joined by others from a Kiowa village, began to collect in ominous numbers on the hills surrounding the battleground.

The fresh warriors, of unknown numbers, placed Custer in a precarious position. Captive women confirmed Godfrey's report that they came from big villages downstream. Although Quartermaster Bell crashed through an attacking force of Indians to reach the battleground with the ammunition wagons, the vital but weakly defended supply train approached somewhere on the back trail, vulnerable to seizure by a strong enemy body. Of more pressing concern, warriors from the other villages had driven off a small guard and seized the command's haversacks and overcoats, left in the hills in order not to encumber the men in battle.

In keeping with the precepts of total war, Custer's immediate task was to impoverish the enemy. Throwing out skirmishers to fend off the sallies of warriors against his lines, he set the rest of the command to destroying everything of use to the Indians. Troopers knocked down the tipis, set them afire, and heaped the entire contents of the village on leaping bonfires—saddles, clothing, utensils, weapons, ammunition, and the winter supply of dried buffalo meat and other food. Details rounded up the band's ponies, nearly nine hundred, and cut their throats or shot them down with pistols. Warriors on the hillsides howled in rage, and one party tried to slip within rifle range but was driven off. As the men pursued their grim assignment, they also found and laid before Custer photograph albums, unopened mail, and other household items that testified to the romps of Black Kettle's young men through the Kansas settlements.

Speculation over Elliott's whereabouts ran through the command. In the afternoon, as the destruction of the village and pony herd continued, Custer ordered Captain Myers to scout down the valley in search of the missing party. Myers reported riding two miles be-

low the village without finding any sign of them. Under attack by
growing numbers of enemy fighters, Custer decided that he must
pull out without further delay.

As dusk approached, Custer mounted the regiment. With colors
flying and the band playing "Ain't I Glad to Get Out of the Wilderness," the companies advanced boldly down the Washita Valley toward the other Indian villages. Disconcerted, the warriors quickly
drew off to defend their homes. As darkness fell, Custer suddenly
turned and countermarched. A forced night march brought the
column of shivering troopers to their supply train by the next morning, but not until the middle of the afternoon did they finally settle
into camp.

From this camp couriers set forth with official reports. They also
carried a private letter to Sheridan. "We have cleaned Black Kettle
and his band out so thoroughly that they can neither fight, dress,
sleep, eat or ride without sponging upon their friends," Custer wrote
triumphantly. "It was a regular Indian 'Sailor's Creek,'" he added,
referring to the destruction of much of Lee's army on the eve of
Appomattox.

On December 2 the Seventh Cavalry marched proudly into Camp
Supply. The Osage Indian scouts, the contingent of white scouts,
and fifty-three captive Indian women with their children preceded
the command. Company after company, sabers flashing at the salute,
the Seventh Cavalry passed in review before Sheridan and his staff
as the band again gave forth the lilting strains of "Garry Owen."

Only the mystery of Major Elliott dampened the elation. Custer
had convinced himself that, without a guide, Elliott had become lost
and would ultimately find his way back to Camp Supply or Fort
Dodge. Sheridan regarded this "a very unsatisfactory view of the
matter" but conceded that it was "altogether too late to make any
search for him." Sheridan's judgment clouded the effusive congratu-
lations he had first showered on Custer.

Aside from the Elliott matter, Custer had in fact dealt the Cheyennes a severe blow in blood and treasure. Although he reported 103
dead warriors counted on the battlefield, the "count" actually consisted of estimates by company commanders. Based on what Indians
told him, moreover, Custer later raised the toll to three hundred
people killed, wounded, and missing. Indian calculations—a dozen
warriors and twice as many women and children killed—are as im-
probably low as Custer's are high. Equally devastating, Custer's de-

struction of property, especially the slaughter of the ponies, inflicted destitution on Black Kettle's band at the onset of winter, stunned and grieved all the Indians, and scared other groups inclined to stand up to the soldiers. Finally, Custer's dramatic demonstration that soldiers could operate during the winter came as a demoralizing revelation to the Indians.

Now, Sheridan recognized, it remained to finish the job by hounding all the rebellious bands into submission. The Nineteenth Kansas had finally arrived, much worn after wandering, lost, in snow-choked gorges of the Cimarron River. The force now numbered seventeen hundred. On December 7, with Custer in immediate command, Sheridan led the expedition south through winter storms and freezing temperatures.

On the Washita, Sheridan and Custer took a small detachment and examined the battleground of November 27. They found the horribly butchered bodies of Elliott and his men and pieced together the story of how they died. Downstream, the officers inspected the other village sites. Littered with camp gear and provisions in evidence of hasty flight, they extended for six miles along the river. In one some troopers found the body of a white woman and her child, obviously killed when the soldiers attacked the Cheyenne camp upstream. She had been shot in the forehead at close range, her skull smashed, and her scalp taken. Her child had probably been dashed against a tree. The woman was Mrs. Clara Blinn, seized by Arapahoes in October on the Arkansas River in Colorado.

Although Indian trails pointed to the south and west, one led down the Washita River. Because it would take them to Fort Cobb in a little more than a hundred miles, Sheridan and Custer chose that direction. Approaching the fort on December 17, they flushed a large party of Kiowas under Satanta and Lone Wolf. At the same time, however, a courier from Fort Cobb brought a message from Colonel Hazen identifying these and all other Indians in the vicinity as peaceful.

Sheridan thought this "a pretty good joke," although neither he nor Custer laughed. They were certain that the warriors of Satanta and Lone Wolf had fought Custer at the Washita. They had just followed a big trail all the way from those villages to Fort Cobb. Moreover, they had brought along three of the women captured at the Washita. One, Black Kettle's sister Mahwisa, had turned out to be a voluble storehouse of information, and she had blamed the killing of Mrs. Blinn on none other than Satanta. Sheridan and Custer both wanted to attack the Kiowas, but Hazen's certificate of good conduct made that out of the question.

In actuality, Hazen was right. Mahwisa had been slanting her statements to Sheridan and Custer to try to protect her people at the expense of others. A few Kiowa warriors had ridden up to help the Cheyennes when Custer attacked but without sanction of the leadership. After the battle, at a grand council on the North Fork of Red River, west of the Wichita Mountains, the Cheyennes and Arapahoes had tried to persuade the Kiowas and Comanches to join in open war against the soldiers. They had refused, and some had begun to move hesitantly to Hazen's sanctuary when Sheridan and Custer appeared in their midst.

Badly frightened, the Kiowas prepared for flight. Although convinced that they richly merited chastisement, Sheridan contented himself with ordering Lone Wolf and Satanta to move their village at once to Fort Cobb. They acted duplicitously, the general thought, so he had them seized as hostages. Still, even after the column reached Fort Cobb the next day, the village did not come in. He then "put on the screws." The chiefs would be hanged if their people had not surrendered within forty-eight hours. Although not all the Kiowas complied, enough appeared to allow Sheridan to lift the ultimatum.

As Jim Bridger had warned, winter operations had their drawbacks. As soaking rains fell, Sheridan's unwieldy force slopped about in the mud of Fort Cobb while their horses, combined with those of the Kiowas and Comanches steadily drifting in from the west, stripped the countryside of the thin winter grass. Early in January 1869, soldiers and Indians alike moved thirty miles to the south and bivouacked in a more pleasant setting at the eastern foot of the Wichita Mountains. Sheridan began construction of a new post, which he named Fort Sill.

The move did not alleviate supply problems. Rations for the men trickled in over the long, muddy road from Forts Gibson and Arbuckle, but forage did not come in sufficient quantity to keep the cavalry horses from growing so weak as to inhibit operations. The crippling logistical failings dramatized the perils of campaigning in winter far from established bases.

The Cheyennes and Arapahoes had their own logistical problems. Sodden in their winter camps west of the Wichita Mountains, they were hungry, destitute, and disheartened by the Washita disaster. Through Mahwisa, early in January Custer enticed some of the chiefs in for talks. They told of the distress of their people and promised that all would soon be in to surrender.

They did not come in. Impatient, Custer found forty horses strong enough to do service, mounted forty of Cooke's sharpshooters, and late in January made a circuit around the Wichita Mountains. He found sixty-five lodges of Little Raven's Arapahoes and started them in. But the skittish Cheyennes, visions of the Washita fresh in their memory, had limped off to the west, into the Texas Panhandle.

Sheridan resolved to temporize no longer but once more to set Custer on the obstinate Cheyennes. By converting the Nineteenth Kansas into infantry, Custer succeeded in mounting most of the Seventh. On March 2, 1869, he led the two regiments, fifteen hundred strong, out of Fort Sill, determined to run down the Cheyennes and make them fight or surrender.

Custer's expedition soon bogged down in mud, exhaustion, and hunger. The Cheyennes easily gave him the slip, scattering up the narrow creek valleys toward the eastern escarpment of the Staked Plains, in the Texas Panhandle. With almost no trail to follow, Custer sent half the command to camp on the Washita and mounted the rest, elements of both regiments, on the strongest horses. Doggedly stalking the trace of a single lodge, he watched it grow as other lodges joined until finally, on March 15, it led to two villages, one of two hundred lodges under Medicine Arrows, the other of sixty under Little Robe, laid out on Sweetwater Creek, in Texas.

Far in advance of the worn-out command, Custer and Lieutenant Cooke made first contact with the Indians. In a brazen and dangerous gamble, the two officers accompanied their warrior escort into the village. Around a fire in the center of the chief's lodge, Custer, Medicine Arrows, and a holy man engaged in a pipe ritual and other incantations and ceremonies that Custer did not understand. Actually, Custer was sitting beneath the Cheyenne medicine arrows, the tribe's most powerful and sacred objects, and the medicine man was none other than the keeper of the arrows. Tapping ashes from the pipe bowl on the toe of Custer's boot, the keeper told him, in Cheyenne, that if he acted treacherously toward the Indians, he and all his command would be killed.

By this time the cavalry had come up. The Kansans could hardly be restrained from launching an immediate attack. They believed that the Indians held two white women taken captive in Kansas. The brother of one had accompanied the expedition to search for his sister, and the men of the Nineteenth had campaigned in hopeful anticipation of liberating them. One recorded in his diary that the volunteers branded Custer "a coward and traitor to our regiment."

While in the village Custer had learned that the Indians did indeed have the women. He did not want a repetition of the killing of Mrs. Blinn, which would inevitably occur if the troops attacked. Subsequently, Little Robe and a Cheyenne delegation came to Custer's bivouac, and the chief openly admitted that the village contained the two women. To hasten a resolution of the issue, Custer ignored Little Robe's truce flag and had three of his party seized as hostages. Three days of tense negotiation followed, climaxed with a threat to hang the hostages if the captives were not freed. With ropes strung to the limb of a large willow and the condemned standing by, the Cheyennes finally relented, gave up their prisoners, and promised to come to Camp Supply as soon as their ponies grew stronger.

Although Custer had heard that promise before, he had little choice but to consent. He could see that the Indian stock was in no condition to move rapidly, and his own short rations and forage, combined with horses dying by the score from starvation, decreed that he end the march as speedily as possible. As incentives for the Cheyennes, he retained his three hostages and also promised to free the women captured at the Washita, now held at Fort Hays, once the people had surrendered at Camp Supply. On March 28, ragged and exhausted, the troopers limped into Camp Supply.

The winter campaign did not end decisively. Although the Kiowas and Comanches had been settled on their new reservation at Fort Sill and the Arapahoes subdued, the Cheyennes failed to live up to their promise to report at Camp Supply. Most favored peace, but they could not bring themselves to surrender. The war element, chiefly the militant Dog Soldier band, headed back to Kansas for another summer of chasing buffalo and raiding settlers. On July 11, 1869, the Fifth Cavalry, under Major Eugene A. Carr, attacked Tall Bull's Cheyenne camp at Summit Springs, near the South Platte River in northeastern Colorado, and inflicted a severe defeat. Summit Springs ended the Cheyenne war, and by autumn most Cheyennes had settled on their new reservation near Camp Supply. The tract of plains between the Platte and the Arkansas had at last been swept free of troublesome Indians.

The Battle of the Washita and the ensuing winter campaign marked a critical turning point in the career of George Armstrong Custer and the evolution of the Seventh Cavalry. It also revealed much about Indian warfare in general and the Sherman-Sheridan concept of total war in particular.

The Battle of the Washita awarded Custer what he had told Libbie he needed most—the "regular Indian 'Sailor's Creek'" that would unite his regiment and give him a new public image. It gave him the latter, for the Washita was the foundation of his stature, contemporary and posthumous, as the nation's preeminent Indian fighter. It did not give him the former, for the Washita not only failed to heal old wounds but opened new ones that would fester in the Seventh Cavalry until the day of his death.

The fate of Major Elliott and nineteen troopers inflicted the new wounds. Critics (including even Sheridan) faulted Custer for leaving the battlefield without learning what had happened to Elliott. Defenders replied that further search would have jeopardized the rest of the regiment, that Elliott was already dead, and that anyway he had flown off on an independent glory-seeking expedition without orders or permission. When the regiment returned to the battlefield, the horribly mutilated remains of the victims made the issue painfully personal for all.

Within weeks the issue broke into the open and laid the basis for bitter and lasting factionalism. A letter written by an anonymous participant in the battle appeared in a Saint Louis newspaper. In emotional language it portrayed the death of Elliott and his men as the result of callous abandonment by the regimental commander. Furious, Custer summoned his officers to a tense confrontation and vowed to horsewhip the culprit. Captain Benteen shifted his pistol and stepped forward to claim authorship. Custer backed down.

The open break between Custer and Benteen, dramatizing a mutual aversion dating from their first meeting, deepened factionalism in the officer corps. It fed on the issue of Major Elliott and drew force, too, from personality conflicts, petty jealousies, strains between West Pointers and volunteers, and Custer's favoritism and nepotism. Benteen stood at the center of the opposition to Custer, a first-rate company commander but a sour, crotchety, eternally carping troublemaker with character flaws as unbecoming as those he charged to his commander. The specter of Elliott would haunt the Seventh Cavalry for eight years and darken the thoughts of more than one officer as the fateful events of June 25, 1876, unfolded along the Little Bighorn.

Beyond the Elliott question, honestly debatable in military terms, the Washita illumined some important truths about Indian fighting and about Custer's potential as an Indian fighter.

At the Washita, Custer violated a fundamental military precept: he attacked an enemy of unknown strength on a battlefield of unknown terrain. A prudent commander would have conducted a thorough enough reconnaissance to allow an estimate of enemy numbers and to disclose terrain features that might affect his tactics. As it turned out, the Seventh Cavalry overwhelmingly outnumbered the fighting men in Black Kettle's village, and no unforeseen terrain factors disrupted the attack plan. As it turned out too, however, the unsuspected villages farther east contained large numbers of warriors who changed the battlefield equation and dramatized the lack of adequate reconnaissance.

But Custer had learned, or perhaps instinctively sensed, that the precepts of conventional warfare did not always apply to Indian warfare. Possibly intuition combined with lessons gained from the Indian and white scouts with whom he had been thrown into intimate association for six weeks gave him an understanding that had eluded him a year earlier. He seems to have been more fascinated by their stock of plains lore, more appreciative of their skills, and more willing to listen and learn than in 1867. From the Osage guides and trailers and such white scouts as Ben Clark and California Joe Milner, he may have absorbed critical insights into his new profession.

One insight was that the hardest task in Indian warfare was catching the Indians, not defeating them once caught. Given the chance, Indians would almost always flee, especially if their families were threatened. They rarely fought unless clearly favored to win, and even then not if casualties seemed likely. For the soldiers, victory, even battle, thus depended on surprise. Hence Custer's anxiety to find the enemy as speedily as possible and hit without warning; hence his forced march once he found a trail and his stealthy approach as he neared the objective.

Custer did not allow prudence to jeopardize surprise. A reconnaissance of Black Kettle's village and its surroundings, especially one wide-ranging enough to have uncovered the downstream villages, would have risked discovery and flight before Custer's companies had reached their assigned attack positions. Better to risk the uncertainties of terrain and enemy strength than premature discovery.

In Indian warfare, moreover, such uncertainties did not entail as serious risks as in conventional war. Psychological factors figured more importantly and usually outweighed disparity of numbers. If surprise could be achieved, demoralized flight could be expected no matter what the odds, especially if women and children were present. Also, Indians fought as individuals, each pursuing his own aims and instincts, not as organized, disciplined bodies obedient to the orders of a leader. Because of this style of combat, small but disciplined teams of mediocre soldiers could hope, in favorable circumstances, to overwhelm large but undisciplined masses of individually superior Indian warriors.

The Washita typified a reality of Indian warfare that all frontier commanders had to face, staining their public image and, for most, inducing personal stress through shaken moral codes. Total war subjected women, children, and old people to death or cruel suffering. Surprise attack on an Indian village, centerpiece of the strategy of total war, inevitably struck down noncombatants. Women and children were killed at the Washita, rarely deliberately, except by the Indian scouts, but accidentally in the tumult of combat and in self-defense. The destruction of property, food, and transportation, followed by weeks of fearful flight to avoid the soldiers, forced women and children to endure terrible hardship. Most officers, including Custer, lamented such measures but believed them a necessary evil.

The Washita and the subsequent dispute over the character of the Kiowas also exposed the fallacy of neat classifications of peaceful and hostile. No chief claimed a deeper or more consistent commitment to peace than Black Kettle, yet his young men raided in Kansas. Satanta and Lone Wolf and all their people refrained from hostilities along the Arkansas yet did not regard their continuing raids in Texas as inconsistent with their dedication to peace. In this as in all other confrontations between whites and Indians on the frontier, Indian groups defied simple categorization that could serve as the basis for decisions of war and peace.

Like other successful Indian fighters, therefore, Custer bore the bitter fruits of the complexities and ambiguities of his new profession. Extolled in western and military circles for a brilliant victory, he drew the abuse of humanitarians, who castigated him for attacking a peace chief and slaughtering women and children. Compelling evidence revealed Black Kettle's people to have been less pacific than their chief and most of the slain noncombatants to have been honestly mistaken for warriors, or indeed themselves fighting as warriors. Yet Custer saw himself compared with the merciless Colonel Chivington and the Washita with Sand Creek. Although Sherman and Sheridan rose to the defense, forever after, in life as in death, Custer would be judged by many as an indiscriminate butcher of innocent, peaceful Indians.

But he emerged from the Washita Campaign a new man. Fame, even diluted by controversy, had touched him again, feeding his hungry ego and giving him renewed purpose in life. Military success, contrasting with his sorry performance in 1867, allowed the general to regain mastery over the adolescent that had dragged him down. Boy and man would always vie within this complex personality, but never again would the boy gain the ascendancy of 1867. Now he had a new identity and a new public persona, one firmly locked to the frontier West rather than the Civil War East: shrewd and skilled Indian fighter, mighty hunter, and master plainsman.

Projecting the image sharply and drawing vivid contrast between old and new persona, the blue and gold of the Civil War had given way to the buckskin jacket and trousers of the frontier—elaborately fringed in imitation of his scouts, decorated with a double row of brass buttons in recognition of his military station. Henceforth, he would be a cavalier in buckskin.

Armstrong Custer as a West Point cadet, 1861. "Fannie" Custer's pranks kept his comrades constantly amused but earned almost enough "skins" to wash him out of the academy. His academic record fared no better. (National Portrait Gallery, Smithsonian Institution.)

Boy General. Custer's first portrait (right) as a brigadier, in the autumn of 1863. He also posed (below) with his mentor, General Pleasonton, in October 1863, shortly after returning from the leave in which he proposed to Elizabeth Bacon. (National Portrait Gallery, Smithsonian Institution, and Custer Battlefield National Monument.)

Libbie's father and stepmother visited the newlyweds for the 1864 holiday season at General Custer's headquarters near Winchester, Virginia. On Christmas Day they joined with staff and orderlies for a picture. Judge and Mrs. Bacon stand behind the general, Libbie to his right. Tom Custer sits on steps at left. (Custer Battlefield National Monument.)

In January 1865, Sheridan and some of his generals posed for Matthew Brady in Washington, D.C. Left to right: Major General Philip H. Sheridan, Brigadier General James W. Forsyth (Tony, as distinguished from Sandy), Major General Wesley Merritt, Brigadier General Thomas C. Devin, Major General George A. Custer. (Custer Battlefield National Monument.)

Custer's favorite portrait of himself, taken by Matthew Brady in Washington, D.C., on May 23, 1865, the day of the Grand Review. Featured are his red tie and sailor's shirt. Below, Custer poses with Libbie and Eliza on April 12, 1865, three days after Appomattox. Later, Libbie's military costumes set the style for the Seventh Cavalry wives on the frontier. (Smithsonian Institution and Custer Battlefield National Monument.)

Sherman and Sheridan. William Tecumseh Sherman (left) commanded the Division of the Missouri from 1866 to 1869 and then moved up to head the army as general-in-chief. Philip H. Sheridan (right) commanded the Department of the Missouri from 1867 to 1869, when he filled in behind Sherman as lieutenant general and commander of the Division of the Missouri. Custer owed much of his professional advancement to the patronage of "Little Phil" Sheridan, but in the ugly political clash with President Grant in the spring of 1876 Sherman proved more his friend than Sheridan. (National Archives and Library of Congress.)

The Hancock Expedition made an impressive sight at Fort Harker, Kansas, in April 1867, but succeeded only in driving the Cheyennes and Sioux into a summer of hostility. The campaign was Custer's introduction to Indian fighting. (Kansas State Historical Society.)

Custer (above) emerged from the Washita Campaign of 1868–69 with a new public stature as an Indian fighter and plainsman. His field gear projected the image of "cavalier in buckskin." For Major Joel H. Elliott (below left) and Captain Louis M. Hamilton (below right), however, the Washita brought death in battle. (All Custer Battlefield National Monument.)

In January 1872, Custer participated in a buffalo hunt General Sheridan staged for the Russian Grand Duke Alexis. They liked each other immensely and had their picture taken together (right). At the same time Sheridan and his staff and Custer (below) posed for a Topeka photographer. Left to right: Custer, Major George A. ("Sandy") Forsyth, Sheridan, Major Morris V. Asche, Major Nelson B. Sweitzer (2d Cavalry), Lieutenant Colonel Michael V. Sheridan, Lieutenant Colonel James W. ("Tony") Forsyth. (Custer Battlefield National Monument.)

En route to the Yellowstone in March 1873, the lieutenant colonel of the Seventh Cavalry donned his dress uniform and sat for a Memphis photographer. (Custer Battlefield National Monument.)

The mighty hunter and the "King of the Forest," the huge elk he killed on the Yellowstone, September 6, 1873 He prepared the carcass for mounting and hauled it in a wagon back to Fort Lincoln. (Custer Battlefield National Monument.)

Fort Abraham Lincoln, Dakota Territory, Custer's base from 1873 to 1876. This view looks southeast along the rear of officers' row (right), with the Custer home third from left. Barracks for enlisted men face the officers' quarters from across the parade ground. (Custer Battlefield National Monument.)

Sitting Bull. The influence of this Hunkpapa Sioux extended beyond his tribe to all the Teton Sioux and also to the Northern Cheyennes. He was a political and religious leader as well as a war leader, and his influence held together the "nontreaties" who remained in the unceded territory after the Treaty of 1868. To force the Sitting Bull bands onto the reservation was the objective of the campaign of 1876. (Custer Battlefield National Monument.)

Rain-in-the-Face. Custer had this noted Hunkpapa warrior arrested for the murder of Honsinger and Baliran during the Yellowstone Expedition of 1873. He escaped and, says legend, swore a vengeance that he exacted on the Little Bighorn. Longfellow immortalized the myth in "The Revenge of Rain-in-the-Face." (Custer Battlefield National Monument.)

Six officers of the "royal family" that enjoyed Custer's patronage. (All except Weir, Custer Battlefield National Monument.)

Captain Myles Moylan. A "ranker" promoted from sergeant major in 1866, Moylan owed his commission to Custer. He served as regimental adjutant from 1867 to 1870 and as captain of Company A from 1872 to 1892. At the Little Bighorn, he fought under Major Reno.

Captain Thomas W. Custer, the general's younger brother. Tom was a good troop leader and superb fighter, a ladies' man, and a hard drinker and gambler when away from Libbie's restraining influence. He commanded Company C at the Little Bighorn and fell near his brother on Custer Hill.

Captain George W. Yates. A good and reliable soldier, Yates commanded Company F, the "band box troop," from 1866 to 1876. He had served with Custer in the Civil War and died with him on Custer Hill.

First Lieutenant James Calhoun. "Jimmi" married Custer's sister Margaret, served as Custer's adjutant on the Yellowstone and Black Hills expeditions, and died at the Little Bighorn on Calhoun Hill.

First Lieutenant William W. Cooke. A tall, muscular Canadian, Cooke served Custer faithfully for a decade and, as regimental adjutant, died near him on Custer Hill. Cooke's Dundreary whiskers attracted wide admiration and grew ever longer with passing years.

Captain Thomas B. Weir. Tom Weir served with the Seventh Cavalry throughout the Custer era. Libbie Custer and other ladies of the regiment enjoyed his quick mind and wit when he was sober but lamented his frequent bouts with the bottle. Captain of Company D at the Little Bighorn, he precipitated Reno's move toward the sound of the firing from the Custer battlefield. After helping Frederick Whittaker with his biography of Custer, Weir died from the effects of his drinking in December 1876. (B. William Henry Collection.)

For the "royal family" gathered around the Custers, pages 92–94, life at Fort Lincoln was a lively scene replete with close relationships and gay social affairs. (All Custer Battlefield National Monument.)

Officers and their ladies pose on steps of the Custer home in November 1873. This house burned to the ground three months later. Left to right: Lieutenant Nelson Bronson (6th Infantry), Lieutenant George D. Wallace, Lieutenant Colonel George A. Custer, Lieutenant Benjamin H. Hodgson, Elizabeth B. Custer, Mrs. Thomas McDougall, Lieutenant Thomas M. McDougall, Dr. J. V. T. Middleton, Mrs. Annie Yates, Captain George W. Yates, Charles W. Thompson, Mrs. Margaret Calhoun, Miss Agnes Bates, Captain John S. Poland (6th Infantry), Lieutenant Charles A. Varnum, Lieutenant Colonel William P. Carlin (17th Infantry), Mrs. Myles Moylan, Lieutenant Thomas W. Custer, Captain William Thompson, Lieutenant James Calhoun, Mrs. Donald McIntosh, Captain Myles Moylan, Lieutenant Donald McIntosh.

Picnic in a cottonwood grove along the Heart River, near Fort Lincoln, July 1875. Left to right: Lieutenant James Calhoun, Leonard Swett, Captain Stephen Baker (6th Infantry), Boston Custer, Lieutenant Winfield S. Edgerly, Miss Emily Watson, Captain Myles W. Keogh, Mrs. Margaret Calhoun, Mrs. Elizabeth B. Custer, Dr. Holmes O. Paulding, Lieutenant Colonel George A. Custer, Mrs. Nettie Smith, Dr. George E. Lord, Captain Thomas B. Weir, Lieutenant William W. Cooke, Lieutenant Richard E. Thompson (6th Infantry), Miss Nellie Wadsworth, Miss Emma Wadsworth, Lieutenant Thomas W. Custer, Lieutenant Algernon E. Smith.

A social gathering (above) around rented piano in Custer parlor, July 1875. Left to right: Boston Custer, Mrs. Margaret Calhoun, Lieutenant Winfield S. Edgerly, Mrs. Elizabeth B. Custer, Leonard Swett, Lieutenant Richard E. Thompson (6th Infantry), Miss Nellie Wadsworth, Lieutenant Thomas W. Custer, Lieutenant Colonel George A. Custer, Miss Emma and Miss Emily Watson.

The celebrated author (right) at his cluttered desk in his Fort Lincoln study, November 1873.

For the Seventh Cavalry, the Black Hills Expedition was a summer's romp, hugely enjoyed by all. But it led, two years later, to the Little Bighorn.

Custer's wagon train in Castle Creek Valley. (National Archives.)

Custer's first grizzly. In reality Captain Ludlow (right) and Bloody Knife (left) also fired bullets into the bear. (Custer Battlefield National Monument.)

Custer with his Ree scouts. Bloody Knife points to map. The spacious wall tent was a gift of the Northern Pacific Railroad, whose stencil appears to right of entrance. (Custer Battlefield National Monument.)

In French Creek Valley, where gold was discovered, the officers assembled for a group portrait. Custer reclines in front of tent, with Sandy Forsyth seated behind his head and Major Tilford behind his feet. Bloody Knife stands in tent's doorway. On left are Ludlow, Yates, Tom Custer, McIntosh (standing), and Calhoun (reclining). Benteen is third from right. (Custer Battlefield National Monument.)

George Armstrong Custer, in one of the portraits made at his last sitting before a camera, April 1876. He was thirty-six. (Custer Battlefield National Monument.)

Elizabeth B. Custer, as she appeared at roughly the same time, in 1876, the year of Autie's death. She was thirty-four. (Custer Battlefield National Monument.)

The columns of Terry, Crook, and Gibbon converged on the Sioux country in 1876. None of the commanders performed very efficiently. After they retired from the field, it remained for "Bear's Coat" Miles to run down the Indians in a winter campaign and force them to surrender. Miles and Custer were friends and similar in temperament and ambition. Miles rose to command of the army.

Brigadier General Alfred H. Terry. (Custer Battlefield National Monument.)

Brigadier General George Crook. (John M. Carroll Collection.)

Colonel John Gibbon. (National Archives.)

Colonel Nelson A. Miles. (Montana Historical Society.)

Major Marcus A. Reno, Custer's second-in-command at the Little Bighorn. A mediocrity, he enjoyed little respect in the Seventh. Both in the valley and on the bluffs he displayed poor leadership of the companies that fell under his command. Drink cost him his commission and ultimately his life. (Custer Battlefield National Monument.)

Captain Frederick W. Benteen. Commanding a battalion at the Little Bighorn, Benteen dawdled on the trail when he should have rushed to join Custer. Although a fine company commander, he was a cranky complainer who disliked Custer and almost all the other officers of the regiment. (Custer Battlefield National Monument.)

Of the hundreds of last-stand paintings, only a few can pretend to historical accuracy. Among the better representations of what might have happened on Custer Hill is one of several paintings by Nick Eggenhofer (overleaf, courtesy John M. Carroll). Far more consequential in exciting the public imagination and adding to the legend of George Armstrong Custer were the great canvases of the late nineteenth century. No portrayal is better known to the world than the Adams-Becker rendition that graced thousands of saloon walls in behalf of the products of the Anheuser-Busch Brewing Company (above). Also well known to exhibition visitors was John Mulvany's "Custer's Last Rally." (Custer Battlefield National Monument.)

CHAPTER 5

Iron Horse

IN the Washita Campaign, Custer had laid the groundwork for his new reputation as an Indian fighter and for his new public image as a cavalier in buckskin. His dedication to his fresh prospects, however, remained tepid. He continued to have trouble deciding what he wanted to do in life.

The army still held appeal, as he discovered upon returning to the frontier in the autumn of 1868. Arriving at Fort Leavenworth, he wrote to Libbie in Monroe: "I experienced a home feeling here in garrison that I cannot find in civil life."

But love of the army did not necessarily mean love of the West, with its dearth of amenities and its separations from Libbie. Like most officers of the frontier army, from subaltern to colonel, he strove for something higher or, at least, better.

All officers confronted disheartening prospects. Men still in their twenties or thirties occupied most of the billets on every grade level. Lieutenant Colonel Custer was not alone in his youth, merely one of the youngest. Sheridan was only thirty-eight in 1869, Sherman not yet fifty. Short of another war, promotion promised to stagnate for a generation or more. Not for another eight or ten years could Custer expect seniority to bring him the eagles of a full colonel.

Cuts in the size of the army aggravated the problem. In 1869 Congress slashed the number of infantry regiments from forty-five to twenty-five (the black infantry from four regiments to two) and limited the line brigadiers to eight instead of ten. From fifty-four thousand under the 1866 act the army dropped to about thirty-seven thousand. More reductions came in 1870, both in line generals (to three major generals, six brigadiers) and enlisted men (to thirty thousand). Finally, beginning in 1874, the annual appropriation acts fixed still more stringent ceilings, yielding an army of slightly more than twenty-seven thousand officers and men. With each new curtailment officers saw chances of promotion grow dismayingly dimmer.

In such an environment politics potently influenced an officer's
fortunes. Although seniority generally governed promotion through
the grade of colonel, the president appointed all generals. Officers
who hoped to wear stars therefore assiduously cultivated congress-
men, senators, and governors who would work for them when one
of the active generals retired or died. Among the colonels and lieutenant colonels, who alone could seriously nurture such exalted ambitions, the pursuit of patrons reached brazen extremes.

Not just for promotion were patrons essential. Choice assignments
also frequently depended on influential friends, inside the army and
out, and so did the coveted transfers from the line to a staff corps.
Thus did politics seep downward to the newest second lieutenant, as
officers sought details to comfortable eastern cities or to department
or division headquarters. Since all line commissions were in a regiment, every such detail deprived a combat unit of an officer.

In the quest for political backing, Custer's Democratic leanings in
a time of Radical Republican ascendancy imposed a handicap. During the Civil War, however, his success with the Michigan Brigade
had endeared him to the Michigan congressional delegation, and his
fight in 1864 for senate confirmation of his brigadier's appointment
had given him experience in the perilous arena of partisan politics.
In particular, he (and perhaps even more, Libbie) had forged links
to Michigan's powerful Senator Zachariah Chandler.

What Custer lacked in outside political support he made up for in
the patronage of General Sheridan, now even more powerful in military circles. Grant's inauguration to the presidency had lifted Sherman to the four-starred command of the army. To the resentment of
more senior major generals such as Meade, Sherman's three stars as
lieutenant general went to Sheridan, who assumed command of the
Military Division of the Missouri and established his headquarters
in Chicago.

For Custer the Washita Campaign cemented even more solidly his
ties to Sheridan and gave promise of opening pathways to something
better. While still in the field, in January 1869, the two concocted a
scheme for Custer's advancement. What he hoped for is unknown,
but political conditions seemed propitious.

At this stage of the Washita Campaign both Sheridan and Custer
planned to go east for Grant's inauguration on March 4. Asking Libbie to reserve a room at the National Hotel in Washington, on the
same floor as Senator Chandler, Armstrong explained darkly: "I dare

not trust it to paper what is planned but if everything works favorably Custer luck is going to surpass all former experience, and you will be as greatly surprised as my greatest enemy. There are but two persons besides Gen Sheridan and myself who know what is contemplating." (Sherman and Grant?) As it turned out, the Cheyennes prevented both Sheridan and Custer from attending Grant's inaugural, but as Sheridan prepared to leave Camp Supply for the East on March 2, 1869, he wrote to Custer: "I will push your claims on the subject of promotion as soon as I get to Washington, and, if anything can be done, *you may rely on me* to look out for your interests."

Whatever they plotted failed to materialize, and six months later Custer tried again to break free of the West. Old A. J. Smith retired, and seniority elevated Samuel D. Sturgis, major general by brevet, to the colonelcy of the Seventh Cavalry. As a young officer before the war Sturgis had served efficiently against Indians; but his Civil War record had gone sour, and now, a portly forty-seven, he seemed most interested in taking his ease and enjoying his family. He assumed command of the regiment, however, and this relegated Custer virtually to the role of supernumerary. Pointing out that the Seventh did not need him, Custer wrote to General Sherman on June 29, 1869, asking to be detailed to West Point as commandant of cadets. Although Sturgis endorsed the application, the appointment went to Lieutenant Colonel Emory Upton, a cerebral young theorist destined to leave a deep imprint on America's military policy.

For nearly two years, diverted only by light official duties, the Custers pursued such pleasures of garrison and camp as the Kansas frontier offered. In the summers of 1869 and 1870, with part of the regiment, they camped on Big Creek, near Fort Hays. During the winter of 1869–70 they threw themselves into the sparkling social life of Fort Leavenworth.

The Big Creek camp afforded new opportunities for Custer to add luster to his reputation as hunter and plainsman. In 1869 the Kansas Pacific Railroad pushed into Colorado and in 1870 reached Denver. Hordes of excursionists came by train to sample the Wild West and thrill to the hunt. Eagerly the tourists sought a glimpse of the renowned General Custer. A favored few followed the great hunter and his yelping dogs in a breathless chase after buffalo, thus acquiring memories they would cherish for a lifetime. For two summers English noblemen, eastern industrialists, and eminent political leaders enjoyed the tented hospitality of the buckskinned celebrity and his charming wife. The nation's hunting fraternity vicariously shared the adventures in graphic letters that Custer penned for *Turf, Field and Farm*.

"What a party it was!" recalled a young woman who had participated in one such excursion. "General Custer was the hero of all who knew him, and Mrs. Custer, who attended in a carriage, was like a queen, surrounded by her court." Of a futile dash after an antelope, she drew a picture typical of the many that filled in the outlines of consummate sportsman: "Custer, ahead, was seen to rise in his saddle, with his long, golden hair flying in the wind, his heavily fringed buckskin suit matching the color of his hair. He gave the Indian war-whoop—every horse and dog understood it meant a dash—a run at full gallop."

Despite appearances, these were not carefree times for the Custers, for the storybook marriage had run on hazardous shoals. While Libbie brooded alone at Fort Leavenworth, Armstrong spent Christmas 1869 with family and friends in Michigan. In a letter of December 20 he touched on their problems: "While I am absent you may perhaps think kindly of me and remember much that is good of me but when I return that spark of distrust which I alone am responsible for first placing in your mind but which others have fanned into a flame, will be rekindled and little burning words will be the result." Most men, he observed, "feeling the greatest disappointment of their lives had overtaken them, that the love of the one person whose love alone was desirable was surely but slowly departing from them, would endeavor to hide or drown their troubles by drink or dissipation. I am not so inclined." How he was inclined, he failed to explain, other than a resolution not to meet the burning words with anger or profanity. But, he ended, "you are and ever will be that one single object of my love."

This was not the first sign of a troubled marriage. Late in 1866, probably during his trip to Washington to be examined for his lieutenant colonel's appointment, he had written a similar letter to Libbie. It expressed contrition over some indiscretion committed during their holiday in Saint Louis en route to Fort Riley, mourned the perceived loss of Libbie's love, and professed his own undying love.

Now another rift had disturbed their relationship. What caused it? The answer, in whole or part, may be marital infidelity. Custer had been athletically sexual ever since adolescence. The correspondence between him and Libbie, especially in the first two years of marriage, implies their intimacy to have been as sexual as emotional and intellectual.

Gossip connected Custer to other women as well. How much the gossip revealed truth or simply dislike or jealousy cannot be known. Captain Benteen, prince of gossipers as well as Custer's bitter enemy, declared that "at this time it was notorious that Custer was criminally intimate with a married woman, wife of an officer of the [Fort Leavenworth] garrison; besides, he was an habitue of demimonde dives." Benteen added that Libbie knew about these peccadillos, which, he said, "rendered her—if she had any heart (?) a broken-hearted woman." Benteen also labeled Eliza, who followed Custer's headquarters without interruption from 1863 to 1869, as her master's "concubine."

However nebulous this gossip, more substantial evidence linked Custer to a Cheyenne woman captured at the Washita. In the days after the battle, Interpreter Raphael Romero acted as procurer for a number of officers, in token of which they dubbed him Romeo. Custer's companion was Monahsetah, a young woman not yet twenty, the daughter of Chief Little Rock. In his book Custer described her as a maiden of rare beauty but did not disclose that she was about seven months pregnant when captured. He saw to it that she accompanied the expedition, with two other women, throughout the winter, and in truth she performed valuable service as an intermediary with her people. Early in January 1869, Custer wrote Libbie that "one of the squaws that I have here as a prisoner had a little papoose," and he promised to bring the infant home for Eliza.

That Monahsetah shared Custer's bedroll throughout the winter is attested not only by Benteen but by the chief scout of the expedition, Ben Clark. The story is also common in Cheyenne oral history, which alleges further that she bore Custer's child. She may have. She had three months with him after the birth of the "little papoose," and tradition hints of another infant late in 1869.

Libbie herself may have had a wandering eye, its attraction Lieutenant Thomas B. Weir. He was a likable fellow, possessed of greater intellectual depth than his comrades, and a favorite with the ladies of the regiment. Libbie found him appealing, although his fondness for liquor probably discouraged more than a nonphysical electricity.

Again, Benteen is the authority. He asserted that the dash across Kansas in 1867 that earned Custer a court-martial was prompted by an anonymous letter, written by Lieutenant Charles Brewster at Eliza's urging, that he had better hurry back and "look after his wife a little closer." "It is said," Benteen asserted, "that Custer 'tackled Weir' at Harker making him beg for his life on his knees." Invented or exaggerated (certainly the latter if not the former), Benteen's account finds a fragment of substantiation in a letter from Custer to Libbie early in 1869: "The more I see of him [Weir] Little one, the more I am surprised that a woman of your perceptive faculties and moral training could have entertained the opinion of him you have."

Whether or not the rumors were true, or caused the fracture in the relationship, the marriage weathered the crisis. Subsequently, Armstrong found at least one occasion to lecture Libbie about improprieties in relations with other officers, and a muted testiness of language sometimes crept into their letters. But such storm signals were all but submerged in page after flowery page of ardor and esteem. Whatever dalliances had occurred, or still occurred, the two had worked out an accommodation that preserved one of history's most intimate and glowing love matches.

Even when diverted by real or imagined hurts, the two were immersed in each other. In fact, in addition to the role of wife, Libbie came more and more to take on the roles once played by half-sister Ann—surrogate mother and confidant. More and more his letters to Libbie, besides the usual effusions of adoration, captured these two themes, so prevalent in earlier letters to Ann.

Gradually, the relationship came to have no place in it for children. At first they both eagerly looked forward to parenthood. By 1868, however, either from biological causes or deliberate decision, they had convinced themselves of the advantages of a childless marriage. "I am delighted and overjoyed that my little darling bride is having an opportunity of really seeing and determining how troublesome and embarrassing babies would be to us," Armstrong wrote from Kansas in October 1868, when Libbie was visiting a Michigan household teeming with children. "Our pleasure would be continually marred and circumscribed." For this product of a large, rowdy family, a childless household may have found compensation in obsession with pets—dogs, horses, assorted wildlife captured on the plains, and once even a pelican.

Coincident with the strain in his marriage, Custer indulged another of his frequent bouts of self-analysis. He prided himself on his self-control, on imposing his will on himself and his environment. In 1861 he had vowed never again to taste an intoxicant, and he never had, even though his career constantly surrounded him with hard drinkers and even drunkards. Much of his Civil War success he owed to this same stubborn determination. Yet despite repeated resolutions, he had failed to conquer the compulsion to gamble. In December 1869, however, at the very time his tension with Libbie peaked, he made a thirtieth-birthday resolution. "From the day I leave Fort Leavenworth next spring to go on the plains," he informed Libbie, "I cease so long as I am a married man to play cards or any other game of chance for money or its equivalent."

Money occupied Custer in ways other than gambling. Memories of his adventures in New York City in 1866 remained tantalizingly vivid—dinner at Delmonico's, the theater and opera, beautiful women, the congenial society of wealthy capitalists, and, above all, the fantasy of himself as one of them. Early in 1871 the imminent reassignment of the Seventh Cavalry to Reconstruction duty in the South once again opened the question of whether to leave the army and pursue fortune on Wall Street. Obtaining a leave of absence, Custer set forth to scout the prospects while Libbie went home to Monroe. Extended through repeated applications, the leave ultimately lasted seven months, until September 1871.

In New York, Custer applied most of his energies to promoting a mining scheme in which he had become involved with a Michigan friend late in 1870. With his characteristic excess of optimism, he looked upon the Stevens silver mine, near Georgetown, Colorado, as the platform for launching a rise to wealth. "Can it be that my little Standby and I who have long wished to possess a small fortune, are about to have our hopes and wishes realized?" he wrote to Libbie in April 1871. "If I succeed in this operation as now seems certain, it is to be but the stepping stone to large and more profitable undertakings."

It seemed certain because Custer had cultivated some of New York's leading financiers. Among his friends were John Jacob Astor, August Belmont, Levi Morton, Leonard Jerome, Jay Gould, and Jim Fisk. He persuaded a few to buy some of the greatly watered stock floated to raise working capital for the Stevens Lode. Belmont, for example, subscribed fifteen thousand dollars, Astor ten thousand. Custer himself, according to the company's prospectus, subscribed thirty-five thousand dollars. Almost certainly he commanded no such sum; instead, he had sold his name in what turned out to be a vain hope of attracting enough other investors to make the mine pay.

After several years of frantic manipulation, he saw the enterprise collapse.

Custer's friends belonged not only to the financial elite but the political and social elite as well. Belmont, publisher of the *New York World*, headed the conservative wing of the Democratic Party. James Gordon Bennett, Jr., editor of the *New York Herald*, also championed politics agreeable to Custer. Courted and flattered by such leading Democrats, including his old commander General McClellan, Custer openly mingled with political elements hostile to the Grant administration, an association that could not have gone unnoticed in Washington.

He also pursued a heavy social schedule. Nattily turned out after a series of fashionable purchases at Brooks Brothers, he attracted constant public and press attention at parties, lavish dinners, the theater, faro casinos (though he swore he had not broken his resolution about gambling), yachting excursions, and the Saratoga races. As always the society of attractive women enchanted him. As in 1866, he described his experiences with women in letters to Libbie, spelling out the more titillating aspects in minute and sometimes anatomical detail. Always he reassured her of the central role she played in his life and affections, on one occasion perhaps unconsciously letting slip the essence of their conjugal relationship: "All the women are but as mere toys compared to you."

For the second time New York failed to furnish Custer with an acceptable alternative to the army, and early in September 1871 he returned to active duty. The Seventh Cavalry had been scattered among little stations in Kentucky, South Carolina, and Louisiana. Custer took command of a two-company contingent at Elizabethtown, Kentucky, near Louisville. Duties were light and routine, chiefly suppressing Ku Klux Klan activity, chasing moonshiners, and inspecting horses purchased for the cavalry.

Blue Grass breeding farms and racetracks provided some diversion but could not prevent Kentucky from paling. "Autie would like to be on the Frontier," Libbie wrote to an aunt, "but spends his leisure reading and writing."

The writing signified a continuing ambition to publish. He had set aside his war memoirs and now worked diligently on a series of articles about his frontier adventures. The first, an account of the Hancock campaign of 1867, appeared in the January 1872 issue of *Galaxy* magazine. Ultimately, the series carried his plains experiences through the Washita Campaign. In 1874 the publishers of *Galaxy* consolidated the articles into a book, *My Life on the Plains*, and George Armstrong Custer emerged as celebrated author in addition to soldier, Indian fighter, hunter, and plainsman.

The Kentucky interlude afforded one opportunity for a return to the frontier. Late in 1871 the Russian Czar's third son, the Grand Duke Alexis, visited the United States, and to General Sheridan and staff fell the task of treating him to a buffalo hunt on the Plains. The inclusion in the ducal party of General Custer, Buffalo Bill Cody, and a band of Sioux Indians gave the excursion a fitting tone. The gala affair, in January 1872, went off perfectly. The twenty-one-year-old Alexis liked Custer so well that he and Libbie were invited to join the ducal entourage for a sojourn in New Orleans. Well publicized by the press, the Grand Duke's buffalo hunt reminded the public of Custer's stature as premier outdoorsman.

Armstrong and Libbie both wanted out of Kentucky. If they could not have New York, the West seemed not so bad after all. At least it held the possibility of excitement, adventure, and perhaps another military feat like the Washita. As Libbie observed, "a true cavalryman feels that a life in the saddle on the free open plain is his legitimate existence."

Notice of the Custers' return to "the free open plain" came at last in February 1873. Behind their reprieve from Kentucky, unsurprisingly, stood General Sheridan, and behind him the voracious demands on the army of that instrument of conquest the Indians called the "iron horse."

"No one measure so quickly and effectually frees a country from the horrors and devastations of Indian wars and Indian depredations generally," observed Custer, "as the building and successful operation of a railroad through the region overrun."

Custer spoke not only for himself but all officers who had served on the frontier. Sherman and Sheridan had recognized the importance of railroads ever since 1866. Sherman called them, simply, "the solution of the Indian problem." Railroads moved troops and supplies quickly and cheaply. Railroads split the great buffalo herds on which the Plains Indians relied. Railroads brought immigrants to settle on the lands the Indians roamed, and with the newcomers came agriculture, commerce, and industry. As a military measure alone, therefore, railroads deserved all the aid the army could extend.

Sherman and Sheridan both made protection of railroad builders a prime responsibility of department commanders. "The safety of the line of the Pacific Rail Road from Omaha to Utah is your first responsibility," Sherman informed the commander of the Department of the Platte in 1870. Guardian forts sprang up along the Union Pacific in Nebraska and the Kansas Pacific in Kansas. From 1866 to 1869 troops defended surveyors, graders, and tracklayers of both railroads. The Indians, alarmed by the advance of the iron horse, harried survey parties but usually gave the completed road a wide berth.

Now another railroad crept out onto the Plains and aimed for Indian country. Projected to connect Duluth, Minnesota, with the Pacific Northwest, the Northern Pacific began to lay rails into northern Dakota Territory in the early 1870s. Surveyors ranged far in advance to stake out a line across the Little Missouri Badlands and up Montana's Yellowstone River Valley.

Sherman and Sheridan stood ready to furnish the Northern Pacific as much help as they had the Union Pacific and Kansas Pacific. "That Northern Pacific Road is going to give you a great deal of trouble," Sherman wrote to Sheridan in 1872, "and I expect to stand back and do the hallowing whilst you or younger men go in." "The Indians will be hostile in an extreme degree," he predicted, "yet I think our interest is to favor the undertaking of the Road, as it will help to bring the Indian problem to a final solution."

No more intractable "Indian problem" existed in the West than on the northern Plains as the new railroad approached. This was the domain of the Teton Sioux and the allied Northern Cheyennes and Northern Arapahoes. Six separate tribes made up the Tetons—Hunkpapa, Oglala, Brule, Miniconjou, Sans Arc, and Blackfoot. A proud, strong people numbering more than twenty thousand, the Tetons had fought their way westward from Minnesota in the eighteenth century, brushing aside weaker tribes and clamping a mighty supremacy on the northern Plains. By the middle of the nineteenth century, with their Cheyenne and Arapaho friends, the Tetons ranged freely from the Missouri River on the east to the Bighorn Mountains on the west, from the Platte River on the south to the British Possessions on the north.

Like the Medicine Lodge treaties, the Fort Laramie Treaty of 1868 left Indian affairs in the north confused and ambiguous. Ostensibly, it represented a victory for the Sioux, who under Red Cloud and other chiefs had successfully fought off government attempts to open the Bozeman Trail to the Montana goldfields. In abandoning the Bozeman Trail and its guardian forts, however, federal officials also secured the agreement of the signatory chiefs to settle on a vast new reservation, where they would be provided with rations and other needed provisions but also subjected to government controls. For this purpose the treaty set aside all of present South Dakota west of the Missouri River as the Great Sioux Reservation.

The majority of the Sioux, about fifteen thousand, drifted onto the reservation and gradually grew dependent on the rations handed out at the agencies. Among those who settled into the new life were two of the most powerful chiefs of the Sioux, Red Cloud of the Oglalas and Spotted Tail of the Brules.

Not all Indians, however, went to the reservation or accepted the treaty. To gain any agreement at all, negotiators had to acquiesce in an "unceded territory" west of the Great Sioux Reservation, where the Indians might hunt so long as the buffalo ran. This unceded territory—the Powder River basin and the eastern flanks of the Bighorn Mountains—proved a source of endless trouble. Distant from government authority, it afforded a haven for the "nontreaties." These people had not signed the treaty, indeed had scorned it. Intolerant of the restraints of reservation life, they followed the free life of the chase in the unceded territory.

These hunting bands, or "northern Indians," numbered about three thousand Sioux and four hundred Cheyennes. The various bands, representing all the Teton tribes, followed their own leaders— such noted chiefs and warriors as Black Moon, Four Horns, Gall, Crow King, Lame Deer, Black Eagle, and the incomparable Crazy Horse. One commanding presence, however, towered above all: Sitting Bull of the Hunkpapas. A leader of forceful personality, superior intellect, and personal magnetism, Sitting Bull inspired a unity among bands and even tribes rare in Indian life. In the eyes of Indians and whites alike, the bands in the unceded territory came more and more to be identified as Sitting Bull's people.

Although roaming at will far to the west, the Sitting Bull bands bedeviled the Indian agents. Groups frequently visited their kinsmen on the reservation and even attached themselves for a time to the agencies to draw rations. While there they defied the agent's authority and spread discontent among the reservation Indians. Also, the nontreaties in the unceded territory provided a refuge for reservation Indians disgruntled with government regulations or simply yearning

for a sample of the old freedom. Each summer Indians left the reservation to join their relatives to the west, returning in the fall to the
agencies and the regular meals to be obtained there. Thus the number of Indians in the unceded territory swelled in summer and shrank
in winter.

The Sitting Bull bands regarded the Yellowstone Basin as Sioux
country, whatever the elegant words used to describe it in the Treaty
of 1868. They had wrested it from the Crow Indians a century earlier,
and they did not intend to let a railroad violate it without a fight. In
actuality the treaty left vague whether the unceded territory extended as far north as the Yellowstone, and anyway it explicitly sanctioned railroads anywhere in the region, even across the reservation
itself.

Such legalisms meant nothing to the Sitting Bull Indians. They
had not accepted the treaty and knew little, if anything, that it said.
When surveyors and their soldier escorts appeared in the Yellowstone Valley in 1871 and 1872, therefore, the Sioux made abundantly
clear their attitude toward the railroad. War parties constantly ha-
rassed the invaders and on several occasions boldly attacked them.

Responsibility for the Northern Pacific fell to the Department of
Dakota, headquartered in Saint Paul and embracing the state of Minnesota and the territories of Dakota and Montana. General Hancock
commanded. At the close of the 1872 field season, he alerted Sheridan
to the implications of the gunfire rattling up the Yellowstone Valley.
"It is evident that more troops will be needed if the railroad is to be
run into the Yellowstone and Gallatin Valleys," he warned. Except
for four companies of the Second Cavalry at Fort Ellis, in western
Montana, infantry manned all the posts in the department. Therefore, declared Hancock, "Cavalry is especially needed."

Sheridan knew which cavalry he wanted for the task. The Seventh
had already been alerted for movement to Texas, but at Sheridan's
request the orders were changed. In March 1873, from all over the
South the companies of the Seventh converged on Memphis, Ten-
nessee, and prepared for the journey to Dakota Territory. Colonel
Sturgis established the regimental headquarters in Saint Paul, leaving
Lieutenant Colonel Custer, as Sheridan surely intended, to command the companies in the field.

For the final leg of its journey the Seventh Cavalry marched from
railhead at Yankton, capital of Dakota Territory, up the Missouri
River to Fort Rice. The trek hardened men and animals for a sum-

mer of fieldwork and also brought the regiment back together after its two-year dispersal in the South. Happy in the old camaraderie, the officers also faced old dissensions, discontents, and factionalism.

An officer new to the regiment, Lieutenant Charles W. Larned, noted that Custer surrounded himself with a "royal family." It consisted mainly of Tom Custer, Yates, Moylan (now a captain), "Fresh" Smith, and a new addition, "Jimmi" Calhoun. At Fort Leavenworth, early in 1870, Custer's sister Margaret had fallen in love with the tall, blonde "Adonis," an infantry officer. In anticipation of their marriage, Custer had arranged his assignment to the Seventh Cavalry, with promotion to first lieutenant thrown in. The wedding had taken place in March 1872. Now Calhoun served as Custer's adjutant.

Lieutenant Larned did not belong to the royal family and spoke for others denied membership. "Custer is not making himself at all agreeable to the officers of his command," Larned wrote to his mother. "He keeps himself aloof and spends his time excogitating annoying, vexatious, and useless orders which visit us like the swarm of evils from Pandora's box, small, numberless, and disagreeable. However, we are enjoying ourselves hugely."

So was the royal family, for Libbie Custer and Maggie Calhoun rode at the head of the column with their husbands, while other wives traveled on an accompanying steamboat. When they finally reached Fort Rice, however, there was no place for the wives to live during the summer. The fine new fort that most of the Seventh was to garrison had yet to be built, and the ladies rode the Northern Pacific out of Dakota. Libbie and Maggie returned to Monroe.

The Seventh's new station was Fort Abraham Lincoln. Located on the west bank of the Missouri River, across from and three miles below the Northern Pacific's railhead at Bismarck, the fort had been established as an infantry post in 1872. The advent of cavalry made extensive new construction essential. While the regiment took to the field, therefore, carpenters, mechanics, and other civilian craftsmen labored to have the post ready for occupancy by the end of the summer.

The Seventh's assignment for the summer was to protect yet another railroad survey west of the Missouri River into Montana. Tracklayers still toiled east of the Missouri, but much engineering work remained to be done to the west in staking an exact line for the graders, bridgers, and tracklayers.

The Yellowstone Expedition of 1873 served unmistakable notice

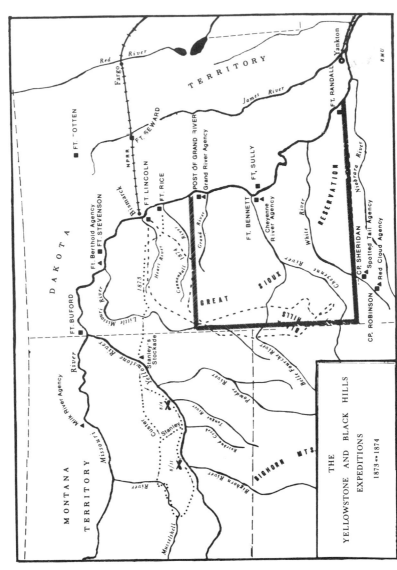

The Yellowstone and Black Hills Expeditions, 1873–1874

of the government's resolve to push the Northern Pacific Railroad through the Indian country. As in 1872, David S. Stanley, colonel of the Twenty-second Infantry and major general by brevet, commanded. Custer and ten companies of the Seventh Cavalry provided an offensive capability lacking the year before. (The other two companies of the Seventh, under Major Marcus A. Reno, spent the summer escorting surveyors marking the international boundary with the British Possessions.) Nineteen infantry companies marched in defense of the Northern Pacific's engineering party. Two Rodman cannons formed the artillery. Nearly three hundred mule-drawn wagons hauled provisions, while seven hundred beeves comprised a mobile commissary. With white and Indian scouts and attached civilians, the Yellowstone Expedition numbered more than fifteen hundred men.

The column pushed off from Fort Rice on June 20, 1873, to the good wishes, among others, of the new department commander. Brigadier General Alfred H. Terry had succeeded Hancock. A tall, heavily bearded officer, kindly and soft-spoken, Terry had been a lawyer before the war. He had done so well as a general of volunteers, however, that he had received a brigadier's commission in the regular army.

Slowly the column made its way across the western half of Dakota. Although hail, rain, and windstorms caused trouble, the march, as General Terry had predicted, turned into a "big picnic." The Seventh's regimental band furnished the musical backdrop.

A profusion of antelope, elk, and deer challenged the hunting skills of everyone. Anointed "chief huntsman," Custer led a daily detail of twenty-five men that kept messes well supplied with game and spared the cattle herd for leaner times. "I have done some of the most remarkable shooting I ever saw," he boasted to Libbie only six days out, "and it is admitted to be such by all." Thereafter, in letter after letter, he treated her in almost endless detail to his repeated feats of marksmanship, the exploits of his ever-present pack of hounds, and the record-setting dimensions of his kills.

His own mess fared exceptionally well, for he had his black cook with him. Eliza had dropped out of the Custer family in 1869. ("She got on a spree & was insolent," according to Libbie; later, she married and, as Eliza Denison, renewed her friendship with Libbie in the years after "the Ginnel's" demise.) Eliza's place had been taken by

Mary Adams, who proved a wizard at conjuring a feast in the midst of the wilderness.

Although Custer delighted in his royal family, to his distress they extended the picnic far into each night, drinking heavily and gambling for high stakes. The spectacle of the usually steady Captain Yates, drunk and out of his mind for several days, disgusted Custer and prompted pity for his talented wife, Annie (daughter, incidentally, of the chief engineer of the Northern Pacific). Watching Calhoun go bankrupt at cards, Custer congratulated himself "that I have told Satan to get behind me as far as poker goes."

Other pleasures occupied Custer's time. Besides hunting, he pursued two new hobbies, both learned from men in the "scientific corps." One was taxidermy, at which he worked in his tent by candlelight until late at night, much to the vexation of orderlies required to help but who needed more sleep than he. The other was paleontology, for which the badlands between the Little Missouri and Yellowstone rivers furnished a lush laboratory. By summer's end wagons bulged with the fruits of his work—crates of fossilized animal and fish parts, petrified wood, and an array of heads, horns, and hides of deer, elk, antelope, bear, and buffalo prepared for mounting, including the entire carcass of his prize elk, a great beast dubbed "King of the Forest." He intended the Audubon Club, the University of Michigan, and other such institutions to benefit from his scientific diligence.

Custer found another source of pleasure in the big, bluff southerner who headed the Northern Pacific engineering party. Tom Rosser had been Custer's fast friend at West Point, had fought him as a Confederate cavalry general, and now served as chief engineer of the Northern Pacific's Dakota Division. In the evenings, while others partied, Custer and Rosser lay on a buffalo robe exchanging war stories.

Custer also discovered pleasant society in young Fred Grant, the president's son. Graduating from West Point two years earlier, he had been commissioned a second lieutenant of cavalry. His mother, however, had so insistently pressed for something better that Sheridan finally added Fred to his staff, with the rank of lieutenant colonel. Custer found Colonel Grant a frank, modest, likable youth. When he left the expedition to go east, by way of Monroe, Armstrong wrote to Libbie to meet him at the depot and invite him for dinner. Also, "Have his father's portrait hung in the parlor."

Predictably, as with Sully in 1868, Custer clashed with Stanley almost at once. It was largely a war of trivia but was rooted in Stanley's drinking and Custer's desire for freedom from supervision. Normally a genial, considerate gentleman, Stanley was also an inebriate. When sober he could not remember what he had said or done when drunk. This not only produced confrontations between the two officers but ensured that Custer would ultimately prevail. The feud peaked when Stanley placed Custer under arrest and relegated him to the rear of the column. Two days later a sober colonel lifted the arrest and asked forgiveness.

Stanley thus ended the dissension, but so too did he virtually abdicate his command. Despite a promise to "turn over a new leaf," he continued to drink copiously; and as he drunkenly spawned delay and disruption, actual leadership fell increasingly to Custer. As Captain Benteen summed up, "Now Stanley was stupidly drunk at the time, and that is how Custer got away with him."

Fresh provisions awaited the expedition in the Yellowstone Valley. The army had chartered two steamboats, the *Key West* and the *Josephine*, to haul supplies up the Missouri and Yellowstone rivers. As the command neared the Yellowstone, Custer "volunteered to go on a 'steamboat hunt.'" With two companies he forced his way through twisted badlands and reached the river. A search located the *Key West*. On the south bank of the Yellowstone, eight miles above the mouth of Glendive Creek, the troops threw up a fortified supply depot, dubbed "Stanley's Stockade."

Leaving Captain Benteen with two companies of the Seventh and one of infantry to guard the supply depot, the expedition moved up the Yellowstone Valley into an area roamed each summer by the Sitting Bull bands of Sioux. With a small force Custer usually rode in advance each day, pioneering routes for the wagons and selecting the evening's campsite. His favorite scout, the Arikara Bloody Knife, pointed out fresh Indian sign and warned him to be on the alert for an attack.

On August 4, a scorching day that told severely on men and animals both, Custer's advance consisted of the companies of Moylan and Tom Custer, about ninety officers and enlisted men. As they lazed through the noon break in a grove of timber nearly opposite the mouth of Tongue River, a half-dozen mounted warriors whooped down the valley and tried to stampede the cavalry horses. The troopers sprang to arms, repelled the attack, and then mounted for the chase. With Tom, Calhoun, and twenty troopers, Custer took up the gallop. Moylan followed more slowly with the balance.

A two-mile ride up the valley left little doubt that the Indians were decoys. Even so, as a decoy stratagem of his own, Custer and his orderly got out in front of the pursuers. Opposite another patch of timber the trap snapped shut. A swarm of warriors burst from concealment. "Mounted and caparisoned with all the flaming adornments of paint and feathers," as Custer later wrote, they bore down on the cavalry.

The officers hastily formed their men into a dismounted skirmish line to meet the charge. Custer and his orderly raced back to the skirmishers, reaching them barely in time to avoid being cut off. Beside him Custer heard two Irish troopers exchange comments: "Say, Teddy, I guess the ball's opened." "Yis, and by the way thim rid nagurs is comin' it's openin' wid a grand march." "Teddy, if we only had the band here, we could play 'Hail to the Chief' for their benefit." Three volleys broke the charge, prompting the Indians to dismount and, concealed in the tall grass, try to creep toward the blue line on foot. Moylan came up with the rest of the command.

Custer saw that he might be overrun if he did not find cover. He therefore formed a skirmish line completely around the led horses and slowly retreated to the protection of the timber downstream. Here the troops spread out behind the natural parapet of an old riverbank and held the Sioux at bay throughout the hot afternoon. Hoping to burn out the defenders, the Indians fired the valley grass, but no wind rose to drive it into the timber. Late in the day, with ammunition almost exhausted, the begrimed troopers glimpsed the rest of the cavalry galloping through the smoke to the rescue. Mounting, they joined the charge and ended the fight by chasing their assailants several miles back up the valley.

Custer had shown that he still could fight Indians. Badly outnumbered by some three hundred warriors, his two companies, in the hands of less cool and spontaneous leadership, might well have been overrun in the first rush. Instead, in more than three hours of hard fighting, they drove their assailants from the field.

Although Custer had sustained no loss beyond one man shot in the arm and two horses wounded, the Indians did not pull off without victims. The regimental veterinarian, Dr. John Honsinger; the sutler, Augustus Baliran; and two soldiers had left the main body to ride through to Custer's advance party. While they rested beside a spring, a handful of Sioux pounced upon them and killed Honsinger, Baliran, and Private John H. Ball. The second soldier escaped to bring word to the troops.

Moving on up the Yellowstone Valley, on August 8 the command discovered the site of the village from which Custer's antagonists had ridden forth on August 4. Bloody Knife estimated that it consisted of four to five hundred lodges; if so, it harbored either most of Sitting Bull's following or a lesser part augmented by summer visitors from the agencies. In any event, that number of lodges meant that as many as a thousand warriors might be in the neighborhood.

With Stanley's blessing Custer at once set forth on a night pursuit with all eight companies of the Seventh and the Arikara Indian scouts. A forced march of thirty-six hours led the column up the valley on the trail made by the village until, three miles below the mouth of the Bighorn River, it ended on the river's shore. The Indians had crossed to the south side of the Yellowstone. All day on August 10, men tried to make a lodgment on the other bank that would enable the command to cross in pursuit, but the river ran so swift and deep that all efforts failed.

At daybreak on August 11, before the troops could renew their attempts to cross the Yellowstone, large numbers of warriors gathered among cottonwood trees on the other shore and opened fire on the cavalry. Behind them the old men, women, and children of the village clustered on the bluff tops to watch the fight. Other warriors crossed the Yellowstone above and below the bivouac of the troops and rode to the attack.

Custer reacted swiftly. Posting sharpshooters in the timber to return the fire across the river, he deployed the balance of the command facing the bluffs on his side of the river. To meet the threat of Indians crossing the river, he sent two companies under Captain Thomas H. French down the valley and two companies under Captain Verling K. Hart up the valley. In turn, Captain Hart posted twenty men under Lieutenant Charles Braden on a brow of benchland rising from the valley on his left.

Braden had no sooner reached his position and spread out a skirmish line than he confronted what to him "looked like the whole Sioux Nation." About a hundred "painted and feathered" warriors, astride racing ponies, bore down on his little platoon and almost overran it before the troopers got their carbines into operation. Another hundred followed the first. Four times the skirmishers turned back thrusts at their line. A bullet shattered Braden's leg and sent him tumbling down the slope to the valley, critically wounded.

As Braden held back the Sioux on the west, Captain French also stopped the Indians who had crossed on the east. Other contingents dispatched by Custer flushed groups of warriors who had worked into the cover of ravines and opened a galling fire into the valley. Within twenty minutes Custer had all of the command saddled, mounted, and formed into two bodies for attacks on the left and in the center. The band moved in behind the formations and at Custer's signal struck up "Garry Owen." The companies surged forward in the charge. Downstream the pressure on French relaxed as Stanley's infantry hove into view, and a courier galloped to French with authority for him to return and join in the charge of the other companies.

"Our evil-disposed friends tarried no longer," recalled Lieutenant Larned, "but fled incontinently before the pursuing squadrons. We charged them eight miles and over the river, only returning when the last Indian had gotten beyond our reach." In the meantime Stanley had arrived on the field and had ordered his Rodman guns unlimbered and thrown into battery. Artillery shells bursting in the timber across the river drove the Indian sharpshooters from their positions and ended the Battle of the Yellowstone.

Once more Custer had won an Indian battle. In this fight he had commanded about 450 cavalrymen against Sioux warriors in excess of 500 (some participants estimated enemy strength at more than double that figure). Indian losses, in Custer's reckoning, totaled about 40 in the fights of August 4 and 11. In the second action, besides Lieutenant Braden badly injured, he had lost 4 men killed, 3 wounded, and 8 horses hit. Again Custer had handled his command with calm deliberation and sound tactical instinct.

Only once more did Indians show themselves. On August 16, six warriors rode down to the riverbank, fired a volley into a frolicking group of swimmers, and scattered naked infantrymen, frightened but unhurt, up the opposite bank. Otherwise the Sioux caused the expedition no further trouble.

The clashes gave Custer and other officers some lessons to ponder, had they been inclined. First, the Sioux fought more daringly and aggressively than customary in such high-risk situations, a measure of their outrage at the invasion as well as of their warrior prowess.

Their behavior expressed the bellicose temper, above all the defiant independence, of the so-called "nontreaty" bands that followed Sitting Bull. Secondly, the encounters showed the Indians to be well armed with Henry and Winchester repeating rifles and to have ample ammunition. This unusual firepower testified to the ease with which the means of war could be obtained from traders at the Indian agencies, chiefly Milk River, along the Missouri River. Finally, the military might have drawn meaning, and embarrassment, from the facility with which the Indians, whole families as well as warriors, crossed and recrossed a river that the cavalry never succeeded in fording.

The balance of the Yellowstone Expedition proved routine. Surveyors and escort pushed on up the Yellowstone another thirty miles, as far as the looming stone landmark of Pompey's Pillar. Then they crossed northward to the upper reaches of the Musselshell River before turning about for the march back to Stanley's Stockade. From here, early in September, Custer and six companies of cavalry escorted surveyors eastward into the Badlands for additional work before continuing on the backtrail to the Missouri River. Stanley and the infantry followed more slowly in the rear.

"Welcome home," read the telegram from General Sheridan handed to Custer as the Seventh Cavalry marched into camp at Fort Abraham Lincoln. The nation also proclaimed its welcome. The *New York Tribune* and the *Army and Navy Journal* published his official report in full, and newspapers everywhere praised the "Glorious Boy," as one called him, for his Indian victories, his exploratory achievements, and his hunting deeds. Fittingly coinciding with the appearance of his *Galaxy* articles, Custer's exploits on the Yellowstone paraded him before the American people more prominently and favorably than at any time since the Washita. "What a history and reputation the 7th has achieved for itself," he enthused to Libbie.

All but unnoticed amid the tumult of Custer's return, Colonel Stanley and the plodding infantry also found their way back to Fort Lincoln. Stanley quietly returned to his home post of Fort Sully, down the Missouri River a comfortable distance from the flamboyant new presence at Fort Lincoln.

Custer posted six of his cavalry companies at Fort Lincoln. Four, under Major Joseph G. Tilford, took station at Fort Rice, twenty-five miles down the Missouri. The other two, Major Reno's northern boundary survey escort, were assigned to Fort Totten, to the north-east on Devil's Lake.

Custer delighted in the gratitude of the Northern Pacific Railroad. "My little durl never saw people more enthusiastic over the 7th and her dear Bo than are the representatives of the R.R.," he wrote Libbie.

The Yellowstone Expedition marked only the beginning of a fruit-ful relationship, for Custer's new assignment positioned him, offi-cially and personally, to continue helping the Northern Pacific. He commanded not only the new post of Fort Lincoln, established spe-cifically to serve railroad interests, but also the Middle District of the Department of Dakota, which included three other Missouri River posts as well.

The Northern Pacific needed all the help it could get. Even as the Yellowstone Expedition disbanded in September 1873, the failure of Jay Cooke's banking house plunged the railroad into bankruptcy and touched off the Panic of 1873. For six years end of track remained stalled at Bismarck while capitalists sought to reassemble the com-pany and resume the advance toward the Pacific Northwest. Illustrat-ing the identity of interests and aims between the army and the trans-continental railroads, Custer aided materially in the enterprise.

The fiscal revival and solvency of the Northern Pacific depended on settling the lands through which it ran. The company's principal asset, especially after the financial collapse, was millions of acres of public domain granted by the federal government. Until these lands could be sold to immigrants and an agricultural way business cre-ated, the railroad could not expect to turn a profit. As financial agent for the Northern Pacific, Jay Cooke understood this necessity, and his publicists portrayed the northern plains as a "Fruitful Garden," blessed by fertile soil and gentle climate.

In Custer's eyes, which magnified nearly everything, much of the country he saw on the Yellowstone Expedition, although perhaps not so bounteously endowed as Cooke's promoters claimed, could indeed be turned into a fruitful garden. Except for the Badlands, he judged the Dakota plains and the Yellowstone Valley congenial to wheat growers and stockmen.

One who thought differently was the commanding officer of Fort Buford, high on the Missouri River opposite the mouth of the Yel-lowstone. William B. Hazen, brevet major general and colonel of the

Sixth Infantry, had differed with Custer, and Sheridan, in the past. At West Point, in 1861, Lieutenant Hazen had placed Custer in arrest. With Sheridan he had quarreled over battle honors at Missionary Ridge in 1863. With Sheridan and Custer he had quarreled over whether the Kiowas at Fort Cobb in December 1868 were peaceful or hostile. A truculent controversialist, Hazen was not one to bury old feuds or smooth over disagreements. His assignment to remote Fort Buford in 1872 represented a barely concealed banishment ordained by Sheridan.

Jay Cooke's promotional literature incensed Hazen, who had endured enough of Fort Buford to have a pessimistic view of the country's agricultural future. He set his opinions to paper and mailed them to the *New York Tribune*. WORTHLESS RAILROAD LAND, headlined the *Tribune* in its issue of February 7, 1874. In the article Hazen scored the Northern Pacific for "shameless falsehoods" and characterized the railroad's so-called "Northern Tropical Belt" as an arid waste, sunblasted in summer, frozen in winter, that on its merits could not command a "penny an acre."

To meet the "effusion of the gallant Col. of the '6th Foot,'" the Northern Pacific's Tom Rosser called on his friend Custer. Citing his own observations the previous summer and drawing heavily on Northern Pacific literature, Custer prepared a rebuttal. Published in the *Minneapolis Tribune* of April 17, 1874, it drew as bright a picture as Hazen's was bleak. "Dashing Cavalry General Goes for Scalp of Hazen," proclaimed the *Bismarck Tribune* as the newspaper war heated up.

Colonel Hazen fought back. A lengthy article appeared in the January 1875 issue of *North American Review*, and he followed the same year with a book, *Our Barren Lands*. Also in 1875, broadening the feud with Custer, Hazen prepared and privately published a pamphlet, "Some Corrections of 'My Life on the Plains,'" in which he dissected Custer's published history of the Washita Campaign and refuted the Sheridan-Custer contention that the Kiowas of Lone Wolf and Satanta richly deserved punishment.

The Northern Pacific thanked Custer profusely. Alfred B. Nettleton, agent for the company's bankruptcy trustees, wrote Custer an appreciative letter promising to have his article reprinted and widely circulated. Like Rosser, Nettleton was an old friend and admirer; he had commanded an Ohio regiment in the Third Division. As with all the transcontinental railroads, the Northern Pacific enjoyed personal bonds, rooted in the Civil War, between its builders and its military guardians.

The Northern Pacific showed its gratitude in other ways as well. Custer's favorite field shelter, a spacious wall tent, bore the stenciled label, NPRR. He and Libbie rarely boarded an N.P. passenger coach without a pass that relieved them of any cost. On occasion they traveled in a private car, and in at least one instance the company provided a special train and then made heroic efforts to free it from snowdrifts in which a winter storm imprisoned it.

In such exchange of favors, later generations would see conflict of interest at best, blatant corruption at worst. Gilded Age standards, however, condoned these transactions. Practitioners on both sides did not regard their honor or integrity compromised or any services purchased that would not have been freely extended anyway as a matter of duty. Most army officers, from Sherman down, firmly believed it a national purpose and a military responsibility to help the railroads in every way possible; and most army officers, and their families, traveled free on the railroads without the least stirring of guilt. Within this ethical context Custer served the Northern Pacific.

The military aid received by the Northern Pacific testified not only to the army's assessment of strategic importance and institutional self-interest but to the truly national character of all the transcontinental lines. Also receiving federal land grants, federal financial backing, and federal charters, they were public enterprises dedicated to public purposes as well as private profit. If the army helped enrich the capitalists who built the roads, which it did, it also helped attain the national purposes of conquering the West and bringing the Indians under control.

And, in fact, no single force proved more decisive in the conquest of the Indians than the railroads. Ever the realist, General Sherman clearly understood the significance of the railroads. Reflecting on the tranquility that lay on the frontier at the time of his retirement in 1883, he observed: "The Army has been a large factor in producing this result, but it is not the only one. Immigration and the occupation by industrious farmers and miners of lands vacated by the aborigines have been largely instrumental to that end, but the *railroad* which used to follow in the rear now goes forward with the picket-line in the great battle of civilization with barbarism, and has become the *greater* cause."

For Custer that result lay in a future he would not live to see. His service to the Northern Pacific, however, did not end with his rejoinder to Hazen. Even as his letter set off a national newspaper debate in the spring of 1874, Custer made ready to embark on another adventure, one in which he would give further aid to the railroad while also embracing an equally powerful force in the conquest of the American West—gold.

CHAPTER 6

Gold

THE Dakota winter had already begun to set in when, late on a November afternoon in 1873, the train bearing the Custers pulled into the Northern Pacific depot at Bismarck. An army ambulance conveyed the couple, together with Maggie Calhoun and a young lady friend of Libbie from Monroe, out on the ice that had already begun to form on the Missouri River. A rowboat tossing precariously on the swift current transferred them, to Libbie's unforgettable terror, to the ice extending from the west bank. A short walk across the ice brought them to shore, where Lieutenant Tom Custer packed them into another ambulance for the short drive to the fort.

"In the dim light I could see the great post of Fort Lincoln," remembered Libbie, awed by the transformation wrought since she and other wives had viewed the barren site the previous spring, before parting with their husbands for the summer. The fort occupied a broad level plain between the river and gentle slopes rising to table-land on the west. Like most other frontier posts, it was not fortified but was rather groupings of buildings arranged with military precision around a parade ground. Officers' row, a line of seven frame houses, edged the parade ground on the west, at the base of the plateau. Facing the officers' line from the east side of the parade ground were three barracks for enlisted men, with attached kitchens and mess halls. Completing the rectangle on north and south were commissary and quartermaster storehouses, adjutant's office, guardhouse, and hospital. Behind the barracks, near the river, sprawled stables and corrals for the cavalry horses. "Suds Row," the rude habitations of laundresses and their soldier husbands, hid behind the corrals. On the brow of the hills to the north, the original site selected for the post in 1872, stood a cluster of buildings that now housed the garrison's infantrymen.

On a sketch map sent to Libbie in September, Custer had drawn a large square in the center of officers' row and labeled it "Weuns."

This was the commanding officer's quarters, a roomy two-story house with an inviting veranda, more imposing than its neighbors and pronounced by its builder to be the finest on the frontier. Before journeying back to Monroe to get Libbie, Armstrong and Mary had furnished the house, but Libbie had been left to expect a cold and empty edifice that she would have to make into a home.

As the ambulance bearing the Custer party swung onto the parade

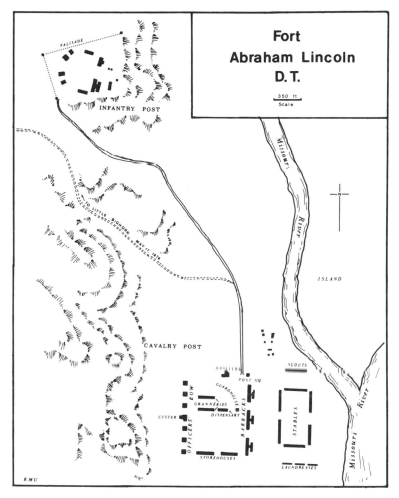

Fort Abraham Lincoln, D. T.

ground in the frigid dusk, the big house glowed with light. Fires danced in the fireplaces. A feast prepared by Mary laden the tables. The regimental band struck up "Home Sweet Home." Then, to the lilting strains of "Garry Owen," the officers and wives of Fort Lincoln boisterously welcomed the commanding officer and his lady to their new home.

The new home did not stand for long. It had been insulated with a highly touted "warm paper" that caught fire late one freezing February night in 1874. The house with most of its contents swiftly burned to the ground, leaving the occupants homeless. Another, equally grand, rose in its place, and from here, for the next two years, the Custers reigned over the social scene of Fort Lincoln.

A gay and lively scene it was, long remembered by those who shared it. Autie and Libbie almost always had one or more of Monroe's young beauties as long-term guests, an enticement that ensured the frequent presence of the post's bachelor officers and stimulated the robust matchmaking proclivities of the Custers. Evening entertainments centered on tables spread with the bounty of Mary's kitchen and on a piano rented in Saint Paul. Charades consumed endless hours and prompted great hilarity. Much thought and planning also went into the inventive practical jokes that the Custers had always inflicted on family members. Calhoun, dour and humorless, was a favorite target. "How they do tease and devil Mr Calhoun," Autie marveled.

Beyond the Custer household the garrison at large strove with equal diligence to conquer boredom with creative entertainment. Festive balls and hops, theatrical performances, concerts by the regimental band, and other indoor amusements competed with summer pastimes of riding, shooting, hunting, horse racing, baseball, and picnics amid a shady grove along the Heart River. Officers and enlisted men had their separate recreation, and on occasion the two intersected. Monthly company balls staged by the enlisted men included officers and their wives. Dramas and minstrel performances contrived by enlisted men played to front benches reserved for officers and wives.

The Custers also entertained visiting friends and dignitaries and even, as in Kansas, the excursionists to end of track who wanted to shake hands with the famous General Custer. To all who came, the Custer home and the post at large projected an aura of close-knit intimacy, good cheer, and a cordiality rare in military garrisons. In the big house in the middle of officers' row, recalled a visitor, "one was permitted to receive the courtesies of the happiest home I ever saw, where perfect love and confidence reigned." Beyond, he noted, "The whole regiment with one or two exceptions seemed imbued with the spirit of its commander, and in fact so close was he to his officers, that when off duty one would be led to think that all were brothers, and happy brothers at that." Years later an old paymaster recalled Fort Lincoln as the scene of the pleasantest experiences of his career. "So many memories cluster about Fort Lincoln," he wrote.

Relationships at Fort Lincoln may in fact have been as friendly as visitors perceived. Custer had retained with him companies officered by his intimates, while posting companies containing such uncongenial men as Captain Benteen to Fort Rice. With two of the regiment's majors, Tilford and Reno, Custer's relations were cool; with the third, Lewis Merrill, they were actively hostile. But all three remained agreeably distant—Tilford at Rice, Reno at Totten, and Merrill on detached service in the East and did not disturb the world Autie and Libbie created at Fort Lincoln. For the most part this world consisted of the royal family and those compatible with it.

Complacency did not reign unchallenged, for Indians kept the garrison constantly on guard. The infantry post on the hill attested to the Indian danger. The barracks, quarters, and other structures had been erected behind a log palisade with projecting blockhouses designed to ward off direct attack. Indians almost never attacked a military fort, but in 1872 and 1873, before the arrival of the cavalry, the infantry skirmished with bold raiding parties and twice had to beat off attacks on the fort itself.

Most likely the aggressors came from the Grand River and Cheyenne River agencies, where Hunkpapa, Miniconjou, and Sans Arc Sioux drew rations. Some, however, may have been from the hunting bands of Sitting Bull, who often gravitated as far east as the Missouri in periodic visits to their kin at the agencies. For the Sioux the appeal of this area lay not in soldiers and neighboring ranchers but in the Mandan and Arikara (or Ree) Indians, hereditary enemies, who lived upstream at the Fort Berthold Agency.

The restive disposition of the Sioux, as their agents reported, reflected the approach of the Northern Pacific Railroad. At the Milk

River Agency, high on the Missouri in Montana, elements of Sitting Bull's followers complained bitterly of the surveying activity along the Yellowstone and its effect on the game. People from the hunting bands also frequented the agencies of the Oglala and Brule Sioux. These two agencies were located in northwestern Nebraska rather than on the Missouri, where the government wanted them. The cantankerous (and rival) chiefs for whom the agencies were named, Red Cloud and Spotted Tail, so stubbornly insisted on remote locations that the Indian Bureau gave in.

Large numbers of people from the Sitting Bull bands showed up at these two agencies in the autumn of 1873, just after their battles with Custer on the Yellowstone. They were "exceedingly vicious and insolent," reported the Red Cloud agent, and kept the agency in turmoil all winter. In February 1874 one of them murdered the agency clerk. At the same time, farther west, a roving party shot and killed a lieutenant and a corporal out of Fort Laramie. At once Sheridan dispatched a strong force from Fort Laramie to impose order on the agencies. Nearby the troops built Camps Robinson and Sheridan.

The turbulence on the Sioux reservation continued to wash shock waves into Custer's district. Isolated ranchers fell prey to marauding Sioux, and residents of the forts dared not venture beyond the post limits. On April 23, 1874, a raiding party stampeded a civilian herd of eighty mules grazing within sight of the Fort Lincoln parade ground. Custer had "Boots and Saddles" sounded with such repetitive urgency that all six companies of cavalry tumbled in pursuit, leaving the ladies to endure a day of defenseless terror. Custer pressed the Indians so closely that they abandoned their loot, but they suffered no damage beyond one man wounded. Again in late May, Custer took to the field, attempting to head off a Sioux foray against the Rees and Mandans, but the quarry eluded him.

Despite occasional incursions of Sioux warriors, Custer's district remained on the far edges of the world of the Sioux, only mildly threatened compared with the menace and bloodshed that had led to the dispatch of troops to Red Cloud and Spotted Tail agencies. Even before the founding of Camps Robinson and Sheridan at those agencies, however, General Sheridan had concluded that a more strategically located post was needed to discourage the Indians at Red Cloud and Spotted Tail from raiding the Nebraska settlements and travel routes to their south. A post to their north would meet this purpose, he decided: "By holding an interior point in the heart of the Indian country we could threaten the villages and stock of the Indians, if they made raids on our settlements."

Sheridan's new fort would thus fall somewhere in the vicinity of the Black Hills. These invitingly wooded mountains sprawled over the western portion of the Great Sioux Reservation, remote, mysterious, and imperfectly known to the outside world. The Sioux treasured the Black Hills as their "Meat Pack," rich in game, with sheltered valleys and abundant firewood, ideal for winter camping. Drawn by these resources, they had seized the hills from the Kiowas almost a century earlier and had jealously guarded them against whites and other Indians ever since.

Sheridan knew that a reconnaissance would be necessary to find a suitable site for his fort. In the autumn of 1873 he discussed the matter with President Grant, the secretaries of war and the interior, and General Sherman. All concurred. At first Sheridan intended to launch the expedition from Fort Laramie, only a hundred miles southwest of the hills. But the belligerent temper of the Sioux at Red Cloud and Spotted Tail (combined with some pointed hints from his old friend at Fort Lincoln) led to a change of plans. An approach from the north, even though three times as far, would be less likely to disturb the Indians. Thus the assignment to explore the Black Hills fell to George Armstrong Custer.

Officially, from beginning to end, the objective of the Black Hills Expedition of 1874 remained the search for a suitable site to build a military post. Friends of the Indian scored the operation as a violation of the Treaty of 1868, which barred whites from the Great Sioux Reservation. Generals Sherman and Terry, both members of the commission that negotiated the treaty, scoffed at such a notion, pointing out that government officers in discharge of their duties were explicitly excepted and that three military posts had already been established on the reservation without protest from anyone.

Although somewhat labored, this interpretation was honestly debatable. Less debatable was another purpose of the Black Hills Expedition of 1874, a purpose never officially acknowledged, one with serious implications for the integrity of the treaty, and one that as a grievance in the minds of the Sioux would eclipse the Northern Pacific Railroad. That purpose was gold.

"If the whole Army of the United States stood in the way, the wave of emigration would pass over it to seek the valley where gold was to be found." So declared Senator John Sherman, the general's brother, to his congressional colleagues in the summer of 1867. Thus it had always been—in California, the Pacific Northwest, Nevada, Montana, Colorado, and the Southwest. No alarm more surely set off Senator Sherman's "wave of emigration," more surely condemned Indian land to white conquest, more surely demoralized, displaced, or even destroyed the Indian inhabitants, than the cry of gold. It was a potent factor fueling the westward movement and dooming the western Indians.

In the imagination of Americans the Black Hills offered the last great mining frontier of the West. For almost half a century rumors of gold in the Black Hills had periodically tantalized the nation and stirred boomlets in frontier towns. But the region remained unexplored and unknown, the haunt of Indians who turned aside all comers or made certain that none who entered succeeded in departing. In Yankton and Bismarck, "Dakota promoters" championed the Black Hills as essential to the territory's prosperity, and the legislature petitioned the federal government to conduct a geological survey that would prove or disprove the persistent rumors.

The Treaty of 1868 infuriated Dakotans, for it unmistakably confirmed the Black Hills as Indian domain, part of the Great Sioux Reservation and therefore barred to all white settlers and even travelers. The "abominable compact with the marauding bands," as a Yankton paper put it, did not dampen enthusiasm for opening the hills. On the contrary, impoverishing thousands, the Panic of 1873 kindled new ardor. "As the Christian looks forward with hope and faith to that land of pure delight," rhapsodized the *Bismarck Tribune*, "so the miner looks forward to the Black Hills, a region of fabulous wealth, where the rills repose on beds of gold and the rocks are studded with precious metal."

Stirred by such seductive visions, would-be prospectors organized gold-hunting forays. Threatening military action against any who trespassed on the Sioux reservation, the government headed them off. But as the *Tribune's* editor pointed out in a comment reminiscent of Senator Sherman, "the time has come when the entire army could not much longer keep the country from being over run by the invincible white man—by the hardy pioneer."

The time had already come, and even then, in May 1874, the army had begun to side with the "hardy pioneer." Across the Missouri River from the *Tribune's* office, Fort Abraham Lincoln whirred with preparations as the Seventh Cavalry made ready for a second summer in the field. As in 1873, the "scientific corps" contained engineers, topographers, and other specialists needed to classify and map the country and fix a suitable site for a fort. But on hand as well, by invitation of Custer, were two "practical miners," men who knew pay dirt when they saw it in their pan. Personifying the second, unadmitted objective of the Black Hills Expedition, William McKay and Horatio Nelson Ross also represented the army's sensitivity to public opinion. In view of the clamor about gold in the Black Hills, no military expedition could have entered the hills for any purpose without also looking for gold.

Besides McKay and Ross, other personnel reflected interests beyond the purely military. Three journalists went along—William E. Curtis for the *Chicago Inter-Ocean* and the *New York World*, Samuel J. Barrows for the *New York Tribune*, and Nathan H. Knappen for the *Bismarck Tribune*. Botanist A. B. Donaldson and a teamster, James P. Power, filed dispatches to the two Saint Paul papers. A Saint Paul photographer, William H. Illingworth, hauled his cumbersome gear in the service of the chief engineer of the expedition, Captain William Ludlow (the same Ludlow whose fisticuffs had got Custer in trouble at West Point in 1861; he was now chief engineer of the Department of Dakota and had also accompanied the Yellowstone Expedition of 1873).

Two staff officers showed up as observers for General Sheridan. One was Major George A. ("Sandy") Forsyth, hero of Beecher's Island. The other was Lieutenant Colonel Fred Grant, son of the president, to whom Custer had taken a liking on the Yellowstone the year before.

The Black Hills Expedition marched out of Fort Lincoln on July 2, 1874. The Seventh Cavalry band, sixteen musicians mounted on white horses, played "The Girl I Left Behind Me" as the column shook itself into formation for the dusty trek to the Black Hills.

The command made an imposing sight. All of the Seventh Cavalry except the two companies on the northern boundary survey had been concentrated for the mission. Custer formed them into two wings, one under Major Tilford, of Fort Rice, the other under Sandy Forsyth, pressed into service to help make up for the shortage of officers of the Seventh. On the open plains the train of more than a hundred canvas-topped wagons traveled in four parallel lines, with the cavalry of Tilford and Forsyth on the far flanks. Two companies of infantry marched close by the wagons. In front three rapid-fire Gatling guns and a Rodman cannon clanked behind condemned cavalry horses. Sixty-one Indian scouts, mostly Arikaras, rode far in advance. Among them, again this year, was Custer's favorite, Bloody Knife. In all the expedition counted more than a thousand men.

The first phase of the march was a 227-mile trek of two weeks over parched, sunblasted plains. The route lay southwest across the Cannonball and Grand rivers to the upper reaches of the Little Missouri. Here, in welcome relief, the country turned pleasantly wooded and well watered, and the temperatures cooled. Entering the Black Hills from the northwest, the troops found themselves in a wonderland of forested slopes, grassy valleys, and alpine meadows exploding with wild flowers. The cool, pulsing streams teemed with trout, and the hills came alive with antelope, deer, elk, and game birds. "We have discovered a rich and beautiful country," Custer wrote Libbie.

The expedition had set forth amid speculation that it would have to fight its way into the hills. With cavalry, infantry, and artillery, it went amply prepared. Even before entering the hills, troops spotted parties of warriors tracking the command's progress, and signal smokes spread a tense readiness through the companies.

Not for another two weeks did anyone see more Indians. Then, shortly after entering the hills, the troops came face-to-face with Sioux: five lodges standing forlornly in Castle Creek Valley. Surrounding the little village with a company of cavalry, Custer went in under a flag of truce. He found several surprised and frightened families of Oglalas, twenty-seven people in all, up from Red Cloud Agency on a hunting trip. Custer and the leader, Chief One Stab, smoked a peace pipe and talked about the country. Custer invited him to bring his people to the military camp for presents of sugar, bacon, and coffee.

Next day the Indians responded to the invitation. But the Ree scouts, angry that Custer would not let them kill all the Sioux, dressed for war and behaved so menacingly that the guests took fright and stampeded. One scuffled with a scout and was shot at as he fled; blood later found on the ground showed that the bullet had hit either the Indian or his mount. All but One Stab lost themselves in the hills, abandoning their tipis as they ran. The chief was not so fortunate. As Custer wrote disarmingly, "I have effected arrangements by which the Chief One Stab remains with us as a guide."

No more Sioux showed themselves, and the excursion through the Black Hills turned into even more frolicsome a picnic than the Yellowstone outing of 1873. As on the Yellowstone, Custer reveled in the presence of his "clan." Calhoun served as adjutant again, "Fresh" Smith as quartermaster. Tom Custer, Moylan, and Yates commanded companies. Present this year for the first time was a third Custer brother, Boston, age twenty-five. The quartermaster rolls bore his name as "guide." "Bos takes to life on the plains as naturally as if bred to it," Autie proudly informed Libbie.

The profusion of game inspired Custer to new hunting feats. The ubiquitous pack of hounds bounded in all directions and filled their lord with pride over their marvelous achievements. The antelope herds in particular suffered fearful casualties; but for the master hunter the zenith of the summer came shortly before the column left the Black Hills. "I have reached the highest rung on the hunters ladder of fame," he wrote Libbie. "I have killed my grizzly after a most exciting hunt & combat." To support the claim, he enclosed a photograph taken by the expedition's photographer. It pictured the hunter and his prize, together with his orderly, Captain Ludlow of the engineers, and Bloody Knife. What Custer did not divulge was that the carcass contained not only two bullets from his own Remington but three bullets fired by Ludlow and Bloody Knife.

Another incident also shed light on Custer's pride in his reputation as a marksman. George Bird Grinnell, one of the scientists, took a saddle of deer to Custer's tent for his evening meal. Grinnell's assistant, scout Luther North, had shot it during the day. "Captain North did some remarkable shooting today," Grinnell explained. "He killed three running deer in three shots." Custer's response: "Huh, I found two more horned toads today."

The toads formed only part of Custer's personal scientific trove, for the Black Hills proved almost as rich a field for his collecting instincts as the Yellowstone badlands. "Antelope Fred" Snow drove his personal ambulance and "had charge of his collection of curiosities." While the "professors and bug hunters," as Snow called them, made their official collections, Custer filled his ambulance not only with fossils and other interesting specimens but also with wildlife destined for Central Park's zoo. In September the New York City

Department of Parks thanked him for his gift of rattlesnakes, a badger, a porcupine, two marsh hawks, and a jackrabbit.

"There has been no drunkenness on this trip and no card playing," Custer happily informed Libbie. He had written her similar assurances in 1873 even when letter after letter had already recounted drunkenness and gambling in his own inner circle. Again this year he either simply lied or wrapped himself in typical self-delusion. Like the Yellowstone Expedition, the Black Hills picnic did not want for alcoholic lubrication, as diarists and even the expedition photographer documented.

Tirelessly, with two or three hours of sleep a night, Custer played many roles besides hunter and collector. "I have been Commanding Officer and everything else particularly guide since the expedition started," he told Libbie. As in 1873, he blazed each day's trail himself, through country far more difficult than on the Yellowstone. Even in the most tortuous defiles he usually found a route. As a trooper remarked, Custer was "not used to being thwarted, even by nature." Antelope Fred struggled to keep up with the ambulance, aided by a twelve-man detail that lifted it over obstructions and, unhitched from the team, lowered it by ropes down mountainsides. A pioneer corps followed to make way for the command and the wagon train. At night, as others fell into exhausted sleep, Custer sat in his candlelit tent penning long letters to Libbie, drafting official reports, and even, on one occasion, composing a forty-five-page dispatch for the *New York World*.

As the command moved south and east through the hills, Ross and McKay panned the streams without result. The end of July found them working upper French Creek, a stream that flowed southeast to Cheyenne River and the plains below. In one of his pioneering scouts Custer had located this pleasant glade, of which one of the scientists recorded: "After much entreaty, his modesty as far gave way as reluctantly to consent to the request of the topographical engineer that the name be Custer Park." Here in Custer Park, on July 30, 1874, Horatio Nelson Ross spotted the glint of gold in his pan.

The first discovery was so nominal as to stir little excitement. Even later, when flecks of gold continued to show up in the pans, the explorers found more engrossing interests. As the command tarried, they slept, strolled the countryside, played baseball, applauded the band's rendition of "The Blue Danube" and the perennial "Garry

Owen," and, for officers only, relished a lavish champagne party thrown by Major Tilford. Custer climbed Harney Peak, the highest point in the Black Hills, and Captain Ludlow, the topographer, named two lesser peaks in honor of Generals Terry and Custer.

Ross and McKay kept at it, and gradually the color improved. On August 1 they estimated that a hard day of panning, under ideal conditions, might net a prospector fifty to seventy-five dollars. Though scarcely a bonanza appraisal, the miners' judgment finally caught the expedition's attention, and next morning men lined the creek with every conceivable implement and utensil to try their luck. Twenty banded together in the Custer Park Mining Company and recorded claims near the discovery site.

Coincidentally or not, Custer chose this moment to send a messenger to the outside world. "Lonesome Charley" Reynolds had been engaged for this very purpose. A scout of exceptional competence combined with pronounced taciturnity and modesty, he had performed a similar mission for Custer in 1873. Leaving a base camp on French Creek, Custer sent two companies to reconnoiter to the southeast while he, with Forsyth's five companies, struck off to the south accompanied by Reynolds. At Cheyenne River, on the southern edge of the hills, the command turned back while Reynolds continued the ninety miles to Fort Laramie.

On August 7, Custer abandoned his base camp on French Creek and pointed the command northward. After hard marching in country almost impassable for wagons, he broke free of the hills on August 14 and camped near Bear Butte, a solitary mountain rising from the level plain. Here, before beginning the hot and difficult march back to Fort Lincoln, Custer penned another official report. He dwelled at length on the lushness and beauty of the hills, their immense potential for agriculture, and the likelihood of mineral riches. Neither here nor elsewhere, however, did he discuss the ostensible purpose of the expedition—to locate a site for a fort. In 1878, Fort Meade would be built near Bear Butte.

"We all leave the Black Hills with regret," Sandy Forsyth wrote in his journal on August 14, "for we have enjoyed them very much. The scenery is beautiful, grass splendid, water fine, and climate delightful. I hope to see the day when there will be any number of brave settlers and fine farms there." Two weeks later, on August 30, 1874, the Seventh Cavalry paraded smartly onto the Fort Lincoln quadrangle. To the strains of "Garry Owen," the Black Hills picnic drew to an end.

Already the Dakota frontier rocked with an excitement ignited by the contents of Charley Reynolds's saddle pouch. In a long official report written on French Creek, Custer for once had controlled his addiction to embellishment. He mentioned that gold had been found, probably in paying quantities, but cautioned that "until further examination is made regarding the richness of gold, no opinion should be formed." Some of the press dispatches that Reynolds filed at Fort Laramie, however, showed less restraint. "They call it a ten dollar diggin's," wrote the *Inter-Ocean's* Curtis. "From the grass roots down it was 'pay dirt.'" Although the New York papers treated the reports warily, the *Inter-Ocean* and the Dakota journals had all they needed to trumpet a boom. "Rich Mines of Gold and Silver Reported Found by Custer," proclaimed the Yankton editor. "This immense section," declared Bismarck's editor, "bids fair to become the El Dorado of America."

Throwing aside his earlier restraint, Custer joined in the jubilation. The Black Hills contained a rich mining district, he told a reporter two days after reaching Fort Lincoln. "The reports are not exaggerated in the least; the prospects are even better than represented." The best outfitting point for the hills, he added, was Bismarck (which one reached, not coincidentally, on the Northern Pacific Railroad).

Men infected with the gold fever rushed to jumping off points on the Missouri and the Platte. Companies organized to hurry to the mineral district, others to outfit them. One party actually reached the hills during the autumn of 1874 and threw up a stockade to sit out the winter. Bismarck, Yankton, Sioux City, Omaha, and other frontier towns vied with one another in boosterism.

For the time being, boosterism offered the principal outlet for the frenzy, for El Dorado lay within the Great Sioux Reservation. The Interior Department proclaimed the Black Hills closed to whites because of the Treaty of 1868; President Grant ordered intruders kept out; and General Sheridan issued a widely publicized directive for the army to intercept all trespassing groups, burn their wagons, and hold the offenders at the nearest military post.

Faithful to the law and their orders, military officers nevertheless left no doubt of their sympathies. Sheridan himself set the tone even as he announced orders to apprehend all mining parties. If Congress extinguished the Indian claim, he said, he would "give cordial sup-

port to the settlement of the Black Hills." Custer was equally explicit.
"The military will do its duty," he told the *Bismarck Tribune*. But
once Sioux ownership had been eliminated, the army would help
prospective settlers in every way possible. "I shall recommend extinguishment of Indian title at the earliest moment practicable for military reasons."

These military reasons brought Custer from gold back to the
original rationale for the Black Hills Expedition and revealed how
easily military strategy could be summoned to the support of political expediency. In Custer's thinking, the Black Hills served the Sioux
in two ways. They were "a sort of back-room" in which to hide after
committing depredations on the Nebraska settlements and travel
routes. And they were a conduit for communication between the
agency Indians and the "hostile tribes" in the unceded territory. In
actuality they were neither, but the solution was plain: "The extinguishment of the Indian title to the Black Hills, and the establishment of a military post in the vicinity of Harney's Peak and another
at some point on the Little Missouri will settle the Indian question
so far as the Northwest is concerned."

Amid the torrent of strident demands for opening the Black Hills,
a controversy broke out over whether gold had even been discovered.
Newton H. Winchell, chief geologist of the Custer Expedition, expressed doubt, even suggesting that the "gold in the grassroots" had
been planted by Custer's "practical miners." Young Fred Grant sided
with Winchell. He had seen no more than three dollars' worth of
gold during the entire march, and he thought that this might have
been imported. Eastern newspapers ridiculed the gold mania as a
hoax, manufactured by the Northern Pacific Railroad to revive its
flagging fortunes.

Ever the friend of the Northern Pacific, Custer rushed to the defense. Composing a long rebuttal, he had it published in the *New
York World* early in December 1874. "Why Professor Winchell saw no
gold," he concluded, "was simply due to the fact that he neglected
to look for it."

Clearly an authoritative answer had to be sought, first, to settle
the debate over whether the hills contained gold, and second, if they
did, to fix a price tag to the much-discussed "extinguishment of title." The investigation would be conducted by a corps of civilian
scientists headed by Professor Walter P. Jenney of the New York

School of Mines and operating under the auspices of the Interior Department. But they would need a military escort, and everyone assumed that Custer would lead the Black Hills Expedition of 1875.

Custer assumed so, too, and through March and April 1875 he concentrated supplies and transportation at Fort Lincoln. Among other preparations, he invited Captain Yates's brother-in-law, just graduated from Lafayette College, to serve as his "private secretary." That Custer wanted such an assistant, unknown to military tables of organization, may have arisen from a letter received early in April from James Gordon Bennett of the *New York Herald*. Praising Custer for his writing style, Bennett invited him to serve the *Herald* as a paid correspondent with his own command, either openly over his own name, or anonymously.

But Custer did not lead the expedition. "Political influence and red tape," according to his prospective secretary, "caused the 1875 expedition to be abandoned." In actuality General Sheridan had shifted the base for the operation to Fort Laramie and assigned another officer to command Jenney's escort. Sheridan may have considered Custer too conspicuously identified with the mining interests or simply too unpredictable for a mission with such inflammatory political implications. Also, General Terry, Custer's superior as department commander, championed Indian rights and appeared more intent on severe treatment of white intruders than on discovering new fuel for the gold rush. Although the Black Hills lay in Terry's Department of Dakota, they were more accessible from the Department of the Platte, now headed by a general to whom Sheridan felt closer than to Terry.

He was Brigadier General George Crook, West Point classmate and trusted friend of Sheridan. Like Custer, Crook had emerged from the Civil War a brevet major general and lieutenant colonel of regulars. He had done so well against the Paiutes of Oregon, however, that President Grant, jumping him over all the colonels in the army, had made him a brigadier. Crook had promptly cowed the formidable Apaches and brought calm to bloody Arizona, which led Sheridan to ask for him on the northern plains. With a thick, blond beard, forked and sometimes braided, canvas suit, and durable mule, Crook projected an image of homespun simplicity. He was a reticent, unpretentious man who rarely shared his thoughts or plans with even his closest aides.

Sheridan assigned principal responsibility for dealing with the hills to Crook. As the twelve hundred miners in the hills discovered in July 1875, his sympathies lay with them, and he carried out his orders by instructing them to leave and then looking the other way when they returned. To Custer's disappointment, it made sense to Sheridan also to put protection of the Jenney survey under Crook's oversight rather than Terry's.

The Jenney party spent most of the summer of 1875 scrutinizing the hills. Without objection from the military escort, swarms of illegal prospectors accompanied Jenney's experts and provided "great assistance in prospecting the country." The scientists tested the streams, analyzed rock outcroppings, and definitively confirmed the presence of gold. It was not the fabulous bonanza portrayed by the newspapers and did not lend itself to prospecting in the "primitive manner with pan or rocker," but it promised ample reward to organized labor backed by moderate capital. Far from cooling the gold fever, the Jenney Expedition gave it new life.

Even as the Jenney survey examined the Black Hills, the government moved to open negotiations for their sale. Chiefs Red Cloud and Spotted Tail visited the capital in May 1875, but turned aside all attempts to talk about the hills. In June, therefore, the secretary of the interior appointed a commission to take the question to the Sioux at their agencies.

In September 1875, the Allison Commission confronted some five thousand Sioux at a council grounds near Red Cloud Agency. The commissioners handled their task ineptly and never put forth a clear, easily understood proposal. Mutual understanding suffered from bad translation. For their part, the Indians were belligerent, unruly, and fragmented into feuding factions. Large numbers of bellicose young warriors from the Sitting Bull bands had come down for the conference. Irate over the Northern Pacific Railroad and the invasion of the Black Hills, they threatened violence to any chiefs who gave in to the commissioners. For more than a week chaos dominated the daily councils. Testily the commissioners broke off the meeting and returned to Washington.

As the ordeal of the Allison Commission demonstrated, the violation of the Black Hills infuriated the Sioux. "Thieves' Road," they branded Custer's trail to the hills. The growing influx of more thieves and the army's failure to keep them out inflamed Sioux tempers still

more. Added to the festering resentment over the Northern Pacific
Railroad, the Black Hills stirred a dangerous and abiding rancor in
the agency bands as well as the Sitting Bull bands.

Yet, strangely, the Sioux did not lash out with violence. For the
Nebraska settlements and travel routes, Montana's exposed Gallatin
Valley, and the Missouri River frontier watched over by Custer, 1875
passed in almost eerie calm. The Indians might vent their rage in
stormy tantrums, but they did not, as in recent years, commit any
depredations. For Custer, 1875 did not even provide the excitement
of a chase after stolen mules.

One bit of excitement, however, did vary the dull military routine
of Fort Lincoln. Early in December 1874, Scout Charley Reynolds
visited the Standing Rock Agency, the old Grand River Agency now
relocated some forty miles upriver from the previous site. While
there, he overheard a prominent Hunkpapa warrior named Rain-in-
the-Face boast that he had killed three white men on the Yellowstone
River two summers earlier. The deed clearly referred to the slaying
of Veterinarian Honsinger, Sutler Baliran, and Trooper Ball as Custer fought off a Sioux war party on August 4, 1873. Alerted by
Reynolds, Custer determined to seize Rain-in-the-Face and have him
tried in the civil courts for murder.

Through deep snow, in temperatures as low as fifty below zero,
Captain Yates and Lieutenant Tom Custer set forth with a company
of cavalry. At Fort Rice they picked up Captain Thomas H. French's
company and continued to Standing Rock. There, on December 14,
the daredevil Tom took Charley Reynolds and five picked troopers
into the trader's store, filled with Indians heavily blanketed against
the cold. When one dropped his blanket enough to reveal himself as
Rain-in-the-Face, Reynolds signaled and Tom pounced. After a brief
scuffle Tom seized his captive's rifle and, with help from the soldiers,
bound his hands behind his back. Yates and other soldiers burst in,
covered the other Indians, and through an interpreter explained the
situation. Tom, meantime, spirited the prisoner out of the building,
lashed him to a horse, and got him safely to the military camp.

At Fort Lincoln, Custer lodged his celebrity in the guardhouse.
There he remained for more than three months. Custer interrogated
him at length and succeeded in extracting a confession that he had
indeed led the party that killed Honsinger, Baliran, and Ball. What
to do next, however, raised practical as well as legal questions, as

invariably happened when officials decided to try an Indian for murder in the white man's civil courts.

Rain-in-the-Face himself solved Custer's problem. His cell contained two Bismarck residents caught stealing army grain. On the night of April 18, 1875, confederates cut through the guardhouse wall and liberated their friends. Rain-in-the-Face also escaped, registering a vow, according to legend, that would inspire Henry Wadsworth Longfellow to poetic heights in describing the bloody vengeance wrought on the "White Chief with the yellow hair."

Throughout 1875, even though the Sioux gave no serious offense beyond declining to do the Great Father's bidding, sentiment built for a military solution to the Black Hills dilemma. The army felt increasing distress over the unpopularity and impossibility of preventing the white invasion of the hills. In their frustration Generals Sheridan, Crook, and Custer, if not General Terry, believed that the time had come for a military showdown with the Sioux. In preparation Custer wanted a fort in the Black Hills and one on the Little Missouri. Sheridan went even further. In June 1875 he sent staff officers up the Yellowstone by steamboat to look for good locations in the heart of the Sitting Bull country, and he recommended a fort at the mouth of the Tongue and another at the mouth of the Little Bighorn. President Grant leaned toward the thinking of his generals.

For a change, so did the Department of the Interior, whose cooperation was essential. Unless Interior asked for military intervention, the War Department remained powerless. Zachariah Chandler, longtime Michigan senator and friend of Custer, had just been named secretary of the interior. Unlike his predecessor, he did not look upon himself as a defender of Indian rights. Indeed, he may even have been appointed in a move to bring Interior into line behind the generals.

At the same time, in October 1875, the Allison Commission returned from Red Cloud Agency bristling with pugnacity. In their report they urged Congress to fix a fair value for the Black Hills and "then notify the Sioux Nation of its conclusion," which should be "presented to the Indians as a finality." If the Indians rejected it, all rations and annuities should be cut off. Moreover, thought the commissioners, no settlement seemed likely until the Sioux were made to feel the power of the United States.

The sentiment for a forceful policy crystallized in a meeting in the executive mansion on November 3, 1875. Present were President Grant, Secretary Chandler and his commissioner of Indian affairs, Secretary of War William W. Belknap, and Generals Sheridan and Crook, summoned from the West by the president. (General Sherman was not invited; he could be expected to dissent from any scheme that he saw as dishonest or illegal, and anyway, in a continuing feud with Secretary Belknap, he had moved his headquarters to Saint Louis.)

The meeting produced two presidential decisions. First, although the orders to bar miners from the Black Hills would remain in effect, the army would no longer try to enforce them. Second, the troublesome Sitting Bull bands would be compelled to abandon the unceded territory and settle on the reservation. Both decisions, of course, promoted the "extinguishment of title" that all sought, the first by filling up the Black Hills with white settlers and confronting the Indians with a *fait accompli*, the second by curbing the independence of the Sitting Bull Indians and thus their power to obstruct the sale of the hills.

The first purpose was self-fulfilling. By the winter of 1875–76, fifteen thousand white settlers occupied the Black Hills. The second purpose, getting the year-round roamers out of the unceded territory, posed a more difficult challenge. The Treaty of 1868 gave them every right to be there, and for a year no offense sufficient to warrant full-scale war could be blamed on them.

Nevertheless a scenario for launching the process was contrived, probably at the presidential meeting of November 3. Six days later Indian Inspector Erwin C. Watkins, recently returned from a routine inspection of Missouri River agencies, submitted a report on the "wild and hostile bands" in the unceded territory. Damning these Indians more by pejorative language than particular indictments, he concluded: "The true policy, in my judgment, is to send troops against them in the winter, the sooner the better, and *whip* them into subjection." The report perfectly reflected military views, a rarity in the correspondence of the Indian Bureau. Watkins's inexperience in his post, ignorance of his subject, and Civil War ties to Sheridan and Crook raise more than a suspicion that the two generals dictated, or even wrote, the Watkins report. Secretary Chandler heartily endorsed his subordinate's assessment of the problem and the proposed solution.

The program that Generals Sheridan and Crook pushed through

to presidential approval reflected the desperation to which the Grant administration had been brought by a political problem of the most compelling magnitude and complexity. On the one hand, the Treaty of 1868 imposed an unarguable legal mandate on the government to preserve the integrity of Indian lands. On the other hand, an over-powering public opinion demanded that the government step aside and allow enterprising citizens to tap the mineral riches locked up by a handful of natives who could never use them. That dilemma led the United States to manufacture a war against a people who for more than a year had withheld the only pretext—aggression against whites—that could have provided persuasive justification for war.

Although Custer had opened the Black Hills, he himself made little contribution toward moving the Sioux crisis from the first violation of the hills to the terrible denouement on the Little Bighorn two years later. He watched those developments from the sidelines, at distant Fort Lincoln, in the congenial drawing rooms of Monroe, or amid the sparkling pleasure resorts of New York City.

Despite his detachment, these events shaped his destiny. George Armstrong Custer blazed the Thieves' Road into the Black Hills, but it would lead ultimately to the Little Bighorn. With more than a shadow of truth, some observed that in the Black Hills he dug his own grave.

CHAPTER 7

Politics

OF the decisions in Washington that were about to trigger an Indian war, Custer knew little. As Sheridan plotted a winter campaign, Autie and Libbie enjoyed their usual winter holiday in New York City. A few hints of impending war cropped up in the press, but no military preparations were visible, and the correspondence that alerted Sheridan's two department commanders, Generals Crook and Terry, remained confidential. During this winter of 1875–76, Custer pursued other activities with which he had filled the year and a half of military idleness since the Black Hills Expedition.

For one, he had applied himself diligently to writing. *My Life on the Plains* had firmly established him as an author of note. A wordy, convoluted, pretentious style would prove tedious to future readers, but his contemporaries hailed the work as an absorbing picture of the frontier West. Who could have predicted, recalled a West Point classmate, that the rough-and-tumble soldier would also become a "scholar of artistic tastes and a writer of graphic contributions to the magazines?" "Your book," General Sherman assured him, "will turn the heads of all the bold spirits of the country."

Heartened, Custer wrote furiously—in hotel rooms, on trains, in his field tent, and at a desk in his study at Fort Lincoln, with Libbie seated next to him. He worked on more articles for *Galaxy*, dealing with his experiences in Dakota and Montana. He also turned to his long-interrupted war memoirs.

Custer's published writings recounted his adventures on the Plains, etched the self-portrait that he wanted the world to behold, and set forth his observations on Indians and Indian policy. On the last, he emerged as an expert in the eyes of the public as well as the men in Washington who made policy. On the eve of another Indian war in which he would play a prominent part, his views held more than passing interest.

Not surprisingly, in this man overflowing with contradictions, inconsistency marked his attitude toward Indians. "Stripped of the beautiful romance" of James Fenimore Cooper's novels, he wrote in *My Life on the Plains*, "the Indian forfeits his claim to the appellation of *noble* red man. We see him as he is . . . a savage in every sense of the word . . . one whose cruel and ferocious nature far exceeds that of any wild beast of the desert."

Thus wrote Custer the Indian fighter. But Custer the romantic delighted in the ways of the Indians, in "their rude interchange of civilities, their barterings, races, dances, legends, strange customs, and fantastic ceremonies." And Custer the plainsman marveled at the warrior's proficiency in horsemanship, personal combat, plainscraft, and hunting—skills in which he himself excelled.

Some who equated the Indians with wild beasts advocated extermination. Custer abhorred such talk. Yet he believed that the Indians must inevitably give way to what he and most others of his time saw as a higher civilization confronting them. They would not yield of their own accord, nor in response to any measure not backed by superior physical force, for they were "capable of recognizing no controlling influence but that of stern arbitrary power." The corrupt politicians of the Indian Bureau, manipulated by visionary idealists and rapacious contractors, could never supply such power. The army, responsible for conquering the Indians in war, should also be charged with managing and "civilizing" them in peace.

Custer never questioned the conviction of his age that the Indian's salvation lay in "civilizing" him, in making him into a Christian tiller of the soil embracing white values. But the prospective transformation was saddening. "If I were an Indian," he wrote in a much-quoted passage of his book, "I often think that I would greatly prefer to cast my lot among those of my people who adhered to the free open plains, rather than submit to the confined limits of a reservation, there to be the recipient of the blessed benefits of civilization, with its vices thrown in without stint or measure."

In his view of the Indian and Indian policy, Custer was not exceptional. Most of the frontier army's leadership shared his attitudes, contradictions included. George Crook, Nelson A. Miles, Ranald S. Mackenzie, Oliver O. Howard, Eugene A. Carr, and a host of lesser-known commanders approached the Indian and the Indian problem with similar ambiguity.

Ambiguity distinguished their service records too. Like Custer, all may be credited with acts of generosity and compassion. Like Custer at the Washita, all may be charged with attacking Indians of doubtful hostility and warring on women and children. In "unconventional" war the distinction between friend and foe, combatant and noncombatant, often grew blurred.

Writing obsessed Custer during the idle year of 1875 but could not contain the restlessness that fed his craving for action. The shift of the second Black Hills expedition to others came as a bitter disappointment. He had also hoped that another summer expedition would be ordered to the Yellowstone, under his command, but instead Sheridan sent staff officers up the river on a steamboat. As he wrote, therefore, Custer turned to another pastime that intrigued him, one in which he was less skilled and less successful—politics.

"My blood boils within me with indignation when I think of the unjust course now being pursued towards our brethren of the south," Custer wrote early in 1875 to his close friend, actor Lawrence Barrett. "But for the glorious results of the last election I would feel that men had good cause to have their faith shaken in the permanency of free popular government." As a conservative Democrat, Custer abhorred the Grant administration's harsh application of Reconstruction measures in the South, and he rejoiced when the Democrats captured the House of Representatives in the 1874 congressional elections.

Prudently, Custer refrained from publicly proclaiming his political convictions. Not so prudently, he did nothing to mask his close ties to the Democratic leadership, especially such moneyed party barons of New York City as August Belmont and Robert Roosevelt. Even less prudently, he played the dangerous game of working behind the scenes to malign the Republican administration and embarrass the president himself. For a lieutenant colonel to trifle so boldly with his commander in chief was dangerous, and his brief but calamitous alliance with President Andrew Johnson in 1866 should have convinced him that he was a better soldier than politician.

Such political sniping commonly took the form of newspaper items, printed without byline or over a *nom de plume*. Custer enjoyed strong bonds with leading Democratic journals, especially after the Yellowstone and Black Hills expeditions, coupled with his growing stature as an author, revived him as a national celebrity. In particular, the *New York World* and the *New York Herald* encouraged Custer to enrich their columns.

"I am often situated where I could telegraph you important bits of interesting items," Custer wrote in November 1874 to Jerome B. Stillson, an old friend from the Shenandoah campaigns who was managing editor of the *World*, "had I only arranged to have done so over another signature than my own." One bit of gossip—that Grant desired a third term—he obtained from within the president's own family (undoubtedly Fred Grant). As another example Custer cited the recent unveiling of a Lincoln statue in Springfield, Illinois, attended by President Grant and other high officials of the administration. The consternation produced in this group by news of the Democratic congressional victories in Ohio and Indiana would have made a good press item, Custer thought.

Also for Stillson, Custer advanced his assessment of the political prospects of Generals Sherman and Sheridan. "Sherman is fishing for a presidential nomination," he surmised, "but I think he is so unstable in his opinions that he would, like Grant did, accept from the first party that offered with any chance of success. Sheridan would make a much stronger radical candidate than Sherman as far as controlling the soldier vote goes. But he would be even more radical in his administration than Grant has ever been."

Custer had correctly appraised Sheridan. On treatment of the South he had been a hard liner from the beginning, as he had amply demonstrated when assigned Reconstruction duties. He had also loyally and uncritically supported the Grant administration despite its descent ever deeper into the morass of corruption and scandal. He had even participated in an attempted whitewash of the president's private secretary, Orville Babcock, in the face of overwhelming evidence of his complicity in the Whiskey Ring frauds.

Less accurate was Custer's estimate of Sherman, soon to utter one of history's most unequivocal refusals to run for president. Personally loyal to Grant the old soldier and horrified at the thought of the party of secession controlling the machinery of government, Sherman nevertheless became increasingly estranged from the administration. This resulted mainly from a bitter feud with Secretary of War William W. Belknap, a big-framed Iowa politician who had done well as a volunteer general under Sherman in the war but, like most of Grant's other appointees, fell woefully short of cabinet stature. Belknap supported the staff chiefs, lords of petty fiefdoms, in the perennial conflict over the powers of the general in chief. Deprived of all control over the staff and retaining little over the line, Sherman moved his headquarters to Saint Louis and virtually abdicated his post as general in chief.

Another of Custer's newspaper friends was James Gordon Bennett, Jr., the vigorous publisher of the *New York Herald*, perhaps the most vociferous of the anti-Grant journals. Custer regularly fed the *Herald* material that was damaging to the administration. He proved particularly helpful in the summer of 1875, when Bennett launched an exposé of official corruption at the forts and trading posts on the upper Missouri.

The assignment fell to reporter Ralph Meeker. As J. D. Thompson, Meeker poked anonymously around Bismarck and the federal outposts scattered along the river. Only Custer, the editor of the *Bismarck Tribune*, and the Bismarck postmistress knew Thompson's true character. From Custer, Meeker received information and leads as well as aid in converting into cash the *Herald* financial drafts that might have betrayed his identity.

Although not well focused, Meeker's investigations uncovered pools of corruption, which he laid bare in a series of revelations printed in the *Herald* from July to October 1875. The frauds grew out of the licensing of the monopoly traderships at the Indian agencies and forts. The former were the patronage preserve of the secretary of the interior, the latter of the secretary of war.

At the Indian agencies the culprit turned out to be not only Secretary of the Interior Columbus Delano but President Grant's worthless younger brother Orvil, who carried influence peddling to new levels of brazenness. In 1874, Delano revoked all Indian trading licenses on the upper Missouri. To get them renewed, traders had to deal with Orvil Grant. Those who failed to meet his terms saw their licenses awarded to others. The tradership scandal was but one of an accumulation of iniquities that brought down Delano in the autumn of 1875 and led to the appointment of Zachariah Chandler.

Similar arrangements for the designation of military post traders had been an open secret on the frontier for several years, as Custer undoubtedly explained to Ralph Meeker in detail. As early as 1872, Custer's literary antagonist, Colonel William B. Hazen, had come perilously close to accusing Secretary Belknap himself of selling the post tradership at Fort Sill, in Indian Territory. Custer knew that the Fort Lincoln trader, Robert Seip, had to pay heavily for his monopoly and that this prodigiously inflated the prices he charged the soldiers for his goods.

Custer suspected Belknap as the ultimate recipient of the kickback. He not only shared his suspicions with Meeker but when Belknap visited Fort Lincoln early in September 1875 greeted him with officially correct coolness. Libbie's charm offset her husband's demeanor, and the secretary did not even know that he had been snubbed. But Custer's complicity with Meeker and the *Herald* would form one of the strands in the rope that almost strangled him.

In the delicate art of extracting kickbacks, Custer himself may not have been a complete innocent. Only Captain Benteen's word (but with his sources of information named) supports a suspicion that Custer played the game. According to Benteen, when the Seventh camped near Forts Hays and McPherson in the summer of 1867, Custer placed them off limits to his command because the local sutlers would not meet his assessments. When soldiers violated his ban at Fort Hays, he had them paraded with shaved heads. At Fort McPherson he had transgressors doused in the Platte River.

At Camp Supply, at the close of the winter operations of 1868–69, an emissary from Custer allegedly solicited a contribution from the post trader. When he refused, Custer moved the regiment a day's march away from Camp Supply before allowing the men to be paid.

In 1873, Custer recruited Memphis gambler Augustus Baliran to serve as sutler to the Seventh on the Yellowstone Expedition. Before falling victim to Rain-in-the-Face, charged Benteen, Baliran had paid Custer eleven hundred dollars. A like partnership supposedly prevailed with John Smith during the Black Hills Expedition of 1874.

Benteen's allegations must be considered in light of their author's hatred of Custer. Other pieces, however, fit into the puzzle. Custer had always been obsessed with money. In promoting the Stevens silver mine, he had engaged in practices common at the time but, even so, more than faintly shady. One of his most reliable young officers suspected collusion between Custer and the captain of the steamboat that accompanied the Seventh up the Missouri in the spring of 1873; in motion the boat earned only the charge for carrying freight, but while tied to the bank it accrued an additional twenty dollars an hour. "This explains why Custer makes such short marches," Lieutenant George D. Wallace wrote to his father.

Most compelling, and most tantalizing, was a letter of August 22,

1875, to Custer from Colonel Rufus Ingalls, a wartime comrade now serving as acting quartermaster general of the army. Ingalls alluded to ambitious plans that he, Custer, and Ben Holladay were concocting. Transportation king of the West, Holladay had been associated with stagecoaches, steamships, and railroads for more than twenty-five years. His name was also synonymous with business skulduggery; anything he touched was apt to be tainted.

"We want to do a big thing in the Black Hills," Ingalls wrote. "Ben wants to put in Stages and be Sutler to new Posts. He has promise of Interior Dept Indian trade. He hopes a Depot, Post, Town &c will be at Cheyenne [River] Agency. Now, what think you? Ben counts much on you. . . . Now, what should he do to be in right *place* at right *time?*"

Ingalls also referred to another project that he and Custer had apparently discussed. This involved adoption of Goodenough horseshoes for the U.S. cavalry. "If I can have control over the whole subject of horse shoes &c.," he wrote, "I mean to ask a Board with yourself as President." All this could be easily managed, he thought, "if—if—if their shoes are actually the *best*, about which I am doubtful more than half the time. What think you?"

The scattered scraps of evidence raise more questions than they answer, and they do not convict Custer of dishonesty or wrongdoing. They are sufficiently complementary, however, to raise suspicions that should be borne in mind when assessing the makeup of George Armstrong Custer.

Ironically, whether his quest for wealth drew on fraudulent practices or not, at the close of 1875 Custer wandered into the fringes of a promising bonanza. The Redpath Lyceum Bureau, which managed the nation's star podium performers, offered him a contract to lecture five nights a week for four to five months, at two hundred dollars a night. Had not the Little Bighorn intervened, he might well have accumulated the modest fortune of which he so insistently dreamed.

Negotiations with Redpath were only part of Custer's activities during the winter leave of 1875–76. He and Libbie rented a room in a boardinghouse across the street from the Hotel Brunswick and kept the frantic social pace typical of their New York visits. Receptions, dinners, dancing, and the theater filled their waking hours. They saw much of their intimate friends, the Lawrence Barretts, and watched the great Shakespearean perform as Julius Caesar. A special treat was lunch with artist Albert Bierstadt in his studio. Everywhere they appeared, admirers flocked around both the general and his wife.

Amid the festivities Custer found time to plunge deeply into the stock market. Apparently he became involved in a wild stock speculation that, over a seven-month period, approached four hundred thousand dollars, an amount he could not have produced had cash been required. By early 1876 his loss stood at eighty-five hundred dollars. On February 10 he signed a promissory note for this amount, at 7 percent interest, to a Wall Street brokerage firm. Significantly, Ben Holladay cosigned the note. When litigation finally brought the matter to the surface seven years later, the judges of the District of Columbia Supreme Court were moved to observe: "It seems to us impossible to read these papers without being impressed with the idea that they refer to an illicit business, with which Custer was rather ashamed to be connected."

This escapade again reveals how desperately Custer wanted riches and how far he would go in their pursuit. Ben Holladay's involvement almost guarantees that the scheme, whatever the particulars, was as shady as the appellate judges later guessed. It may even have been a move toward exploiting the opening of the Black Hills, as forecast by Colonel Ingalls the previous summer. At the least it was a substitution of Custer's name for dollars such as had marked the promotion of the Stevens silver mine five years earlier.

Immediately after the signing of the promissory note, Autie and Libbie headed west, their five-month leave at an end. They departed oblivious to how soon Autie would be back in the East, snared by political coils partly of his own weaving. Those coils nearly saved his life—or, viewed another way, nearly prevented his ascent to glory.

Indian Inspector Watkins's report of November 9, 1875, called for a winter campaign, a Sheridan specialty. Winter had already come to the Great Plains, and Sheridan felt pressed to get started. But the army could not move against the Indians without a public invitation from the Interior Department. The record had to show clearly that the military simply responded to a civilian initiative.

Although Interior Secretary Chandler proved a willing accomplice in what was in truth a scheme hatched by the military, he too worried about the public record. As last-minute dressing for his call for war, therefore, early in December runners set forth from the Sioux agencies carrying an ultimatum to the Sitting Bull bands. If they failed to move onto the Great Sioux Reservation by January 31, 1876, the army would be sent to drive them in.

The implications of this delay disturbed Sheridan. "The matter of notifying the Indians to come in is perhaps well to put on paper," he wrote to Chandler on February 4, 1876, "but it will in all probability be regarded as a good joke by the Indians." If the troops were to move at all, it had to be immediately, while winter immobilized the Indians. "Unless they are caught before early spring," he concluded prophetically, "they can not be caught at all."

Catching them before spring required campaigning in a latitude with more severe winters than Kansas and Indian Territory. In December, Crook had pronounced himself ready to march as soon as he received orders. Terry had been more cautious. If the Sitting Bull bands were wintering near the mouth of the Little Missouri, as reported, they could be reached in a quick cavalry thrust from Fort Lincoln. Unsaid: if farther west, a buildup of troops and supplies would be necessary, and that could not be accomplished until melting snow and ice opened the Northern Pacific Railroad and the Missouri River. By early February, Terry had learned that these Indians were farther west, on the Yellowstone.

By this time the bureaucratic machinery in Washington had produced the required documentation for the war. The Sitting Bull bands had not heeded the order to report to the agencies by January 31. The next day Secretary of the Interior Chandler notified Belknap that "said Indians are hereby turned over to the War Department for such action as you deem proper." Down to Sheridan the word sped, and from him to Crook and Terry.

On February 15, 1876, Custer reported at department headquarters in Saint Paul. He discovered that virtually nothing had been done to prepare for the operation and that Sheridan was displeased that Terry had responded to his wishes less energetically than Crook. Terry, bereft of field experience against Indians, welcomed Custer with relief. Busily they turned to mobilization plans and strategy for the campaign that all, even Sheridan, now understood could not begin until spring, at the earliest.

Terry's strategy was simplicity itself and was probably as sound as any that could have been devised: turn Custer loose. "I think my only plan," the department commander wrote Sheridan on February 21, "will be to give Custer a secure base well up on the Yellowstone from which he can operate, at which he can find supplies, and to which he can retire at any time the Indians gather in too great numbers for the small force he will have." In short, infantry would man supply depots and escort supply trains while Custer led the Seventh Cavalry in probes for the enemy. A repeat of the Washita Campaign seemed in the offing. April 6 was the day fixed for the expedition's departure from Fort Lincoln.

On March 7 the Northern Pacific assembled a special train at Fargo to push Custer over the snow-blocked rails to Bismarck. Three locomotives and two plows drew assorted rolling stock, including a private car for the Custer party. Among passengers jammed into four coaches were men of the Twentieth Infantry chosen to operate three rapid-fire Gatling guns, which had been rolled in among the provisions in the eight freight cars.

The train had scarcely left Fargo when a late-winter blizzard struck. Temperatures plummeted, and drifts piled so high that the plows could not part them. Sixty-five miles short of Bismarck the train stuck fast in the snow. For nearly a week Custer fretted in impatience until Tom Custer (a captain since December) broke through with a mule-drawn sleigh to rescue Autie, Libbie, and the ubiquitous hounds. Not until March 13 did Custer reach Fort Lincoln, and not until a week later did the special train, freed by a thaw, puff into Bismarck with its other passengers.

After casting grave doubt on Custer's April 6 departure date, the blizzard roared southward into Wyoming to acquaint General Crook with the perils of winter campaigning. With eight hundred infantry and cavalry he had marched out of Fort Fetterman on March 1 and pointed up the old Bozeman Trail toward the Powder River. "The worse it gets, the better; always hunt Indians in bad weather," Crook had expounded. But deep snow, subzero temperatures, and driving blizzards wore down the troops. When scouts spotted an Indian camp on Powder River, Crook sent Colonel Joseph J. Reynolds and six companies of cavalry to attack it. On the bitterly cold morning of March 17 the troopers stormed into the village. The surprised Indians scattered, but they rallied and counterattacked. Timidly Reynolds abandoned his prize and fell back to the main column. Angry and discouraged, Crook turned back to Fort Fetterman to outfit for another try—and to bring charges that led to Reynolds's court-martial and retirement from the army.

For Terry and Crook both, weather had wrecked Sheridan's hopes for a winter campaign. Even though Sheridan had prophesied that the Indians must be caught in winter or not at all, his subordinates now aimed for a spring campaign, and even that turned out to be too optimistic.

And for Custer the politics in which he had dabbled suddenly gathered in a dark specter that clouded his participation in the campaign Terry had entrusted to him. On March 15, only two days after Captain Tom piloted the rescue sleigh onto the Fort Lincoln parade, the telegraph brought a summons for Custer to come to Washington as a witness in congressional hearings.

Foreshadowing the interruption in Custer's campaign preparations was a letter that he had received early in January, while still in New York City, from his friend Ralph Meeker, now with the *New York Herald's* Washington bureau. "I saw Orville Grant on the street the other day and friend Belknap," he quipped, "and I have no doubt but they would be glad to see you." Orvil had been loudly proclaiming how much money he had lost on the upper Missouri, said Meeker, but in fact he had invested nothing "in the frontier swindling business." "He gave influence, but he took money." With the Democrats in control of the House of Representatives, "we expect to have lots of fun before the session is over," and "there won't be much room for Brother Belknap or Friend Orville to repent."

Meeker prophesied correctly. Under the leadership of Democrat Heister Clymer and cheered on by the *Herald,* the House Committee on Expenditures in the War Department went after Belknap, and his elaborate house of fraud crashed around him. Colonel Hazen's old charges about the sale of the Fort Sill tradership were dusted off and added to others that left the entire post tradership system reeking of corruption.

The Fort Sill transaction was the only one clearly proven, but it illustrated how the others worked. The appointment as trader went to a middle man, who in turn farmed it out to someone already on the scene, usually the incumbent trader. He in turn paid a yearly kickback to the middle man, who split it with an influence peddler or the secretary (or, in the Fort Sill case, the secretary's wife). According to Custer, the Fort Lincoln trader paid about twelve thousand dollars a year for his monopoly.

As the evidence tumbled out, Belknap took fright. On March 2, while Custer was still in Saint Paul, the secretary hastily resigned rather than face impeachment. The Clymer Committee continued its probe, however, and the House debated whether to ignore the resignation and initiate impeachment proceedings anyway. On a list of possible witnesses supplied by Colonel Hazen, Clymer found the name of George Armstrong Custer and sent forth the summons that reached him on March 15 at Fort Lincoln.

Custer toyed with the notion of trying to get free of the obligation and even sought the legal opinion of General Terry, who thought it could be arranged. In the end, either from a sense of duty or the chance to inflict further damage on the administration, Custer decided to heed the summons. On March 21, the railroad still blocked, he headed east by stage.

In the capital, where Custer stayed with the Ben Holladays, he threw himself wholeheartedly into the Democratic offensive against the administration. He and Congressman Clymer got along famously and, in addition to official relations, socialized visibly. Custer testified before the committee on March 29 and again on April 4. He related what others had told him of the machinations of Belknap and Orvil Grant on the upper Missouri and what he himself suspected. Mostly hearsay, his testimony would not have held up in a court of law. But this was not a court of law, and what he said found corroboration in the testimony of others.

Custer also openly consorted with Representative Henry B. Banning, chairman of the Committee on Military Affairs. In February, Banning and his fellow Democrats had begun extensive hearings on the state of the army and were said to be on the verge of proposing drastic reductions. Custer testified before the Banning Committee and also commented on drafts of legislation.

Dining with Banning, Custer learned that the congressman had prepared a speech for delivery in the House chamber advocating transfer of the Indian Bureau to the War Department. "He told me," Autie wrote to Libbie, "that some of his strongest points were taken from my book, some extracts being taken word for word."

As the weeks of April passed, Custer grew increasingly impatient to start for Fort Lincoln. Clymer had warned him that, if Belknap were impeached, more testimony might be wanted. And, in fact, the House indicted the former secretary for trial before the Senate. None of the charges, however, drew on Custer's testimony, and he easily secured release from appearing as a witness. He left Washington on April 20.

Curiously, instead of hurrying straight to Fort Lincoln, where the

April 6 departure date for the Dakota Column had long since passed,
Custer went to Philadelphia to visit the Centennial Exposition and
then on to New York, where he met with his publishers and dined
with August Belmont, head of the conservative Democrats. There on
April 24, to his chagrin, he received a summons from the Senate
managers of the Belknap impeachment.

Although issued by the Senate, the summons was probably engi-
neered by Belknap's friends, or even by President Grant himself.
Custer's testimony before the Clymer Committee and his flaunted
association with leading Democrats had exasperated the president,
whose dream of a third term collapsed in the wreckage of the
Belknap scandal. Racked by exposés and beset on every side, the
bloodied Republicans lashed out at any target that offered itself.
Belknap may have been the administration's worst embarrassment of
1876 and Orvil the black sheep of the Grant family, but Custer's attack on them signaled a closing of ranks and a counteroffensive.

Custer found himself the object of a campaign of vilification in the
Republican press. All manner of wild accusations showered on him,
including perjury and disparagement of brother officers. The only
brother officer he had disparaged was Major Lewis Merrill, of his
own regiment, about whose swindles while on Reconstruction
duty in South Carolina Custer had testified before the Banning
Committee.

Custer also discovered that Belknap still had friends in the army
and that those who were not felt little disposition to bare their chests
to enemy fire as he had done. Among the former was none other
than General Sheridan, always the administration loyalist. He kept
quiet in consideration of his friend, but not so one of his aides. Lieutenant Colonel James W. Forsyth—"Tony," in distinction to the
other Forsyth, "Sandy"—had been a friend of the Custers since the
Civil War. But now he rushed to Belknap's support. Not a single
officer of the army approved Custer's testimony, he assured the fallen
cabinet officer, who gave the letter to the *Army and Navy Journal*. "It
is nothing but hearsay, which is largely made up of frontier gossip
and stories."

Tony Forsyth also gave Belknap some advice that probably led to
Custer's summons by the Senate impeachment managers. "There is
no use of asking who will go in command of any troops or expedition sent against the Indians in Dakota," Forsyth wrote on April 4,
in unwitting tribute to Custer's military talents, "for if Custer is

available *he is certain to have the command*." Therefore, "If you are
going to want him you had better make your application at once."

Among those hostile to Belknap, and therefore disposed to be-
friend Custer, was General Sherman. The new secretary of war,
Alfonso Taft, had encouraged Sherman to move his headquarters
back to Washington and resume his rightful role as commander of
the army. On March 31, Custer breakfasted with Sherman, who received him cordially and took him to meet the new secretary.

Sherman also reacted sympathetically when the aggrieved Custer
reappeared in Washington on April 27, in response to the new summons. Sherman went to Secretary Taft and induced him to write a
letter to the impeachment managers requesting Custer's release so
that he could assume command of the expedition against the Sioux.
Taft promised to write the letter immediately after a cabinet meeting
scheduled for the next morning, April 28. At this meeting, however,
he mentioned his intention to President Grant. The secretary should
write no such letter, the president directed, but instead designate
another officer to command the Fort Lincoln column.

The telegraph wires linking Washington with Chicago and Saint
Paul hummed with exchanges over how to handle the president's
order. No one available to General Terry had the rank and ability to
take Custer's place, certainly not Major Reno, commanding the Seventh Cavalry in Custer's absence. Sheridan concluded that Terry
himself had to go in command of the Dakota Column.

Grant's action stunned Custer, who could not believe that the
president would knowingly endanger the campaign out of political
retaliation. He himself secured the permission of the impeachment
managers to return to his command, but on April 29, a Saturday,
General Sherman advised him to delay his departure until Monday
so that he could meet personally with the president.

Twice since his arrival in Washington, Custer had gone to the
White House to pay a courtesy call on Grant but had been turned
away. On May 1 he went for the third time, only to be kept sitting in
the anteroom for five hours. Finally his friend Colonel Ingalls happened by and interceded with Grant, who sent word that he would
not see Custer.

Leaving a note expressing regret that the president had denied him
an audience, Custer walked next door to the War Department but
found Sherman absent, in New York City. The general in chief had
already sanctioned Custer's departure, as had the impeachment man-

agers. At the War Department the adjutant general and the inspector general likewise gave their blessings. Custer boarded an evening train for Chicago.

On the morning of May 4, in Chicago, Custer had already settled into the Saint Paul train when one of Sheridan's staff officers handed him a telegram from Sherman to Sheridan: "I am at this moment advised that General Custer started last night for St. Paul and Fort Abraham Lincoln. He was not justified in leaving without seeing the President and myself. Please intercept him and await further orders; meantime let the expedition proceed without him."

The words, of course, were Sherman's, but the content was Grant's. Custer's long telegram to Sherman merely recounted what he already knew: Custer had left Washington with the approval and authority of everyone concerned, including Sherman. But by publicly attacking the president's official and personal family, Custer had lent himself to partisan Democratic purposes, and now everyone fell into line to carry out the president's determination to punish him. The latest blow, moreover, ratified by orders on May 5 direct from Grant, represented the ultimate punishment: Custer could not even participate in the campaign but must watch the Seventh march away under the command of Major Reno.

Sherman, Sheridan, and, above all, Terry badly wanted Custer in the field. Sheridan, ever the loyalist, would do nothing to help his protégé. Sherman, no friend of the administration, had little choice but to do Grant's bidding, however distasteful. As he wrote Terry, Custer's political activity had "compromised his best friends here, and almost deprived us of the ability to serve him."

But Terry, able lawyer and compassionate commander, adroitly took the initiative. Reporting in Saint Paul on May 6, as Terry later confided to intimates, Custer, "with tears in his eyes, begged my aid. How could I resist it?" Not only compassion moved Terry. He had never campaigned against Indians, and none of his other subordinates could boast more than a pale shadow of Custer's experience. Terry needed Custer at his side.

Terry therefore dictated a telegram for Custer to send and an endorsement for his own signature. The former, respectful and shrewdly reasoned, sped through channels to the president himself and ended on a note hard to resist: "I appeal to you as a soldier to spare me the humiliation of seeing my regiment march to meet the enemy and I not to share its dangers." In his own message Terry disclaimed any intent to question the president's orders but suggested that if his reasons did not forbid it, "Lieutenant Colonel Custer's services would be very valuable with his regiment."

Sheridan's endorsement on these messages supported the application, but in negative terms that probably helped to ease Grant's acquiescence. Sheridan regretted that Custer had demonstrated less eagerness to stay at home and prepare for the expedition than he now did to accompany it. He alluded to his application, in 1868, for Custer's return to duty before the expiration of his court-martial sentence. And he hoped that, if granted this time, clemency might restrain Custer in the future from "attempting to throw discredit upon his profession and his brother officers." Custer, of course, except for his testimony against Major Merrill, had done neither; but in the rhetoric of his enemies this had become a blanket cliché for his offenses against the administration.

President Grant had already taken a pounding from anti-administration papers for his harsh, politically motivated treatment of Custer. He could hardly court the censure that would result from ignoring the appeals of Custer's superiors, especially if the Sioux campaign turned out badly. On May 8 word reached Saint Paul that the president had relented. Custer could lead the Seventh Cavalry, but under Terry's immediate oversight.

Suddenly the black cloud that had plunged Custer into despair dissipated. "Custer's Luck" had again come to the rescue. Elated, he left department headquarters and headed for his hotel. On the street he met Captain Ludlow, Terry's chief engineer, who had accompanied the Yellowstone and Black Hills expeditions. Excitedly, Custer blurted out the good news and then, in an act of supreme indiscretion and ingratitude, added that at first chance he would "cut loose" from Terry, that he had "got away with Stanley and would be able to swing clear of Terry."

Swing clear of Terry he did, and detractors have accused him of rushing headlong into battle in order to win a great victory for himself, and himself alone, that would wipe out the degradation to which President Grant had subjected him. Some go even further and charge him with presidential ambitions. A battlefield triumph, runs the theory, might stampede the Democratic convention, meeting in Saint Louis in June, into nominating him for the presidency. The only evidence for this assumption is the recollection of an Arikara Indian scout thirty-seven years later. On the eve of departure from

Fort Lincoln, recalled the Indian, Custer had told the scouts, through an interpreter, that a victory over the Sioux would make him their Great Father in Washington.

Custer had indeed performed notable service for the Democratic party and had been severely bruised for his effort, but that the party's gratitude extended to the presidency transcends absurdity. That Custer fantasized such an absurdity cannot be disproved, of course, but that presidential aspirations governed his tactical decisions demands more weighty evidence than supplied by the Arikara scout.

At the same time, Custer certainly had claims on Democratic generosity. He had been close to the Belmont wing of the party for several years. In April, in New York City, he had dined with August Belmont, and in Washington on four occasions he had sat at the dinner table of Senator Thomas Bayard of Delaware, Belmont's candidate for the Democratic nomination. His association with these men, his services to the *New York Herald* and *New York World*, his high public profile, and, finally, his widely publicized testimony against the frontier frauds of the Grant administration and the Grant family had made him a logical recipient of some preferment if the Democrats gained the White House.

What did he want, if not the presidency? One scholar has theorized that "Great Father" actually meant commissioner of Indian affairs. But the Arikara scout used the terms president and Great Father both, and anyway one has trouble picturing Custer as content to head the Indian Bureau.

More plausible, both from the standpoint of reasonable expectations and of Custer's ambitions, is the star of a brigadier. The president appointed all general officers. When a vacancy occurred, candidates exploited every political advantage to win presidential favor. Seniority did not always govern. For an example Custer had to look no further than George Crook, whom Grant had promoted from lieutenant colonel to brigadier general in 1873. In the spring of 1876, the Democrats seemed to have an excellent chance of capturing the White House in the November elections. For the next brigadier's opening, few of the army's field-grade officers would have a stronger claim on a Democratic president than Custer. As Tony Forsyth wrote to Belknap early in April 1876, "The fact of the matter is that both Hazen, and Custer, are now working to make capital with the Democratic party—*they want stars.*"

CHAPTER 8

Last Stand

ON May 14, 1876, the Seventh Cavalry, all twelve companies brought together for the first time, shivered in a tent city laid out with military precision on the Missouri River flats two miles below Fort Lincoln. Cold rains soaked the valley into a quagmire, immobilizing the heavily loaded supply wagons and casting uncertainty over the departure set for next day. On this wet morning Mark Kellogg, reporter for the *Bismarck Tribune* and also representative of the *New York Herald*, wrote in his dispatch of the day of a newly reenergized Indian fighter:

> Gen. George A. Custer, dressed in a dashing suit of buckskin, is prominent everywhere. Here, there, flitting to and fro, in his quick eager way, taking in everything connected with his command, as well as generally, with the keen, incisive manner for which he is so well known. The General is full of perfect readiness for a fray with the hostile red devils, and woe to the body of scalp-lifters that comes within reach of himself and brave companions in arms.

Kellogg caught the spirit of the Seventh and its leader, dampened only by the rains that delayed the departure of the Dakota Column. Three days later, although still threatening, the weather freed the expedition to head for the Sioux country.

May 17 dawned overcast, with fog resting on the Missouri bottoms. Custer, ever ready for pageantry, welcomed Terry's desire to display the command's strength to the families remaining behind, and the Seventh paraded through Fort Lincoln. With the regimental staff, and accompanied by Libbie and Maggie, Custer led. The blue and gold regimental standard flapped above the headquarters group, together with Custer's personal pennant, the old Civil War design of red and blue with crossed white sabers. A company guidon, swallow-tailed stars and stripes, marked each of the twelve companies that trooped behind in columns of fours. Mounted on white horses, the band played "Garry Owen" as the companies clattered in front of the

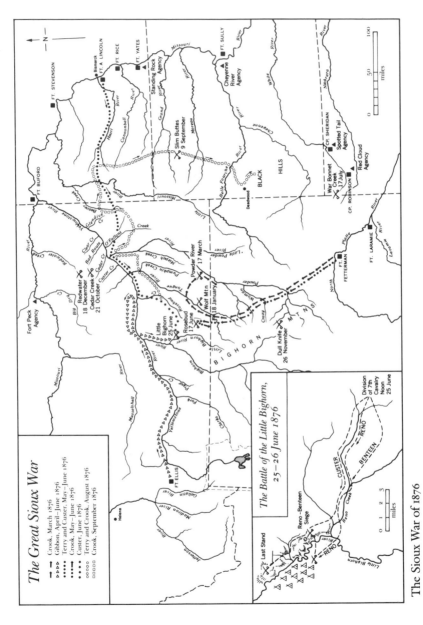

The Sioux War of 1876
The Battle of the Little Bighorn, 25–26 June 1876

quarters of the Indian scouts, with keening women and impassive old men; in front of "Suds Row," with sobbing washerwomen and excited children playing soldier; and, finally, the length of officers' row, families watching in grief from behind closed windows. The procession halted briefly for last goodbyes and then, while the band pumped out the traditional strains of "The Girl I Left Behind Me," obliqued left to crawl up the slope toward the infantry post on the bench.

As the column snaked upward, the sun suddenly pierced the fog. The mist swirled and began to dissipate, a layer clinging to the cold ground. Libbie looked back. "A mirage appeared," she later wrote, "which took up about half of the line of cavalry, and thenceforth for a little distance it marched, equally plain to the sight on the earth and in the sky." Heavy with a symbolism not lost on Libbie and others who saw it, the Seventh Cavalry marched across the heavens to meet its destiny.

On the benchland the expedition spread out in its daily marching formation, organized around the supply train. The train consisted of about 150 canvas-topped wagons. Most of them were ponderous transports drawn by six mules that were owned by the government. The others were light conveyances hitched to two mules that were civilian-owned and under contract to the government. The wagons carried mainly forage and ammunition, the latter in case of battle before reaching the Yellowstone. There the command would meet the chartered steamboats *Far West* and *Josephine* with cargoes chiefly of rations.

Two companies of the Seventeenth Infantry and one of the Sixth marched in close support of the train. The Gatling-gun battery labored cumbersomely behind. On one side of the train meandered a beef herd, on the other a remuda of spare horses and mules. Well out in front and rear and on each flank rode a three-company battalion of cavalry. Under Lieutenant Charles A. Varnum, thirty-nine Indian scouts, mostly Arikaras from Fort Berthold, fanned out in advance.

Altogether Terry's command numbered about 1,000 men, with the Seventh Cavalry alone counting 32 officers and 718 enlisted men. Augmenting the force still further, three companies of the Sixth Infantry from Fort Buford had been ordered to establish a supply base on the Yellowstone, near Stanley's old stockade of 1873.

Custer had divided the Seventh into two wings, of two three-company battalions each, and controlled the regiment through the wing commanders. Reflecting the absence of officers on detached service or leave, the right wing was led by the junior major, Marcus A. Reno, and the left wing by the senior captain, Frederick W. Benteen.

Custer and Benteen had been associated ever since the organization of the Seventh Cavalry. Personally and professionally, Benteen had no use for Custer. Custer respected Benteen professionally but disliked him personally. They usually treated each other with military formality.

Custer and Reno were not well acquainted. Reno had come to the regiment in 1869 and had never served at the same post with Custer. He had a good war record and a brevet of colonel, but his cold personality and social awkwardness repelled fellow officers. He drank too much, misbehaved frequently, and commanded little respect from anyone. He was Custer's opposite in every way, and his unseemly attempts to capture command of the Fort Lincoln Column during the weeks of Custer's disfavor could not have improved his commander's already low opinion of him.

In the ranks the Seventh Cavalry was overwhelmingly a veteran regiment. A recent infusion of recruits made up only 10 percent of the total. Seventy-five percent claimed one or more years of service, while 27 percent had put in at least one five-year hitch. Twelve men had served fifteen or more years, four twenty, and one twenty-five. The average age was twenty-seven, characteristic of the peacetime army but far higher than in the wartime volunteer outfits. German and Irish immigrants made up much of the enlisted complement, especially in the noncommissioned grades. Thirty-two percent were Irishmen.

These men made up in experience what they lacked in the vigor and enthusiasm of the Civil War volunteer. Whatever their limitations, they approached the summer with pride and assurance, as Private Charles Windolph recalled many years later: "You felt like you were somebody when you were on a good horse, with a carbine dangling from its small leather ring socket on your McClellan saddle, and a Colt army revolver strapped on your hip, and a hundred rounds of ammunition in your web belt and in your saddle pockets. You were a cavalryman of the Seventh Regiment. You were part of a proud outfit that had a fighting reputation, and you were ready for a fight or a frolic."

Camp the first night was on Heart River. There Custer allowed the men to be paid; an earlier payday would have left the regiment hung over and reduced by desertions. And, as a private recorded, "we here again meet the blood sucking sutler with his vile whiskey, rotten tobacco, and high priced notions." The sutler was John Smith, the same who had accompanied the Seventh to the Black Hills. Next morning he returned to Fort Lincoln in the party with Libbie and Maggie.

Not all the pay found its way into the sutler's cash drawer. Five weeks later greenbacks fluttered through the grass on the slopes above the Little Bighorn. Some wound up as miniature saddle blankets and other playthings for Sioux children.

General Sheridan's strategy for whipping the Sioux had not been elaborate or imaginative. It consisted solely of ordering Generals Crook and Terry to conduct a winter campaign. Crook had tried but failed. Winter had prevented Terry from even launching Custer, but in March he had sought to meet Sheridan's expectations by organizing a thrust from the west, in Montana.

The task fell to John Gibbon, colonel of the Seventh Infantry and major general by brevet, who commanded the District of Montana. West Point 1847, a battered veteran of frontier and wartime service, Gibbon claimed an outstanding combat record in the Civil War. Past his prime for field service, he might have entrusted the mission to someone else. But his ranking subordinate, Major James Brisbin, was a mediocrity, and Gibbon went himself.

Under orders from Terry, Gibbon concentrated six companies of his own regiment and Brisbin's battalion of the Second Cavalry at Fort Ellis, Montana. On April 3, with nearly five hundred men, Gibbon struck eastward, down the Yellowstone River.

Gibbon's movement was little more than a belated gesture to the concept of a winter campaign. For six weeks, however, as the approach of spring doomed the concept, his Montana Column was the only one in the field. In anticipation of a new offensive from the south by Crook, Terry ordered Gibbon to patrol the north bank of the Yellowstone to prevent the flight of Sitting Bull's Indians northward toward the British Possessions.

Although not deliberately planned, a campaign of converging columns was taking shape, one resembling the successful strategy of the Washita Campaign of 1868–69 and, more recently, the Red River War of 1874–75 against the southern Plains tribes. It did not, however, involve any concert of action. "I have given no instructions to Generals Crook or Terry," Sheridan wrote to Sherman on May 29, the day Crook marched from Fort Fetterman, "as I think it would be unwise to make any combinations in such country as they will have to operate in." "Each column will be able to take care of itself," he added, while "chastising the Indians should it have the opportunity."

Sheridan reasoned soundly, for neither Terry nor Crook knew where the Indians were. None of the generals or their staffs, it turned out, proved adept at analyzing and digesting the intelligence placed before them. In January, Terry believed the Sitting Bull bands to be on the Little Missouri, in February out on the Yellowstone, and in April and May back on the Little Missouri.

Gibbon knew exactly where they were, although he shared his knowledge with no one. On May 16 his Crow scouts, under the able Lieutenant James H. Bradley, spotted the main Sioux and Cheyenne camp in the Tongue River valley. On May 27 the scouts again located the quarry, this time in the Rosebud valley only eighteen miles from Gibbon's position. Gibbon tried to cross the Yellowstone to move on this prize but failed. Unaccountably, in dispatches to Terry, he did not disclose that he knew the whereabouts of the big village that all three columns sought.

As usual the Sitting Bull bands had passed the winter widely dispersed among the valleys of the Powder River country. The village that Colonel Reynolds attacked on March 17, 1876, consisted of about a hundred lodges of Oglalas, Miniconjous, and Cheyennes. After the soldiers withdrew, the warriors reclaimed their tipis and moved down the Powder and then eastward to unite with Crazy Horse and the Oglalas.

The fight on Powder River served unmistakable notice that the soldiers meant war. Little by little, as word of the war sped from one camp to another, the Indians came together for self-defense. As the spring grass greened, they moved slowly westward from the Powder to the Tongue to the Rosebud, their numbers swelling as one group after another joined. By late May, when Gibbon's scouts found them, they had a strength of about four hundred lodges—about three thousand people, including some eight hundred warriors.

The spring grass also set in motion the annual westward movement of agency Indians. From Standing Rock, Cheyenne River, Red Cloud, and Spotted Tail agencies, parties headed for the Powder

River country. Besides the usual lure of a summer's hunt, this year they went in anger over the white people's attempt to seize the Black Hills and the government's ultimatum to abandon the unceded territory. And because of these grievances, this year they went in larger numbers than ever. They moved slowly, waiting for the grass to ripen and their ponies to gain strength.

The lingering westward progress of the agency Indians from Standing Rock and Cheyenne River deceived Terry and Custer. Together with exaggerated reports of Sitting Bull Indians near Fort Berthold, where a dozen lodges had gone to trade for rifles and ammunition, garbled news of the agency Indians in western Dakota gave rise to the notion that all the northern bands waited on the Little Missouri River to do battle with the soldiers. In reality these Indians were 150 miles to the west, almost under Gibbon's nose. Just before leaving Fort Lincoln, however, Terry ordered Gibbon eastward to help fight them on the Little Missouri.

Despite miserable weather, including a heavy snowstorm on June 1–2, the march over Stanley's old trail turned into a frolic similar to those of 1873 and 1874. This year Custer found pleasure in a larger retinue than ever. Captains Yates, Tom Custer, and Moylan and Lieutenants "Jimmi" Calhoun and "Fresh" Smith all commanded companies. So did Captains Myles Keogh and Tom Weir (Libbie's old attraction), Custer loyalists stationed at Fort Totten for the past three years. Lieutenant William W. Cooke, Custer's warm comrade since 1867, served as his adjutant. Brother Boston found his way onto the quartermaster payroll as "guide." Barely eighteen, "Autie" Reed— nephew Harry Armstrong Reed—came out from Monroe for a summer's vacation with his revered uncle. He traveled in the guise of "herder." As in 1873, Mary Adams went along as cook.

The brothers delighted in tormenting one another. Once Armstrong and Tom gave Boston the slip, hid behind some hills, and fired over his head. They had to ride furiously to head him off before he alarmed the command. "I don't know what we would do without 'Bos' to tease," Autie wrote Libbie.

The Little Missouri, with its wild and colorful badlands, revealed no concentration of Indians spoiling for a fight. On May 30, with four companies, Custer scouted twenty-five miles up the valley. Autie Reed provided a hearty laugh when his horse pitched him headfirst into a mudhole, but no sign of Sioux could be found. "All stories about large bodies of Indians being here are the merest bosh," Custer wrote Libbie. "None have been here for six months, not even a small hunting-party."

Swinging southward to check other valleys for sign, the column pushed on toward the Yellowstone, Custer in the lead seeking a route through tortuous country. On June 7, to the amazement of all, the indefatigable trailblazer brought the exhausted soldiers into the Powder River valley.

On that day, as on the Little Missouri scout, he rode fifty miles, only to rise early the next morning and put the finishing touches on his latest article for *Galaxy*. As he wrote Libbie, "Bloody Knife looks on in wonder at me because I never get tired."

While the troops camped here under Custer, Terry hastened down the Powder to the Yellowstone and on June 9 finally met with Colonel Gibbon aboard the *Far West*. Here, for the first time, Terry learned where the Indians actually were—or had been two weeks earlier. How the soft-spoken general vented his annoyance did not find its way into the record, but he ordered Gibbon, who had tarried for a week before heeding Terry's summons to the Little Missouri, to turn back and reestablish himself opposite the mouth of the Rosebud.

Terry now had enough information to plan further operations. Before moving against the village that Gibbon's scouts had discovered on the Rosebud, however, he wanted to make certain that the Sioux had not doubled back to the east. Therefore, he ordered Major Reno with the right wing of the Seventh Cavalry to scout up the Powder and down the Tongue. Custer, with Captain Benteen and the left wing, would march along the south bank of the Yellowstone and join Reno at the mouth of the Tongue. Then, assured of the absence of Indians on the Powder and the Tongue, Terry intended to send Custer back up the Tongue to sweep down the Rosebud while Gibbon, strengthened by three of Custer's companies, advanced up the Rosebud. The Sioux, if still where they were on May 27, would be trapped.

Custer disliked Terry's plan, as he made clear in dispatches he was sending, for publication without attribution, to the *New York Herald*. He thought that the Seventh should move swiftly on the locale where the Indians were last seen, not indulge in a time-consuming scout with only half the regiment through an area where no evidence placed them. By the time the strike forces finally reached the Rose-

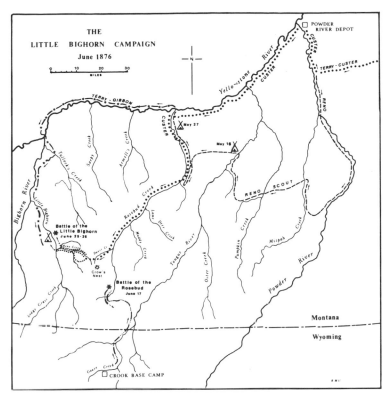

The Little Bighorn Campaign, June 1876

bud, he feared, the Indians would have taken fright and fled. That Terry expected Reno to find no Indians was plain; had there been even a remote chance, he would have sent Custer instead. But the methodical general stood firm, and Custer could only vent his disapproval anonymously in the columns of the *Herald*.

Because the focus of the campaign had shifted farther west, Terry also decided to move his supply depot from Stanley's old stockade on Glendive Creek to the mouth of the Powder. The *Far West*, with the experienced Captain Grant Marsh at the wheel, began shuttling the supplies and soldiers upstream to the new location.

When Custer marched in with the left wing on June 11, he was disappointed to find that the *Far West* had not brought Libbie up from Lincoln to join him. His troopers, by contrast, were elated over the arrival of another passenger: Sutler John Smith. On the bank of the Yellowstone he greeted the Seventh with a makeshift bar of planks and barrels, and the regiment, under the helplessly tolerant eye of its commander, enjoyed an afternoon revel.

Terry decided to cut loose from his wagon train. The wagons would remain at the Powder River base, together with supplies stockpiled by the *Far West* and the *Josephine*. Terry's infantry would man the base, together with the three infantry companies that had marched up the Yellowstone from Fort Buford and about 150 dismounted cavalrymen. The latter consisted of the regimental band, most of the three-month recruits, and a handful of old soldiers for whom the campaign might prove too strenuous. In addition the cavalrymen turned in their sabers, as would Reno's wing at the end of his scout; they were cumbersome, noisy, and useless for the long-range fighting that normally characterized combat with Indians. After three days of struggle to transform draft mules into pack mules, on June 15 the cavalry set forth up the Yellowstone.

On June 19, as Custer and the left wing of the Seventh lay at the mouth of the Tongue, Terry received a message from Reno. The major not only had examined the Powder and Tongue valleys but also had crossed to the Rosebud and scouted up that valley before returning to the Yellowstone, opposite Gibbon's camp. Now Reno was marching down the Yellowstone to rejoin Custer.

Terry was furious at Reno for exceeding orders and, by venturing into the Rosebud valley, jeopardizing the projected pincers movement. Custer, still fearful of the Indians taking alarm and escaping, also severely condemned Reno. In reality Reno had gained crucial information, although he did a poor job of explaining himself. He had found a month-old campsite of four hundred lodges in the Tongue valley and a more recent campsite of the same village on the Rosebud, thus confirming Lieutenant Bradley's sightings. Reno had also learned that the village no longer stood where Terry assumed but had moved up the Rosebud two weeks earlier. That meant that Terry's plan for trapping Sitting Bull on the Rosebud was obsolete and would have to be revised. Despite this service, the general never forgave Reno for overstepping his instructions.

On the afternoon of June 21, Terry called Gibbon, Custer, and Brisbin to the cabin of the *Far West*, moored to the south bank of the Yellowstone at the mouth of the Rosebud. Around a map spread out on a table, they discussed the details of a strategy that Terry had worked out during the morning.

Unlike his earlier plan, Terry's new plan took account of the unknowns. The first plan had contemplated two mobile strike forces of comparable strength maneuvering against a village falsely assumed to have occupied the same location since sighted two weeks earlier. Now, acknowledging the uncertain whereabouts of the quarry, Terry envisioned a strong, swift-moving strike force searching out the Indians and driving them against a less mobile blocking force. Custer, of course, would attack, Gibbon block. "The Montana column felt disappointed," Major Brisbin wrote a few days later, "but General Terry's reasons for affording the honor of the attack to General Custer were good ones."

The strategy reflected the best estimate of where the Indians would be found. About two weeks earlier they were traveling up the Rosebud valley. They could have continued up the Rosebud, or turned east toward the Black Hills, or west toward the Little Bighorn, or north down Tullock's Creek toward the Yellowstone. The general impression was that they would be found on the upper Little Bighorn. Lower down they would approach the Bighorn, the border of Crow country, and thus risk a collision with their longtime enemies.

Terry's plan called for Custer and the Seventh Cavalry to push up the Rosebud on the Indian trail and Gibbon and the Montana Column, with Terry accompanying, to march up the Yellowstone and Bighorn to a blocking position at the mouth of the Little Bighorn. If the Indians turned out to be on the Little Bighorn, Custer would attack from the south and Gibbon intercept any who tried to get away to the north.

But Custer's movements, as all plainly understood, had to be governed by circumstances, for the Sioux might not be on the upper Little Bighorn, or indeed anywhere on the Little Bighorn. Therefore, Custer's written orders, which were to provoke such controversy, laid out his mission in discretionary terms. He was to follow the trail up the Rosebud. If it turned to the Little Bighorn, he was still to continue up the Rosebud before swinging west to the upper Little Bighorn—this to make certain that the Indians did not escape to the south or east and to give Gibbon, with his infantry, time to get to the Little Bighorn. Terry expected him to be there by June 26, but this date had no other significance. The Seventh Cavalry carried rations for fifteen days, and Custer left no doubt that he would use them all if necessary to find the Indians. The notion that Terry meant for him to attack on June 26 arose only after the offensive ended in disaster.

Tactfully but knowingly, Terry couched his written orders to Custer as suggestions, to be followed unless Custer's judgment dictated another course. Proudly Custer repeated the governing passage in a letter to Libbie the next morning: "It is of course impossible to give you any definite instructions in regard to this movement; and were it not impossible to do so, the Department Commander places too much confidence in your zeal, energy, and ability to wish to impose upon you precise orders, which might hamper your action when nearly in contact with the enemy."

Eager for Custer to have every advantage, Terry offered Brisbin's battalion of the Second Cavalry and the Gatling gun battery. The officers on the *Far West* concluded that the cavalry battalion would detract more from Gibbon than it would add to Custer, and that the battery, as the only wheeled vehicles with Custer, would limit his mobility. Unsaid although later implied to his officers, Custer did not want to share credit for the coming victory with another regiment.

More welcome to Custer were six of Gibbon's Crow scouts under half-blood Mitch Bouyer, who knew the country well. "Surely he is being offered every facility to make a successful pursuit," noted Lieutenant Bradley, who had to give up the scouts.

Except as implicit in the discussion of beefing up the Seventh Cavalry, the officers on the *Far West* talked little about enemy strength. The campsites that Reno examined in the Rosebud valley revealed about four hundred lodges, which meant about eight hundred warriors. This represented roughly the magnitude of the Sitting Bull bands, with no substantial infusion of agency Indians. Where they were and whether any had joined the main camp since it had left the lower Rosebud, no one knew, or seems to have cared.

The lack of concern over Indian strength reflected the usual military assumption that the Indians would scatter and run if given the chance. If only they could be caught, Custer often boasted, the Seventh could whip any force of Indians on the Plains. Thus everyone worried not about how to defeat the Indians but how to catch them before they discovered the soldiers and fled in all directions. As Gibbon said, the object of the plan was "to prevent the escape of the Indians, which was the idea pervading the minds of all of us."

At noon on June 22 the Seventh Cavalry passed in review before Terry, Gibbon, and Custer. In the absence of the band, back at the Powder River base, massed trumpets supplied the music. Officers saluted smartly, and the lean, bronzed troopers followed in every variety of costume. Slouch hats, gray or blue shirts, and the regulation sky-blue trousers stuffed into boots predominated. To ease saddle wear, many had lined their trouser seats with canvas. Each man carried a Springfield single-shot carbine and a Colt revolver, with one hundred rounds for carbine and twenty-four for pistol. The packtrain followed, the unruly mules bearing rations for fifteen days and more carbine ammunition. In all the regiment counted 31 officers, 566 enlisted men, 35 Indian scouts, and about a dozen packers, guides, and other civilians.

Amid clouds of choking dust the Seventh Cavalry pushed up the Rosebud, twelve miles the first day, thirty-three the second, twenty-eight the third—roughly the progress that had been agreed at the conference on the *Far West*. Custer had abolished all battalion and wing organization. The twelve company commanders now reported directly to him, although he left everything to them except when to march and when to halt. Each morning he mounted and rode forth, accompanied by Adjutant Cooke, the regimental sergeant major, a detail of orderly trumpeters, and sergeants bearing the regimental standard and his personal banner. This was the signal for the companies to follow. When the headquarters party halted in the evening, the companies scattered for the night's bivouac.

On the second day, June 23, the troops struck the Indian trail that Major Reno had already examined, and by the morning of the twenty-fourth they had reached the limit of his reconnaissance. There they paused at an abandoned village site where the Sioux had staged a sun dance earlier in the month. The frame of the dance lodge still stood, and within hung the scalp of a white man. The Indian scouts observed enough evidence of powerful medicine to make them restive.

Continuing the march, the command suddenly confronted a mystifying development. The Indian trail, hitherto of uniform size and age, abruptly turned larger and fresher. Lodgepole marks cross-hatched the valley in all directions, disturbing older markings and testifying to a sequence of puzzling activity extending to recent days. Some of the pony droppings were no more than two days old, which meant that some Indians, at least, were as close as thirty miles.

The officers speculated over the meaning of the new sign, and Custer sent the Crows forward to gather more information. More skilled at reading sign, the Arikara scouts probably already suspected the explanation.

As Sitting Bull's following made its way slowly up the Rosebud through early June, a scattering of people arrived from the agencies. Others left, however, on hunting forays, to scout the enemy's movements, and even to trade for arms and ammunition at distant points on the Missouri River. The size of the village, therefore, remained about four hundred tipis.

The scouting parties kept watch on Colonel Gibbon and also, to the south, on General Crook. Crook had left Fort Fetterman on May 29 but had paused at the head of Tongue River to wait for Crow and Shoshoni allies. On June 16, Sioux scouts saw Crook break camp and head down the Rosebud. Hurrying back to warn of the danger, they found that their village had crossed from the Rosebud to a tributary of the Little Bighorn that they knew as Sundance Creek but that the whites later named Reno Creek. The next day most of the young men, as many as five to seven hundred, rode back to the Rosebud to head off the soldiers, whose further advance would threaten the village. On June 17, the very day Reno reached the limit of his reconnaissance only forty miles to the north, the warriors swept down on Crook's command, halted for midmorning coffee. In fierce fighting they mauled the troops so badly that the next morning the general countermarched and returned to his base camp on Goose Creek.

On June 18 the chiefs struck camp, moved down Reno Creek to the Little Bighorn, turned south up the valley, and raised their tipis. There they remained for six days, celebrating the victory over the soldiers on the Rosebud. And there their brethren from the agencies finally began to arrive in significant numbers.

On the back trail from the Rosebud down Reno Creek, and down the Little Bighorn itself, the agency Indians converged on their destination. They came in small groups and large, trailing on the ground behind them, in a chaos of size, direction, and age, the marks of their progress. It was this jumble of Indian sign, abruptly intruding on and muddling the easily read trail of the Sitting Bull bands up the

Rosebud, that perplexed Custer and his officers on the afternoon of June 24.

Over a span of only six days Sitting Bull's village more than doubled, from 400 to 1,000 lodges, from 3,000 to 7,000 people, from 800 to 2,000 warriors. In 6 separate tribal circles they crowded the narrow valley of the Little Bighorn. Hunkpapas, Oglalas, Miniconjous, Sans Arcs, Blackfeet, Two Kettles, Brules, and a scattering of Yanktonnais and Santees (Sioux, but not Tetons) made up the 5 Sioux circles, while 120 Cheyenne lodges rounded out the array. Even a handful of Arapahoes cast their lot with their friends.

The tribal leaders had planned to move even farther up the river, toward the Bighorn Mountains (exactly where General Terry had expected to find them). Scouts, however, brought word of antelope herds to the north and west, downstream. On June 24, therefore, as Custer puzzled over the scarred valley on the other side of the Rosebud divide, they moved the village northward, back down the Little Bighorn in the direction from which they had come.

The new location afforded an appealing setting. The upper end of the camp, anchored by the Hunkpapa circle, lay about two miles below the mouth of Reno Creek. The rest of the tipis sprawled along the west bank of the river for nearly three miles downstream. On the west the valley ended in low grassy hills and benches where the huge pony herd grazed. On the eastern edge of the valley, the river, cold and brimming with the spring runoff from the Bighorn Mountains, meandered among thickets of shady cottonwood trees. A series of ragged bluffs rose steeply from the east bank of the river to a height of some three hundred feet.

There in the valley of the pretty stream the Sioux called the Greasy Grass lay a village of unusual size. Such numbers consumed immense quantities of game, forage, and firewood and so could not remain long in one place, or even together in one village. It had come together in this strength only in the few days preceding, and it could stay together for more than a few days or a week only through luck, frequent moves, and constant labor. White apologists, seeking to explain the disaster this coalition of tribes wrought, would later endow it with an immensity it never approached. Still, it was big by all standards of the time, and it was more than twice as big as any of the army officers looking for it had anticipated.

Equally significant, the village contained a people basking proudly in the fullness of tribal power. Contrary to the assumptions and the mindset of the planners aboard the *Far West*, the Indians felt little inclination to avoid conflict. Their grievances united them in a determination to fight against those who would seize the Black Hills and send soldiers to force them out of the unceded territory, where even the white people's paper conceded their right to roam.

The coincidence of timing that brought the Seventh Cavalry to the vicinity of this village during the few days of its peak strength was only the beginning of a run of ill fortune that ended in the utter collapse of "Custer's Luck."

"Passed several large camps," recorded Custer's itinerist, Lieutenant George D. Wallace, as the Seventh Cavalry made its way up the Rosebud on the afternoon of June 24. "The trail was now fresh, and the whole valley scratched up by the trailing lodge poles." The Crows pushed far in advance, seeking more information for the expectant Custer.

Shortly after nightfall the Crows rode into the Seventh's bivouac on the Rosebud. They related exactly what Custer needed to know. Ahead the Indian trail veered to the west and followed a tributary of the Rosebud over a low mountain pass toward the Little Bighorn. Fading daylight had prevented the scouts from learning more. Custer sent them forward, accompanied by Charley Reynolds, Lieutenant Varnum, and six of the Arikaras, to seek further information as the new day dawned.

The Crows had presented Custer with critical intelligence. It placed the Indians on the Little Bighorn, as assumed. But the freshness of the trail meant that they could not be on the *upper* Little Bighorn. They, or a large part of them, had to be on the *lower* Little Bighorn, hardly a day's ride to the west.

Swiftly Custer made a crucial decision. To continue up the Rosebud, as suggested by Terry, made sense only if the Sioux were on the upper Little Bighorn. Now that course would force him to lose touch with an enemy that he had in his immediate front, to make a long detour through country that he knew could not harbor many Indians, and to risk the very possibility that everyone so pervasively feared—the escape of the Indians.

Calling his officers together over a flickering candle, Custer outlined a new plan. Instead of continuing up the Rosebud, he would follow the Indian trail across the divide under cover of night, spend the next day resting the command and fixing the location of the

Sioux village, and then hit it with a dawn attack on June 26, the date appointed for Gibbon to reach the mouth of the Little Bighorn.

Rousted from their blankets at midnight, the troopers groped blindly forward in the darkness, marching about six miles up the rough, rocky valley of a stream now named Davis Creek. At 2:00 A.M., still short of the summit, the weary horsemen halted. As day dawned, they brewed coffee, although the alkaline water made it hardly fit to drink.

Riding bareback around the bivouac, Custer paused at the cook fire of the Arikaras. Bloody Knife was talking. Custer asked the interpreter what he said. "He says we'll find enough Sioux to keep us fighting two or three days." Custer smiled. "I guess we'll get through them in one day."

At this juncture, about 8:00 A.M., two Arikaras rode up with a message from Lieutenant Varnum. With his small party of Crows and Rees the officer had climbed a low mountain known to the Crows as the Crow's Nest. From this lookout, at daybreak, they had scanned the wrinkled landscape to the west. The Indians had spotted telltale smoke rising over the valley of the Little Bighorn and, beyond, an undulating dark smudge that they recognized as the pony herd grazing on the benchland. The whites, with less acute vision, could not pick out the village.

About 9:00 A.M., Custer and several others reached the Crow's Nest. Not surprisingly, he could not see the village either; by this time the sun had risen and a haze had settled over the landscape. But he had no reason to doubt his scouts. His objective lay only fifteen miles to the front.

The scouts gave Custer other information that dampened his elation. During the morning, from their perch high above the surrounding country, they had seen three separate parties of Sioux warriors. That at least one of these groups would discover the soldiers and rush to alert the village seemed probable. Giving point to the anxiety, when Custer returned to the bivouac Tom related that a sergeant had taken a detail on the back trail to retrieve a box of hardtack dropped from a pack mule during the night march. The troopers had come upon several Sioux opening the box and had exchanged fire with them.

Instantly Custer made another crucial decision. All experience pointed to the certainty that he had been discovered. The Indians could hardly be expected to remain in place waiting for the soldiers to find it convenient to fight. The gnawing fear that had ridden with the regiment all the way from Fort Lincoln was about to be realized: the village would break up and flee in all directions. In another stroke of bad luck, Custer could not know that the Sioux in his vicinity were on their way back to the agencies and in fact would not sound the alarm. From his perspective there could be only one proper decision: find the village and strike it as soon as possible.

An attack plan could not be formulated until the exact location of the village had been pinpointed and some impression gained of the surrounding terrain. Therefore, instead of sending out the reconnoitering parties he had planned for this day, Custer advanced in a reconnaissance in force employing the entire regiment. The attack plan would have to take shape as events unfolded.

The noon sun shone torrid in a cloudless sky as the Seventh Cavalry crossed the low divide at the head of Davis Creek and paused on upper Reno Creek. Custer had shed his jacket and wore a dark blue shirt with buckskin trousers encased in boots. A broadbrimmed white hat shaded his bearded, sunburned face. Two holsters on his belt contained a brace of stubby English Webley "bulldog" pistols. His personal flag followed, but the regimental standard remained furled with the packtrain.

There, at the head of Reno Creek, Custer had Adjutant Cooke form the regiment into battalions, to reconnoiter or maneuver for combat as circumstances required. Major Reno commanded one, consisting of Companies M, A, and G—140 officers and enlisted men. Captain Benteen led another, Companies H, D, and K, about 125 strong. Two, E and F under Captain Yates and C, I, and L under Captain Keogh, about 225 horsemen, remained under Custer's direct control. Captain Thomas M. McDougall and Company B guarded the packtrain and brought up the rear.

To Custer the first task was to ensure that no Indians had found their way to the upper Little Bighorn. This not only reflected Terry's concern that the Indians not slip off to the south but had immediate tactical relevance. The early morning sightings of the scouts from the Crow's Nest placed the village on the lower Little Bighorn, below the mouth of Reno Creek. If the Indians were above the mouth of Reno Creek, Custer's attack from the north would drive them south, away from Gibbon's blocking force. Or if the upper valley contained satellite camps, their warriors would be in Custer's rear as he attacked down the valley toward the main village.

Since a ridge blocked the view to the south, Custer assigned Benteen to seek the needed intelligence. He was to oblique his battalion to the left, send a reconnaissance party to the crest of the ridge to scan the Little Bighorn valley, and then rejoin the rest of the command farther down Reno Creek. Twice Custer sent word to Benteen to extend the reconnaissance to other elevations if the first afforded no view of the Little Bighorn.

As Benteen scouted to the south, the rest of the regiment took up the march down Reno Creek, Custer and his two battalions on the right side, Reno with his one on the left. The packtrain and McDougall's B Company fell increasingly to the rear. They were half an hour behind when they met Benteen, returning to the main trail, at a spongy morass in the creek.

Benteen had accomplished his mission. The second ridgeline had afforded a view of the upper Little Bighorn valley, which appeared to be empty of Indians. Benteen neither sent a courier to Custer with this information nor quickened the pace of his march to catch up.

Three miles ahead, where the south fork of Reno Creek joined the main branch, Custer and Reno halted at an abandoned village site, the one from which the Sioux had set forth to attack General Crook a week earlier. A lone tipi remained standing, containing the body of a slain warrior. The Ree scouts gathered around and set it afire. Heeding Custer's signal, Reno led his battalion across the creek, and the two conferred.

A yell from the top of a hill just north of the tipi interrupted the talk. Glancing up, they saw Interpreter Fred Gerard waving his hat and shouting. "Here are your Indians, General, running like devils." Down the creek valley in the distance a party of warriors raced their ponies toward the river. Custer ordered Reno to take the Indian scouts and push forward at a trot. Custer followed with his two battalions. To his right front he could see dust boiling up from behind the high bluffs that hid the Little Bighorn valley.

A trot of about three miles brought the two columns to another fork of Reno Creek, where the north branch joined, and within a little more than a mile of the Little Bighorn. Custer could defer decision no longer. The rising dust meant that he had at last found the village and, coupled with the warriors retreating in his front, that its occupants had taken alarm and were trying to get away. Even though Benteen could not be called upon and the results of his reconnaissance were unknown, the situation demanded an immediate attack.

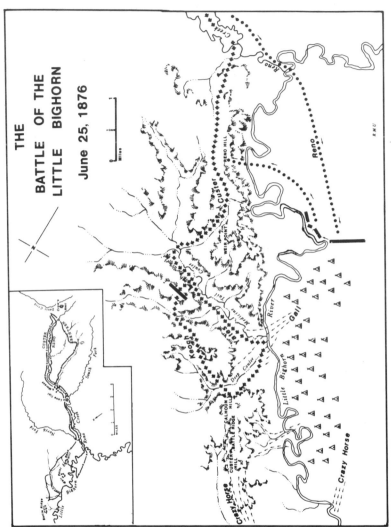

The Battle of the Little Bighorn, June 25, 1876

Custer sent Cooke with orders for Reno: the village lay ahead two miles; the Indians were running away; move rapidly forward, "and charge afterward, and you will be supported by the whole outfit."

As Custer's five companies halted to water their mounts in the north fork of Reno Creek, Captain Keogh and Lieutenant Cooke rode up to Custer. They had accompanied Major Reno to the river crossing at the mouth of Reno Creek and then turned back to rejoin their command. En route, Interpreter Fred Gerard overtook them. The general thought the Indians were running away, he said, but they could be seen riding forth to fight Reno. While Cooke and Keogh were relaying this message to Custer, Sergeant Daniel Kanipe of Tom Custer's Company C glanced toward the bluffs to the right. On the skyline he spotted some sixty to seventy-five mounted warriors. Pointing them out to his first sergeant, Kanipe started the word up the chain of command to Custer.

When the companies remounted, they turned north, up the slope toward the bluffs on which Kanipe had seen warriors. If Custer had intended to follow Reno into battle, as Reno expected, he now changed his mind. Why can only be speculated. He may have hoped to scoop up Kanipe's warriors before turning on the village. More likely, Gerard's news as repeated by Cooke and Keogh decided him to support Reno by falling on the Indians' rear as they fought him in front. This would have the added advantage, if the Sioux were running after all, of cutting off their escape route. In either event, the old Washita gambit of hitting from more than one direction could be expected to strike panic in the enemy.

In parallel columns of twos the five companies galloped up the long, gentle slope toward the bluff tops. After a mile or so they halted short of the brow. Custer, his orderly trumpeter for the day, John Martin, and the Crow scouts rode to the top and looked out over the valley. Just below, the river swung in a wide loop halfway across the valley. "Down the valley," recalled one of the Crow scouts, "were camps and camps and camps. There was a big camp in a circle near the west hills." Below also, related another of the Crows, "we could see Reno fighting. He had crossed the creek [river]. Everything was a scramble with lots of Sioux."

For the first time Custer had exact knowledge of enemy location, enemy strength, and the battle terrain. The village was much larger than expected, but this probably did not daunt him. Reno had not charged into the village but had dismounted and now fought in skirmish formation at its upper end, his right resting in the timber fringing the river bend.

Battle had thus been joined, and Custer had to get the rest of the regiment into it as swiftly as possible. Whatever his initial motive for turning north, he must now have determined to hurry to the next ford downstream and attack the village below the scene of Reno's fighting. Of compelling urgency, too, was to hurry Benteen and the packtrain forward. To fight a village of this size, Custer needed every man of the regiment and the reserve ammunition in the packs.

Back at the command, below the skyline, Custer conferred briefly with Cooke and other officers, including Tom. As the march resumed, Tom rode to his company and, motioning to Sergeant Kanipe, told him to hurry back to Captain McDougall with orders from the general. "Tell McDougall," he instructed, "to bring the pack train straight across to high ground—if packs get loose don't stop to fix them, cut them off. Come quick. Big Indian camp."

As Kanipe turned aside, Custer signaled the advance. Some of the horses became excited and broke into a gallop, out in front even of Custer. "Boys, hold your horses," Kanipe heard Custer shout, "there are plenty of them down there for us all." The command swung to the right, down a long ravine falling away from the heights. It was narrow and forced the formation into a single column. After a mile the ravine opened into a broad coulee now known as Medicine Tail, which ran toward the river and gave promise of ending in a ford. Custer signaled a left turn into the coulee.

Anxious to get Benteen into the fight and worried about ammunition, Custer decided to send another courier. He motioned for his orderly trumpeter, Martin, and barked instructions. Martin had immigrated from Italy, where his name was Giovanni Martini. Adjutant Cooke, distrusting his mastery of English, scrawled a message on a page torn from his memorandum book and handed it to the trumpeter: "Benteen. Come on. Big Village. Be Quick. Bring Packs. W. W. Cooke. P. bring pacs." The final words showed with what haste Cooke wrote.

Spurring his horse up the back trail, Martin glanced over his shoulder. "The last I saw of the command they were going down into the ravine [Medicine Tail Coulee]. The gray horse troop was in the center and they were galloping."

Such is history's last glimpse of Custer and his men in life. The

Crow scouts, released by Custer from the coming fight, watched part of it from a slope overlooking Medicine Tail Coulee from the south, but their recollections were badly garbled. The Indians who fought Custer left equally confused stories. Even so, the Indian accounts are vital pieces of the puzzle. When added to other pieces—the placement of the bodies on the battlefield, the testimony of Reno's survivors, and archaeological evidence plotted on topographical maps—they provide a basis for informed speculation. Indeed, one problem is not too little evidence but too much. Following is what may have happened.

Shortly after sending Trumpeter Martin back for Benteen and the packs, Custer divided his command. He sent Yates's two-company battalion galloping down Medicine Tail Coulee toward the Little Bighorn, and he posted Captain Keogh's three-company battalion on a ridge separating Medicine Tail from the next drainage to the north, Deep Coulee. Keogh's troopers took up dismounted positions overlooking Medicine Tail and the mouth of the ravine they had just descended from the bluff tops.

These dispositions probably reflected news Custer received shortly after reaching Medicine Tail. Boston Custer, who had been with the packtrain, had hurried to join his brothers as soon as it became apparent that a battle was about to take place. Trumpeter Martin met him on the ride back to Benteen. Boston would have informed Custer that Benteen had ended his scout to the left, returned to the main trail, and now, followed by the packtrain, was riding toward the scene of action.

A plausible theory is that Custer intended Yates to hold the ford and threaten the Indians, thus relieving the pressure on Reno, until Benteen could come up and join in a powerful thrust into the village itself. Keogh's mission was to cover Benteen's approach route and then accompany him to the attack position. Whether Custer went with Yates or remained with Keogh is unknown.

Whatever Custer's plans, two crucial developments elsewhere doomed them.

First, Benteen dawdled on the back trail, falling farther and farther behind the rest of the regiment. Sergeant Kanipe, en route to McDougall, told Benteen about the battle taking shape ahead, but that news failed to stir the battalion's pace from a leisurely walk. When Trumpeter Martin dashed up with Cooke's urgent summons, Ben-

teen ordered a trot. Only a gallop would have been responsive to
Custer's expectation, and even that pace might not have brought
Benteen to Medicine Tail in time.

Second, Reno did not hold his position at the upper end of the
village. Flanked on the skirmish line, after fifteen minutes he withdrew into the timber along the river. Then, pressed by Sioux for half
an hour or more, he ordered a retreat. It turned into a demoralized
rout back across the river to the bluff tops from which Custer had
first looked over the valley. The "charge," as Reno termed it, cost
forty dead and thirteen wounded. Among the slain were Lieutenants
Donald McIntosh and Benjamin H. Hodgson, "Lonesome Charley"
Reynolds, and Custer's favorite Ree scout, Bloody Knife.

The actions of his two subordinates left Custer to fend for himself.
Reno's retreat freed all the Indians to concentrate on Custer. Benteen's languor brought him to Reno's hilltop position and thus under
Reno's command. The demoralization of Reno's shattered battalion,
combined with the indecision of the two ranking officers, kept seven
companies and the packtrain, which also reached the bluff tops, out
of action at the most critical moment for the other five.

Yates's two companies reached the Little Bighorn at the mouth of
Medicine Tail Coulee, roughly opposite the center of the Indian
camp. A hot fire greeted them from warriors posted in the brush on
the other side. The bullets flew so thickly, recalled a Sioux participant, "that the head of his command reeled back toward the bluffs
after losing several men who tumbled into the water." Sitting Bull
later described the action succinctly: "Our young men rained lead
across the river and drove the white braves back."

At first only a handful of warriors, perhaps thirty, held the ford
against Yates. But they quickly received help as men returned from
the pony herd with their mounts, and others, freed by Reno's withdrawal, reached the new scene of action. The Hunkpapa Gall rallied
the forces and led them across the river.

Back from the river Yates's two companies retreated, returning a
ragged defensive fire as they rode, dismounting skirmishers to hold
back the Indian advance. The soldiers "held their horses' reins on
one arm while they were shooting," remembered Low Dog, "but the
horses were so frightened that they pulled the men all around, and a
great many of their shots went up in the air and did us no harm."
The line of this fighting retreat lay up the northern slope of Deep

Coulee toward a high ridge that offered the prospect of a better position.

Gall's warriors also hit Keogh, posted on the heights between Medicine Tail and Deep coulees. From dismounted skirmish lines the troopers laid down a heavy fire, including some volley firing, that kept the Indians at bay. Although not seriously threatened, Keogh probably realized that Yates was in trouble and that the Indians gathering in Deep Coulee, to his rear, might isolate the two battalions from each other. After half an hour or more Keogh began to withdraw northward toward a union with Yates.

Gall's warriors pressed closely. On the slope north of Deep Coulee, Keogh dismounted and formed a line. The Indians fired into the horseholders and dropped enough men to stampede the horses and put much of the battalion on foot. With the horses went the extra carbine ammunition. "After this," related Gall, "the soldiers threw aside their guns [carbines] and fought with little guns [pistols]." Dismounted, Keogh's men moved up the slope to join with Yates.

The union occurred on a flat hill, tilted toward the river and overlooking Deep Coulee, that is now named Calhoun Hill, for here Maggie's husband and his company, L, fought and died. Calhoun Hill formed the southern nose of a high ridge extending half a mile northward. This elevation came to be known as Battle Ridge. Commanding a sweeping vista of the river valley and the Bighorn Mountains beyond, Battle Ridge fell abruptly, amid tumbles of steep hills and deep ravines, to the valley below. On the east a narrow ravine heading on Calhoun Hill bordered Battle Ridge and widened and deepened as it ran northward. On Calhoun Hill, Battle Ridge, and the slopes on the east and the west, the final scenes of Custer's Last Stand unfolded.

What role Custer himself played can never be known. Almost certainly no Indian recognized "Long Hair" in the smoke, dust, grime, and excitement of battle, or indeed even knew they were fighting his soldiers. As hinted in some Indian accounts, he may even have fallen, dead or wounded, in the first fire at the mouth of Medicine Tail Coulee and been carried to the spot where his body was found. If he remained in the saddle on Calhoun Hill, he must by now have recognized how desperate, indeed hopeless, his plight. Faced with overpowering numbers of well-armed warriors, caught in rough terrain unsuited to cavalry, partly dismounted, and with no trace of Benteen or the packs on the hills to the south, even Custer's robust self-confidence must have wavered.

If he still commanded, he saw more Indians to his left front, crossing the river at the mouth of a deep ravine draining the western slope of Battle Ridge. From this cover they fired on the command's flank on Calhoun Hill. To counter this threat, Custer advanced one company, either Tom's C or Smith's E. Down the side of the ridge these troopers galloped to the head of the ravine. "The Indians hidden there got back quickly," said the Cheyenne woman Kate Big Head, who watched. The soldiers "stopped and got off their horses along another ridge, a low one just north of the deep gulch." They doubtless meant to fire into the ravine, but suddenly Lame White Man, a Cheyenne, hit with an attack that overran the company and scattered the survivors back to Calhoun Hill.

Northward along Battle Ridge the fighting progressed with growing intensity. While Keogh held Calhoun Hill against the warriors streaming up Deep Coulee, Yates's two companies, probably accompanied by Custer, fought their way along the ridge. From all directions Indians converged in overpowering force.

The warriors made few if any grand mounted charges. Rather, they kept up a long-range fire, mostly from dismounted positions. They took advantage of hillocks, sagebrush clumps, tall grass, and folds and troughs of the terrain. From these hiding places they struck down the cavalrymen with bullets and arrows. Many had rifles, some Winchester and Henry repeaters, others carbines and pistols taken from Reno's dead in the valley, and still others old trade muskets. Arrows took heavy toll. Loosed in high arcs, they fell with deadly effect on clusters of exposed troopers.

The soldiers fought back with a bravery that earned high tribute from Sitting Bull himself. They were veterans, not readily stampeded if they had able leadership. Confusion, scattered pockets of panic, and even a few suicides probably occurred. But the stories of mass suicide and mass hysteria that spared the foe serious casualties flowed from a few self-serving Indian accounts or simply from faulty interpreters. Other Indian testimony, combined with burials discovered in the vicinity of the battlefield and along the Indians' route of retreat, indicate that at least one hundred Indians, and possibly many more, were killed or died later of their wounds.

The fatal blow hit from the north. Crazy Horse had led a large force of warriors down the Little Bighorn valley to a crossing below the village, forded the river, and swept in a wide arc to climb Battle Ridge from the north. They struck the units with Custer and Yates and thrust up the ravine on the east leading to Calhoun Hill. There they crushed Keogh's men against Gall's warriors beyond.

Although each of the companies made its "last stand," the last stand of history and legend occurred at the northern end of Battle Ridge, now known as Custer Hill. There most of Company F, part of E, and remnants of the other companies gathered with the head-quarters group. Whether in panic or deliberate counterattack, a large contingent broke toward the head of the deep ravine in the direction of the river. "We finished up this party right there in the ravine," said Red Horse.

On Custer Hill about forty survivors shot their horses for breast-works and fought until all died. Among them were Armstrong, Tom, and Boston Custer, Autie Reed, Yates, Cooke, "Fresh" Smith, and Lieutenant William Van W. Reily. Myles Keogh fell nearby, in the ravine east of Battle Ridge, with most of his company, I. "Jimmi" Calhoun and L Company died defending Calhoun Hill, half a mile to the south.

The hot June sun hung low over the Bighorn Mountains when the last man fell, possibly two hours after Yates had opened the battle at the mouth of Medicine Tail Coulee. Exultant warriors raced their ponies around the battlefield, dispatching wounded men, firing their rifles in triumph, and raising great clouds of dust. Women and children made their way up the slopes from the village to rob, strip, and mutilate the bodies.

Four miles to the south, a trace of blue appeared atop a peaked hill beyond Medicine Tail Coulee. Hearing firing from the north and irate over Reno's indecision, Tom Weir had simply mounted his company, D, and moved to the sound of the guns. The rest of the command had followed hesitantly. Reaching the high hill later named Weir Point, the troops scanned the rugged terrain beyond. It rose to distant hills and ridges obscured by rolling dust. Indistinctly amid the dust, recalled Lieutenant Winfield Scott Edgerly, "We saw a good many Indians galloping up and down and firing at objects on the ground." Then, as Lieutenant Edward S. Godfrey recalled, "clouds of dust arose from all parts of the field, and the horsemen converged toward our position."

Falling back to their original hilltop position, the seven companies fought desperately until darkness brought relief. During the night they entrenched, and next day they held out as the emboldened Sioux and Cheyennes tried to carry their defenses. Reno displayed weak leadership. Benteen, fearlessly stalking the lines as Indian sharpshooters tried to drop him, inspired the troopers to valiant efforts. By midafternoon the firing had tapered off.

In the valley the Indians fired the dry prairie grass. A wall of thick smoke screened the village. About 7:00 P.M. an immense procession of horsemen, women and children on foot, travois, ponies, and dogs emerged from behind the smoke. Slowly it wound up the slope on the west side of the valley and made its way across the benchland to the southwest, toward the Bighorn Mountains.

Next morning, June 27, a blue column approaching up the valley explained the hasty withdrawal of the Indians. Some on Reno Hill believed it was Custer at last. Others thought Terry. A few even guessed Crook. Two officers rode down to investigate. A short gallop brought them to the leading ranks of the Second Cavalry, General Terry in the van. Both general and lieutenants burst out with the same question: Where is Custer?

Lieutenant Bradley and his Crow scouts brought the answer, and on the morning of June 28 Reno and his men rode down the river to see for themselves. "A scene of sickening ghastly horror," Lieutenant Godfrey remembered. The bodies, many of them stripped, scalped, and mutilated, all grotesquely bloated from the burning sun, lay scattered about the battlefield where they had dropped.

Undiscovered until next day was the body of Mark Kellogg, the correspondent who was to report Custer's great victory over "the hostile red devils." In unintended irony the "scalp lifters" he had ridiculed on the eve of the campaign had repaid the compliment. Except for cutting off an ear, they had not mutilated him. They had only lifted his scalp.

On Custer Hill the knot of fallen men graphically portrayed the drama of the last stand. Although Cooke and Tom Custer had been badly butchered, most in this group escaped severe mutilation. "The bodies were as recognizable as if they were in life," Benteen wrote to his wife.

Although naked, "The General was not mutilated at all," Lieutenant Godfrey later wrote. "He laid on his back, his upper arms on the ground, the hands folded or so placed as to cross the body above the stomach: his position was natural and one that we had seen hundreds of times while [he was] taking cat naps during halts on the march.

One hit was in the front of the left temple, and one in the left breast at or near the heart."

A third wound may have been invisible to Godfrey and the others who looked down on their former chief. The Cheyenne woman Kate Big Head related that two Southern Cheyenne women recognized Custer from his campaign in the Indian Territory in 1868–69. At that time he had been much admired by the women taken captive at the Washita, who had envied Monahsetah her good fortune in gaining the affection of the long-haired white chief. Thinking of Monahsetah, the two women prevented some Sioux men from mutilating the body by explaining that he was their relative. Continued Kate Big Head:

> The women then pushed the point of a sewing awl into each of his ears, into his head. This was done to improve his hearing, as it seemed he had not heard what our chiefs in the South said when he smoked the pipe with them. They told him then that if ever afterward he should break that peace promise and should fight the Cheyennes the Everywhere Spirit surely would cause him to be killed.

CHAPTER 9

Judgments

HOW could it have happened? What flagrant blunders produced so awful a debacle? How could a commander and a regiment widely perceived as the best on the frontier succumb so spectacularly to a mob of untrained, unlettered natives?

The simplest answer, usually overlooked, is that the army lost largely because the Indians won. To ascribe defeat entirely to military failings is to devalue Indian strength and leadership. The Sioux and Cheyennes were strong, confident, united, well led, well armed, outraged by the government's war aims, and ready to fight if pressed. Rarely had the army encountered such a mighty combination in an Indian adversary. Perhaps no strategy or tactics could have prevailed against Sitting Bull's power.

But this explanation exonerates all the military chiefs and yields no scapegoat in blue. George Armstrong Custer is the favored candidate. Driven to win a great victory and wipe out the humiliation inflicted by President Grant, he rushed up the Rosebud and plunged into battle before the cooperating units could get in place. He disobeyed Terry's orders by taking a direct rather than a circuitous route to his destination. He attacked a day early, with an exhausted command and without adequate reconnaissance. Violating an elementary military maxim, he divided his force in the face of a superior enemy and then lost control of all but the element retained under his personal direction, and perhaps, in the end, even of that.

Analysis of this indictment must take account of the character of the evidence on which it rests. No sooner had Custer's body been buried on Custer Hill than all the principals—Terry, Gibbon, Brisbin, Reno, Benteen—began to recompose the history of recent events. Eager to explain the calamity and avert any culpability of their own, they conveniently forgot some things that had happened and remembered some things that had not happened. Their efforts freighted the historical record with firsthand evidence that threw the blame on Custer and powerfully influenced historical interpretation for generations to come.

This self-serving evidence is not without historical value. But only by rigorously comparing it with evidence dating from before the fatal last hour on Battle Ridge can a true understanding of the dynamics of the disaster be reached. A vital step in such an analysis is to strike out of the equation any facts, however plain now, unknown to Custer then. At each critical decision point the test is what he knew and what he could reasonably be expected to foresee.

In such a comparison and analysis most of the charges against Custer collapse. Undoubtedly he hoped to win a great victory for himself and the Seventh Cavalry. But he did not rush up the Rosebud any faster than had been planned on the *Far West*. He did not disobey Terry's orders; they were entirely discretionary and, because of the uncertain location of the Indians, could not have been otherwise. He did not precipitate battle a day before Terry intended, for Terry did not and could not fix any day for the attack; Custer's mission was to attack the Indians whenever and wherever he found them. Custer did not take an exhausted regiment into battle; the men were tired, as soldiers in the field usually are, but no more so than normal on campaign.

That Terry intended Custer to use his own judgment in finding and striking the Indians is made abundantly clear by the written orders, by evidence of what occurred in the conference on the *Far West*, and by the simple logic of what was and was not known to the strategists on June 21.

In addition there is the much-debated affidavit of Mary Adams, Custer's black cook. Until recently most students thought this affidavit spurious because they did not believe that Mary Adams accompanied the expedition. Now she is known to have been with Custer. According to the affidavit she executed in 1878, either on the night of June 21 or the next morning Terry came to Custer's bivouac, and she overheard their conversation. "Custer," said Terry, "I do not know what to say for the last." "Say whatever you want to say," replied Custer. "Use your own judgment and do what you think best if you strike the trail," said Terry. "And whatever you do, Custer, hold on to your wounded."

Custer's first critical decision was to follow the Indian trail over the Rosebud Divide instead of continuing up the Rosebud, as suggested in his orders from Terry. The sudden freshness of the trail on the afternoon of June 24 was all the justification he needed. Plainly, Indians were just over the mountain, a day's march away. His assignment was to find and attack them. The surest and quickest way was to follow the trail.

The fresh Indian sign provided persuasive rationale for what he probably would have done anyway. The judgment to which Terry deferred would likely have kept him on the trail until he overhauled the Indians, wherever they were. A circuit up the Rosebud would have heightened the chances of striking the quarry from the south and driving them toward Gibbon. But it may be doubted that Custer, secure in the conviction that the Seventh alone could handle the enemy, gave much thought to a role for Gibbon or much cared whether he struck from the north or the south. Had the Indians continued their movement up the Little Bighorn, as the chiefs had planned, the attack would indeed have come from the north. Only the chance discovery of antelope herds, prompting the return of the village down the valley, brought Custer in from the south.

The fresh trail also held implications for enemy strength, which Custer failed to note. By the evening of June 24 the Crow and Ree scouts knew that there were more Indians across the Rosebud Divide than anyone suspected. They dropped enough clues that Custer might have taken their worries more seriously and might have questioned them intently in order to bring into the open what they thought and why.

But Custer was not concerned with how many Indians he would encounter, only with preventing their flight. Knowledge of their actual strength would not have changed his dispositions. He had total confidence in the capability of the Seventh Cavalry to whip any number of Indians.

So did all the other generals, from Sheridan down. Most experience with Indian warfare showed that a charge into a village, however large, wrought panic and fleeing Indians, as at the Washita. But this year the Indians were not only numerous but full of fight, as Crook had discovered when hundreds of warriors uncharacteristically attacked him in open battle. News of Crook's defeat on the Rosebud had not reached the Yellowstone, however, and Custer cannot be severely faulted for a mindset shared with his fellow commanders.

It was a mindset, indeed, shared with all his fellow citizens and thus in large part derived from them. That the generals had such contempt for the fighting prowess of their foe as to care little for their numbers was but one symptom of society's attitudes toward Indians. The cultural and racial arrogance of the American people found expression in their generals. Combined with the personal conceit of Custer, this was a deadly mixture. Unquestionably, Custer underestimated his opponents.

Much of what went wrong stemmed from the decision to attack on June 25 instead of the next day, as Custer intended until Sioux were spotted in the vicinity of the command. This decision forced battle before reconnaissance had developed the location of the enemy and the nature of the terrain on which the fight would take place. It prompted Benteen's scout to the left, which would not have been needed had the absence of Indians on the upper Little Bighorn already been established. It led to an afternoon attack rather than the preferred dawn attack. And it decreed a battle plan that had to unfold as information and circumstances unfolded, rather than one conceived in advance.

Despite the consequences, the decision to attack on June 25 was sound. Custer had ample reason to suppose himself discovered and to expect that the village would bolt as soon as alerted. This did not happen because the Indians who observed him continued eastward toward the agencies or were on the way from the agencies to the village. That afternoon the village on the Little Bighorn had perhaps half an hour's warning of the approach of soldiers. Had he known the truth, Custer might still have hidden the regiment, reconnoitered, and struck at dawn on June 26.

Custer drew reproach for dividing the regiment in the face of superior strength. That he faced superior strength, of course, he neither knew nor cared. He formed battalions because of the need to advance in a reconnaissance in force and doubtless also because of his intention, if possible, to attack from more than one direction.

The division of the regiment entailed unavoidable consequences for the impending battle. Because of their seniority Custer had to give battalion commands to Reno and Benteen. Within limits of personal ability they could be expected to do their duty, but not with the enthusiastic, unquestioning loyalty of the favorites in the "royal family." Custer compounded the problem by keeping the most reliable officers with him. Of his inner circle only Weir and Moylan rode with the other battalions.

Custer's decision to order Benteen to the left was sensible. He had to assure himself that the upper Little Bighorn contained no Indians who might fall on his rear in battle or escape southward, as Terry feared. Had the Indians continued up the valley as intended, Benteen would probably have spotted them. If not, the trail would have led to them, and another battle altogether would have resulted.

As it turned out, the scout to the left counted Benteen and three companies out of the critical stage of the battle. It need not have. Benteen counted himself out, as timing factors show. When he came back to the main trail, he was about half an hour behind Custer and Reno. When he neared the mouth of Reno Creek, he was one hour and twenty minutes behind. Had he moved at the same pace as Custer, and had he responded to the message brought by Martin with the swiftness that Custer expected, Benteen might well have fought with Custer. He and his battalion might have perished with Custer, too, but that does not excuse the laggard pace that kept one-fourth of the regiment out of the fight at a decisive moment.

Benteen's course is hard to understand. A possible explanation is distrust of Custer coupled with a rising suspicion that Custer, hoping to keep him out of the fight, had sent him on a useless errand. Keogh or Yates would have signaled a gallop as soon as they received Sergeant Kanipe's report.

Reno also failed Custer, as well as every test of leadership. His retreat freed large numbers of Indians to concentrate on Custer just as he reached the mouth of Medicine Tail Coulee. Had Reno continued to fight in the valley, the pressure on Custer would have been lessened, perhaps decisively. What cannot be known is whether such a course would have awarded Reno the same fate as Custer. Significantly, those who followed Reno into the valley did not condemn the decision to withdraw, only the execution. Some, however, did think that he could have stood firm in the timber, a belief shared by some of the Indian combatants.

Likewise vulnerable is Reno's management of the hilltop operation. He should have rushed to Custer's aid no matter what the odds and even at the risk of disaster to his own companies. The written orders to Benteen, now Reno's by virtue of superior rank, explicitly required such a move. In addition, some of his officers urged this course on him. In fact, Reno made no decision, and his indecision freed subordinates to go off on their own and in the end endangered the entire command. Thereafter, through a night and day of defensive action, he failed to exert effective command. Indeed, there is evidence that he proposed to pull out altogether, abandoning the wounded, a proposition that Benteen indignantly rejected. In fact, no one doubted that Benteen functioned as the true commander. His strong leadership and cool bravery contributed greatly to the successful defense.

On the Custer battlefield itself, nagging questions of leadership arise. Can Indian numbers alone account for Yates's quick repulse from the ford at the mouth of Medicine Tail Coulee? This movement shifted the initiative from the cavalry to the Indians and forced the battle into terrain inhospitable to mounted action. The retreat of both battalions to Battle Ridge also allowed warriors to thrust up Medicine Tail Coulee in strength and thus cut them off from the rest of the regiment.

On Battle Ridge, how to account for patterns of fallen bodies that suggest only one pocket of organized defense—L Company on Calhoun Hill? And how further to account for the concentration of company commanders on Custer Hill? George Yates, Tom Custer, and Algernon Smith fell here. Much of Yates's Company F appears to have died here, but most of C and E perished on other parts of the field.

Whatever Armstrong Custer's failings, combat leadership was not one. Did he take one or two mortal wounds at the Medicine Tail ford? Did that so demoralize Yates's men that they too readily allowed themselves to be driven back from the ford? This move, in turn, led Keogh to yield his position on the heights and fight his way northward to join them on Calhoun Hill. The dead Custer finally came to rest on Custer Hill. Either mortally wounded or dead, he could have been borne there from as far away as Medicine Tail Coulee. No one can ever know, but such a theory would account for much that is puzzling about the fighting on the Custer battlefield.

On the other hand, Adjutant Cooke fell near Custer rather than with Keogh, to the east. Had Custer ceased to function, command would have devolved on Keogh, and Cooke's place would have been with him. Also, there is some indication that expended shells from Custer's Remington sporting rifle were found near his body.

Even more compelling, this theory would force the American people to relinquish the glorious image of Custer's Last Stand that is indelibly burned into their collective memory. That renunciation is as unthinkable as it is impossible.

Could Custer have won? It is a question destined to be forever debated and never settled. Even against the Sioux and Cheyennes in all their numbers and power, however, good arguments support a conclusion that he could have won.

Crucial to this conclusion is the fact that Custer came close to surprising the Indians. The men had little time to prepare for battle. Most of the ponies grazed on the benchland. Several hundred warriors managed to mobilize to meet Reno, but most of the fighters in the village were not ready. Had there been warning, the men would surely have engaged Custer before he got close enough to endanger their families.

In such circumstances Indians usually panicked. Suddenly confronted with soldiers among their tipis, each man turned instinctively to the safety of his family. Thus distracted, the fighting strength could not offer organized resistance, and the village exploded in fleeing family groups. This could be expected to happen even when the Indians enjoyed superiority of numbers.

At the Little Bighorn several scenarios held the possibility of producing such a panic.

First, and most simply, a charge by the eight companies of Custer and Reno into the upper end of the village would almost certainly have stampeded the Indians. The force and momentum of a mounted charge by nearly 350 cavalrymen would have carried into the very heart of the village, striking consternation and chaos and preventing the formation of effective defenses. The attackers would have taken severe casualties, and most of the Indians would have escaped to the north, but Custer would have been left in possession of the village and possibly of much of the pony herd. Benteen and the packtrain would have come up in time to fortify the victors.

Even the two-pronged attack that Custer must have visualized might have worked had Reno not lost his nerve. To continue his charge into the village with 112 men required a fortitude and blind loyalty to Custer that Reno, unlike Keogh or Yates, did not possess. Such an assault, however, could have created enough momentary confusion to win success *if* Custer had driven into the village at the Medicine Tail ford before the Indians could recover and swallow Reno's small command. To achieve this feat, Custer would have had to cover more than three miles, from the bluffs where he overlooked the valley to the mouth of Medicine Tail Coulee, before the Indians crushed Reno. The possibilities of this formula seem slim.

More plausible is Reno holding the timber long enough for Custer to get into the village at the Medicine Tail ford. Although control was difficult in the timber, Reno had taken few casualties when he ordered the retreat. In forming the skirmish line, two horses had bolted and carried their riders into the Sioux. One man had died on the skirmish line and two in the timber. One of the latter was the Ree scout Bloody Knife, sitting his horse beside Reno. A bullet struck his head and spattered blood and brains into Reno's face, an unnerving experience that contributed to the decision to get out of the timber. Had Reno's force remained in place, the warriors here could not have left for Medicine Tail without exposing their families. As it happened, Reno's withdrawal freed them to concentrate on Custer in a strength that forced him back from the river into un-friendly terrain.

Could Benteen have altered the outcome? A swift march on Custer's trail upon receiving Kanipe's report probably would have brought him to Medicine Tail while the action still centered there. His presence might at least have allowed Custer to extricate himself and consolidate the entire regiment on Reno Hill. Had Reno held in the valley, Benteen's timely appearance on Medicine Tail would have given Custer eight companies with which to storm into the village and perhaps carry the day.

The fourth scenario is less a prescription for victory than a remote possibility of staving off defeat. Had Reno and Benteen corralled the packtrain and the wounded on the bluff tops and boldly rushed six companies to the sound of the firing, could they have saved Custer? With a brand of leadership neither had yet displayed, they might have averted the total annihilation of Custer's command. But they would have been badly mauled themselves, perhaps even wiped out. This course should have been tested more promptly and vigorously than it was, but a favorable outcome seems improbable.

Besides the Seventh Cavalry's officers, other campaign leaders are open to criticism but have remained largely immune because of the storm swirling around Custer. Neither before nor after the Little Bighorn did Terry, Gibbon, or Crook gather and use intelligence in a thoughtful way. Gibbon let opportunity slip from his grasp and failed to keep Terry even minimally informed. Crook mismanaged both his March and June offensives, withdrawing on both occasions with dubious justification. The second withdrawal, after the Rose-bud, stopped his movement into the very country that Custer en-tered less than a week later. Had Crook continued his advance, he could not have failed to alter the result of Custer's offensive. Privately, General Sherman believed that Crook bore large responsibility for the failure of the campaign.

And yet, in dissecting strategy and tactics from the perspective of a century later, it is easy to do injustice to the responsible commanders. One cannot know all the circumstances of enemy, weather, terrain, troops, weapons, and a host of other factors great and trivial (Gibbon had a bad stomachache) that influenced judgment and sometimes decisively shaped the final outcome.

But one conclusion seems plain. George Armstrong Custer does not deserve the indictment that history has imposed on him for his actions at the Little Bighorn. Given what he knew at each decision point and what he had every reason to expect of his subordinates, one is hard pressed to say what he ought to have done differently. In truth, at the Little Bighorn "Custer's Luck" simply ran out. Although the failures of subordinates may have contributed and the strength and prowess of the foe certainly contributed, Custer died the victim less of bad judgment than of bad luck.

From blithe unconcern over the number of Indians opposing them, the generals swung to the other extreme. The Rosebud and Little Bighorn traumatized Terry and Crook and all their subordinates. They imagined themselves confronting many times the actual number of warriors that wiped out Custer, and they feared a like fate if they ventured forth without heavy reinforcement.

More troops were on the way. The Little Bighorn had shocked and outraged the American people, and newspapers cried for swift reprisal. Sheridan had fresh troops under orders as soon as he received Terry's first dispatches from the Yellowstone. Although Sheridan impatiently urged Crook "to hit them again and hit them hard," neither general would move without additional units. Not until early August did they begin to arrive.

By this time the great village had fragmented and scattered all over eastern Montana. Some of the agency Indians had begun to creep back toward the reservation, and a few had even reported at their agencies.

On August 10, Terry and Crook joined forces on the Rosebud. The combined command, numbering almost four thousand men, headed east in search of the Indians. Heavy rains drenched the column and turned the prairies to mud. Horses weakened, the shoes of the infantry shredded, morale sank, and sickness and fatigue afflicted the exhausted ranks. By early September the two generals were quarreling over what to do, and at length they simply went their separate ways. On September 9, Crook had a brush with some Oglalas near the Black Hills, but he and his men had lost their ardor for serious fighting.

The campaign accented two truths about Indian warfare. First, ponderous columns could not catch Indians if they did not want to be caught. Second, the logistics of maintaining heavy forces in the field, far from supply depots and transportation routes, were overpowering. Despite hardworking steamboat crews, the generals could never build large enough stockpiles to sustain their operations, and much of their combat strength had to be diverted to moving and guarding supplies.

The campaign pointed up a third truth as well. After Custer's death none of the remaining commanders knew how to fight Indians, at least Plains Indians. General Crook had brought an outstanding record with him from Arizona, where he had perfected innovative and successful techniques for contending with the Apaches. He had refined mule packing to a high art and could move swiftly in the roughest terrain, where wagon trains could not move at all. He had also mastered unconventional warfare, employing Apache methods and Apache scouts against his Apache enemy. Of all commanders he should have appreciated the advantages of chasing the Sioux with light, mobile forces, built around Crow and Shoshoni auxiliaries, that could treat the Sioux to their own brand of fighting. Yet through all the spring and summer campaign of 1876 one searches in vain for a decision that Crook made correctly.

Paradoxically, despite the calamity on the Little Bighorn and the fiasco that followed, the grand scheme to solve the Black Hills problem by ending the freedom of the Sitting Bull bands did not come to grief. A stunned and angry nation insisted on harsh measures. Backed by a stern congressional mandate, a commission visited the Sioux agencies in September 1876 to demand the sale of the Black Hills. This time the chiefs had no choice but to "touch the pen," thus giving spurious legal validity to a transaction that aggressive miners had already made accomplished fact.

Nor in the end did the military effort fail. Because of the Custer disaster General Sheridan easily won authority to impose military rule on the agencies and to build the two forts in the Yellowstone country that he had long advocated. In anticipation of these forts, when Terry abandoned the field in disgust and frustration, he left behind an officer who made up for his own and Crook's deficiencies. Nelson A. Miles, colonel of the Fifth Infantry and major general by brevet, was young and ambitious, a friend of Custer and practitioner of his aggressive, hard-hitting style of war. "The more I see of movements here," he wrote to his wife upon reaching the Yellowstone early in August, "the more admiration I have for Custer, and I am satisfied his like will not be found very soon again."

His like was at once found in Miles himself. Throwing up a rude cantonment at the mouth of the Tongue, the colonel clothed his infantrymen in buffalo overcoats and other cold-weather gear and campaigned all through the hard winter months. "Bear's Coat," the Indians named him. Miles's operations, combined with a winter offensive under Crook in the south, forced the surrender of most of the Indians in the spring of 1877. Only Sitting Bull held out, and he and his immediate following found refuge in the British Possessions.

With Sitting Bull's flight and the surrender of Crazy Horse, the government had won. Never again would the Powder and Yellowstone country harbor unregulated Indians. In the summer of 1877 the army transformed Miles's cantonment at the mouth of Tongue River into Fort Keogh and erected Fort Custer at the mouth of the Little Bighorn, only eleven miles from the Custer battlefield. These forts, representing permanent military occupation, effectively denied the region to Indians, invited white settlement, and ensured that never again would this be Sioux country. In 1881, recognizing the reality, Sitting Bull surrendered at Fort Buford and went to the reservation. He would never truly submit, but he would never again roam the buffalo plains to the west.

Colonel Miles's winter operations of 1876–77 testified impressively to the soundness of the strategy that General Terry had conceived back in February, when first alerted to the decision to move against the Sitting Bull bands. Then he had planned simply to give Custer a base far up the Yellowstone and turn him loose. Now, after months of dismal failure and costly defeat, that strategy had fallen to Colonel Miles, and he had made it work. That he and Custer thought and acted so much alike convincingly suggests that Custer would have made it work also.

Nelson A. Miles went on to become the army's most successful Indian fighter. In the Red River War of 1874–75 against the southern Plains tribes, he had demonstrated his potential. In operations out of Fort Keogh in 1876–80, against both Sioux and Nez Perces, he confirmed his excellence. After thwarting Crook, Geronimo and his Apaches surrendered to Brigadier General Miles in 1886 and ended Apache warfare in the Southwest. On the Sioux reservations in 1890–91, Major General Miles applied an astute mix of menace and conciliation to bring the Ghost Dance troubles to a close after the bloody tragedy of Wounded Knee. No other officer of the frontier army boasted such a record.

Custer might have done equally well, had he lived. Many of the same qualities that carried Miles to the top also marked Custer— ambition, drive, energy, persistence, boldness, self-confidence, courage, capacity for hard work, imagination. Furthermore, they saw Indian campaigning in similar terms: hound the quarry relentlessly, in all seasons, despite all hardships and obstacles, until they wearied and gave up. Also like Custer, incidentally, Miles suffered from some unappealing personality traits that limited his popularity and made him controversial. Miles's example indicates that Custer, with basically the same temperament and methods, might ultimately have lived up to the reputation he enjoyed but did not yet fully deserve—the nation's premier Indian fighter.

That the nation perceived Custer as first among military frontiersmen sprang from two sources. First, he could point to genuine accomplishments. After the summer of failure in 1867, he won the estimable victory at the Washita and went on to the greater, though less dramatic, feat of running down the Cheyennes in the Texas Panhandle and engineering the release of the white women they held captive. Deservedly, the two well-managed battles with the Sioux on the Yellowstone brought more laurels. These exploits, however, represented the sum of Custer's Indian-fighting experience as he went into the Little Bighorn campaign. The record was creditable, better than most of his peers could claim, but not as notable, for example, as George Crook's in Oregon and Arizona or Ranald S. Mackenzie's on the Texas frontier.

What lifted Custer above the competition was publicity. He attracted newspapermen because he made good copy, and on his own initiative he cultivated the press. Then he became his own best publicist, with his articles in *Galaxy* and *Turf, Field and Farm* and his book, *My Life on the Plains*. His writings not only brought his own words to the public, sketching a flattering self-portrait for all to admire, but earned still more notice from the press. His public exposure surpassed that of all the other frontier commanders.

Custer was not totally, or even largely, a product of press agentry. His record formed a solid foundation for the publicity that kept him in the public eye. Verbally decorated, embellished, even exaggerated, the record nevertheless gave an underpinning of legitimacy to the heroic portrait that Americans cherished when news of the Little Bighorn hit their morning papers. Though not the best, as the portrait insinuated, Custer was good, and had he lived he might have given Miles a hard race for best.

Despite his reputation as an authority on Indians, Custer's understanding hardly broke the surface. He could describe the externals—costumes, weapons and implements, shelters, transportation, subsistence, ceremonies—and from the white and Osage scouts in the Washita Campaign he acquired useful knowledge about Indian methods of war. But of the underlying meanings, the cultural content, he remained ignorant. Like most of the nation, he looked down on Indians from a pinnacle of ethnocentrism.

Indian fighters who failed to get inside the Indian mind and fathom how their foe thought and why he behaved as he did could not truly excel at their calling. What was wanted, a later observer pointed out, was not so much Indian fighters as "Indian thinkers"—officers who could think like an Indian and thus fight like an Indian. Whatever his failings in 1876, General Crook dramatized the technique in his Apache campaigns of the 1880s.

Custer never thought like an Indian. With most of his peers, therefore, he was doomed to fight Indians with the techniques of conventional warfare. For a century the army fought Indians as if they were British or Mexicans or Confederates. Each Indian war was expected to be the last, and so the generals never developed a doctrine or organization adapted to the special problems posed by the Indian style of fighting. Indian warfare was unconventional warfare, but the army's answer was no more innovative than the "total war" concepts of Sherman and Sheridan, which of course simply imported the Shenandoah and the March to the Sea to the Great Plains. Total war prevailed often enough, as at the Washita, to inhibit creative thought.

Although the army as an institution never faced up to the issue, some of its officers did. George Crook surpassed all others in his effort to understand his enemies and turn their own methods against them. Nelson Miles learned much about Indian psychology and how to use it to his advantage, as he demonstrated during the Ghost Dance uprising. Custer had been thrown into close enough association with Indians—chiefly Southern Cheyennes and Arapahoes and his Arikara scouts, especially Bloody Knife—to possess the groundwork on which to build toward the insights essential to his profession. But for the Little Bighorn, he might have become an "Indian thinker."

An estimate of Custer's military career has to distinguish between Custer the Indian fighter and Custer the professional soldier. They were not the same. Good soldiers sometimes made poor Indian fighters, and good Indian fighters sometimes made poor soldiers.

Such an estimate must also differentiate between the Civil War army and the frontier army. Volunteer units overwhelmingly made up the Union army. Officers and enlisted men represented a cross-section of the northern populace, pursued a mission of which nearly everyone approved, drew motivation and commitment from popular support and the shared patriotic goal, and wanted to get the job done and go home.

The frontier army, by contrast, filled its enlisted ranks largely from the least educated and intelligent sectors of the population and the lowest social levels. Neither they nor their officers possessed the dedication, the drive, and the sense of purpose that animated the Civil War soldiers. They passed long years of material and social deprivation on the distant frontier, ignored, unappreciated, even derided by society at large. Dull routine dragged them into professional apathy and alcoholic lethargy. Occasionally they took the field, in a land and climate of discomfort and hardship, against an alien people who fought in alien ways.

For a soldier of Custer's makeup, the Civil War army, with its alert, highly motivated soldiery and constant combat, afforded a vehicle greatly superior to the frontier army for achieving and displaying professional worth. He made the most of it. Instinct rather than cerebration endowed him with a rare gift for combat leadership. He personified the cliché of the "born soldier." In battle after battle he shone with a brilliancy that attracted the well-deserved applause of

his peers, the press, and the public. In an army full of generals ranging from mediocre to unfit, he ranked with only a handful who led,
fought, and won with exceptional consistency. As a Civil War general, George Armstrong Custer earns high marks.

The frontier army afforded less fertile ground for Custer's special
talents. There success depended less on instinct than on cerebration.
Custer never methodically and thoughtfully applied himself to building the Seventh Cavalry. This was not entirely his fault, for rarely did
he have more than half of the regiment under his immediate oversight; as usual in the frontier army, the company officers had more
to do with molding units than the colonels and majors. But Custer's
ambivalence about his ambitions played a part too. He never fully
decided whether to be a soldier or a New York capitalist, and his
leaves of absence kept him distant from the regiment, in mind as well
as body, for long periods of time.

Nor did Custer learn how to motivate the human material that fell
to him. On enlisted men he sometimes imposed a harsh, impersonal,
often counter-productive discipline—not an uncommon practice in
the regular army. But his day-to-day influence, like that of any field-
grade officer, filtered through the company officers and thus, however diluted or magnified or transformed, took on the personality of
the officer applying it directly. For the enlisted soldier, therefore,
Custer tended to be a remote figure at post headquarters or at the
head of the column, and the measure of his impact on them lay in
his management of the officers.

In professional skill the Seventh Cavalry's officer corps resembled
that of the other regular regiments—a mix of competence, incom-
petence, and mediocrity. Like most other regiments, too, it suffered
from factionalism. But even in an army noted for factionalism, the
Seventh's prompted remark.

For this rampant factionalism Custer was largely to blame. His
favoritism cut two ways, both harmful: for his inner circle, tolerance
of failings and partiality in the indulgences at his command; for the
excluded, arrogance, rudeness, even malevolence, and penury in the
distribution of rewards. In more or less measure, factionalism influenced the actions of Custer, Reno, Benteen, and Weir at the Little
Bighorn.

Combat, the key to Custer's Civil War success, somewhat offset his
garrison ineptitude and earned him a devoted following in both the

officer corps and the enlisted complement. But on the frontier combat did not happen often enough to make up for his deficiencies of temperament and commitment.

As Civil War general, as frontier commander, and as Indian fighter, Custer's career manifests a notable trend: he grew. His performance improved as he aged and, presumably, matured. At thirty-six he was hardly into middle age when struck down at the Little Bighorn. Had he served until retirement, the trend might have continued. Perhaps, like Wesley Merritt, he would have retired at the turn of the century, a gray-headed major general content in a substantial record extending from the Civil War through the Indian Wars to the Spanish-American War. Then, like Merritt, he could have slipped into an obscurity penetrated only by the inquiries of a handful of historical specialists.

Instead, Custer became one of the mightiest legends in the folklore of the American nation, the embodiment of the Indian-fighting frontier army, and, ultimately, the symbol of the nation's wrongs against its Indian peoples. The embodiment took form in life, spawned by a colorful and controversial persona, an adventurous career as plainsman, hunter, and Indian fighter, and a generous application of publicity. After 1876 the embodiment took on immortality, lifted by legend from contemporary affairs to the national pantheon of heroes.

The embodiment falls short of strict authenticity. He was not the country's greatest Indian fighter, or hunter, or plainsman. But he was enough of each to give solid grounding to the legend and to make George Armstrong Custer an ideal medium for capturing the essence of some significant aspects of America's frontier heritage.

Less substance backs Custer's modern role as national guilt symbol for sins against the Indians. To be sure, he and his men died in the government's service against the Indians. But a truly meaningful guilt symbol, it seems, should fit the stereotype of the bloodthirsty Indian killer in blue, a rampaging and brutish agent of genocide, a fitting victim of his nation's sins. No more nor less than his fellow officers does Custer qualify. Indeed, that a man should be chosen whose principal claim on posterity springs from utter defeat by Indians is ironic. Chivington of Sand Creek would be more appropriate. But he did not fall in battle with Indians, and his name lacks the universality of recognition that a usable symbol demands.

George Armstrong Custer commands both universality and widely perceived symbolic association. The universality is valid, the legacy of a dramatic and controversial career capped by one of the grandest denouements in American history. The associations are invalid, the legacy not of a record or a conception of Indians that sets him apart from contemporaries but rather of the mysterious interaction of history, legend, and myth in the national consciousness.

Well hidden beneath the layers of legend and myth lies a real person. Finding him has challenged several generations of historians, popular writers, pseudopsychologists, and even genuine psychiatrists. They have defined a bewildering array of personalities, but still the quest continues for the real General Custer.

Part of the explanation for the many Custers is simply the inability of evaluators to penetrate the legend and myth, but a large part, too, stems from a personality marked by contradictions. They seem best understood as manifestations of the continuing war between boy and man for control of the person. The Civil War had forced the boy to become a man, to behave like a general. When the war ended, the boy reasserted himself, and for the next ten years the two contended.

The struggle is glimpsed in the contradictions. He imposed rigid military discipline but did not practice it himself. He demanded exact obedience to orders, yet treated orders from superiors with an elasticity overlooked only because of repeated success. Tender and sentimental with intimates, he could be callous, even cruel, toward others. Generosity alternated with selfishness, egotism with modesty, impenitence with contrition, exuberance with solemnity.

Contradictions also mark, and are probably in part responsible for, the range of emotions he aroused in those who knew him. Among them he inspired either deep devotion or bitter hatred but rarely indifference. Men agreed on his courage, stamina, flamboyance, dash, and luck—"Custer's Luck" was a byword in the army for thirteen years. On little else could they agree.

To Colonel Nelson A. Miles, Custer was "the best of friends" and "one of the most enterprising, fearless cavalry leaders the great war produced." A lieutenant testified that "Custer commanded the admiration and excited the enthusiasm of most of the young men in the Army."

Yet Colonel David S. Stanley saw Custer as "a cold-blooded, untruthful, unprincipled man . . . universally despised by all the officers of his regiment except his relatives and one or two sycophants." And Lieutenant Charles Larned wrote his mother from the Yellowstone Expedition: "Custer is not belying his reputation—which is that of a man selfishly indifferent to others, and ruthlessly determined to make himself conspicuous at all hazards."

In reality Custer was all these people, someone whose inconsistencies are more readily recognized than explained. What sort of person he was in life depended, as it still depends today, more on the beholder than the beholden.

Custer may have been more, although we can only guess, or dig for more evidence. He may have been sexually promiscuous, both before and after his marriage. His marriage may not have been the unbroken idyll portrayed by Libbie in her books but may have been periodically marred by mutual suspicion, resentment, jealousy, and moodiness. And his quest for money may have led him into enterprises that stretched or exceeded even the loose ethical standards of the Grant era. On none of these questions is the evidence conclusive, but the scattered scraps fall into patterns that cannot be ignored by anyone seriously seeking to understand George Armstrong Custer.

If the patterns represent reality, moreover, they hold important implications for Custer's character. They convict him of brazen hypocrisy. On the one hand, he posed before the world as a man of honor and integrity. On the other, he engaged in unethical, dishonest, or even unlawful schemes to defraud the government and the public. And unless Libbie knew of and excused his infidelities, even his marriage was hypocritical.

The real Custer, however, is not the significant Custer. The truly significant Custer is the Custer whose death atop Custer Hill (if that is where he died) transformed him into enduring legend. It is this Custer who has captured the fancy and excited the imagination of peoples all over the world. If one measure of historical significance is impact on human minds, then the George Armstrong Custer of legend is a figure of towering significance.

Of the real General Custer all that is mortal rests beneath a monument on the heights above the Hudson River where young Autie was first introduced to the profession of the soldier. This profession he embraced with the passion of a zealot. He loved war, but more especially he loved the laurels that it brought. "In years long numbered with the past, when I was merging upon manhood," he wrote in 1867, "my every thought was ambitious—not to be wealthy, not to be learned, but to be great. I desired to link my name with acts and men, and in such manner as to be a mark of honor, not only to the present but to future generations."

George Armstrong Custer's restless spirit may well rest in content-ment above the Hudson, for in death he achieved his life's ambition.

Sources

THE bibliography of George Armstrong Custer and the Battle of the Little Bighorn is one of the most extensive in American history. Both published and unpublished sources abound. Mentioned here are only those that have proved most useful in the preparation of this book.

Custer letters and other papers exist in the Marguerite Merington Collections at the New York Public Library and the Yale University Library, as well as in the Elizabeth B. Custer Collection at Custer Battlefield National Monument, Montana. Extracts from many letters are set forth in Marguerite Merington, ed., *The Custer Story: The Life and Intimate Letters of General Custer and His Wife Elizabeth* (New York: Devin-Adair, 1950). Unfortunately, the editor saw fit to rewrite and sometimes sanitize these extracts. Extracts of letters still in the Custer family as well as in the Frost Collection are quoted in Lawrence A. Frost, *General Custer's Libbie* (Seattle: Superior Publishing Co., 1976). Finally, extracts from Custer's letters, both surviving and vanished, are set forth in Elizabeth B. Custer's three books: *"Boots and Saddles," or, Life in Dakota with General Custer* (New York: Harper and Bros., 1885); *Tenting on the Plains; or, General Custer in Kansas and Texas* (New York: Harper and Bros., 1887); and *Following the Guidon* (New York: Harper and Bros., 1890). Like Marguerite Merington, Elizabeth Custer edited the portions of the letters she printed. Sometimes she changed meaning slightly to make her husband look better.

Of the many biographies of Custer, the best remains Jay Monaghan, *Custer: The Life of General George Armstrong Custer* (Boston and Toronto: Little, Brown and Co., 1959).

The *Research Review*, periodical of the Little Big Horn Associates, contains much of value that has been used in these pages.

There is a vast literature on the Custer of legend and myth, but see especially the following: Robert M. Utley, *Custer and the Great Controversy: Origin and Development of a Legend* (Los Angeles: Westernlore Press, 1962, 1980); Brian W. Dippie, *Custer's Last Stand: The Anatomy of an American Myth* (Missoula: University of Montana Publications in History, 1976); Bruce A. Rosenberg, *Custer and the Epic of Defeat* (University Park: Pennsylvania State University Press, 1974); Kent Ladd Steckmesser, *The Western Hero in History and Legend* (Norman: University of Oklahoma Press, 1965); and Paul A. Hutton, "From Little Bighorn to

Little Big Man: The Changing Image of a Western Hero in Popular Culture," *Western Historical Quarterly* 7 (January 1976): 19–45.

The best examination of Custer's Civil War career is Gregory J. W. Urwin, *Custer Victorious: The Civil War Battles of General George Armstrong Custer* (East Brunswick, N.J.: Associated University Presses, 1983). Indispensable for understanding the cavalry and for placing Custer in broader context is Stephen Z. Starr, *The Union Cavalry in the Civil War, Volume 1: From Fort Sumter to Gettysburg, 1861–1863 and Volume 2: The War in the East, From Gettysburg to Appomattox, 1863–1865* (Baton Rouge: Louisiana State University Press, 1979 and 1981).

The Texas interlude is treated in John M. Carroll, *Custer in Texas: An Interrupted Narrative* (New York: Sol Lewis, 1975); and Minnie Dubbs Millbrook, "The Boy General and How He Grew," *Montana, the Magazine of Western History* 23 (Spring 1973): 34–43.

For the army on the postwar frontier, including the role of Custer from 1867 to 1876, see Robert M. Utley, *Frontier Regulars: The United States Army and the Indian, 1866–1891* (New York: Macmillan, 1973; Lincoln: University of Nebraska Press, 1984). Also indispensable for understanding the big picture, from both the historical and biographical standpoint, is Paul A. Hutton, *Phil Sheridan and His Army* (Lincoln: University of Nebraska Press, 1985).

For the events of 1866–67 in Kansas, painstakingly researched reconstructions are two articles by Minnie Dubbs Millbrook: "The West Breaks in General Custer," *Kansas Historical Quarterly* 36 (Summer 1970): 113–47; and "Custer's First Scout in the West," *Kansas Historical Quarterly* 39 (Spring 1973): 75–95; the exhaustive footnotes in Brian W. Dippie, ed., *Nomad: George A. Custer in Turf, Field and Farm* (Austin: University of Texas Press, 1980); and Blaine Burkey, *Custer, Come at Once! The Fort Hays Years of George and Elizabeth Custer, 1867–1870* (Hays, Kans.: Thomas More Prep, 1976). A literate, graphic view by a participant is Robert M. Utley, ed., *Life in Custer's Cavalry: Diaries and Letters of Albert and Jennie Barnitz, 1867–1868* (New Haven, Conn.: Yale University Press, 1977; Lincoln: University of Nebraska Press, 1987). The transcript of Custer's court-martial, with other documentation and editorial commentary, is Lawrence A. Frost, *The Court-Martial of General George Armstrong Custer* (Norman: University of Oklahoma Press, 1968). For the formation and early history of the Seventh Cavalry, see Melbourne C. Chandler, *Of Garryowen in Glory: The History of the 7th U.S. Cavalry* (n.p., 1960). For this and subsequent events in the Seventh Cavalry, Captain Benteen's acerbic view is contained in John M. Carroll, ed., *The Benteen-Goldin Letters on Custer and His Last Battle* (New York: Liveright, 1974). With Elizabeth Custer's *Tenting on the Plains*, Custer's own book, *My Life on the Plains; or, Personal Experiences with Indians* (New York: Sheldon & Co., 1874), offers the Custer perspective.

Custer's *My Life on the Plains* also covers the Washita Campaign of 1868–69, as does Elizabeth Custer's *Following the Guidon*. In addition, the following books should be consulted: Stan Hoig, *The Battle of the Washita: The Sheridan-Custer Indian Campaign of 1867–69* (Garden City, N.Y.:

Doubleday & Co., Inc., 1976); Donald J. Berthrong, *The Southern Chey-*
ennes (Norman: University of Oklahoma Press, 1963); and W. S. Nye,
Carbine and Lance: The Story of Old Fort Sill, 3d ed. (Norman: University of Oklahoma Press, 1969). The account of a newspaper reporter
who accompanied the Sheridan-Custer expedition is DeB. Randolph
Keim, *Sheridan's Troopers on the Borders: A Winter Campaign on the*
Plains (Lincoln: University of Nebraska Press, 1985). One of Custer's
officers gave his view in Edward S. Godfrey, "Some Reminiscences, Including the Washita Battle, November 27, 1868," *Cavalry Journal* 37 (October 1928): 481–500. A valuable compilation of official documents is
John M. Carroll, ed., *General Custer and the Battle of the Washita: The*
Federal View (Bryan, Texas: Guidon Press, 1978).

A history of the Yellowstone Expedition is Lawrence A. Frost, *Custer's 7th*
Cav and the Campaign of 1873 (El Segundo, Calif.: Upton & Sons, 1986).
Accounts by participants are George A. Custer, "Battling with the
Sioux on the Yellowstone," *Galaxy* 22 (July 1876): 91–102; Charles
Braden, "The Yellowstone Expedition of 1873," *Journal of the U.S. Cav-*
alry Association 16 (1905): 218–41; George F. Howe, ed., "Expedition to
the Yellowstone River in 1873: Letters of a Young Cavalry Officer," *Mis-*
sissippi Valley Historical Review 39 (December 1952): 519–34; and David S.
Stanley, *Personal Memoirs of Major General David S. Stanley* (Cambridge,
Mass.: Harvard University Press, 1917). For the relationship between
the army and the railroads, consult Hutton, *Phil Sheridan and His*
Army, and Robert G. Athearn, *William Tecumseh Sherman and the*
Settlement of the West (Norman: University of Oklahoma Press, 1956).
For Custer as Northern Pacific publicist, including the Custer-Hazen
controversy, see Edgar I. Stewart, ed., *Penny-an-Acre Empire in the West*
(Norman: University of Oklahoma Press, 1968); and Marvin E. Kroeker,
Great Plains Command: William B. Hazen in the Frontier West (Norman:
University of Oklahoma Press, 1976).

The Black Hills are treated in Donald Jackson, *Custer's Gold: The United*
States Cavalry Expedition of 1874 (New Haven, Conn.: Yale University
Press, 1966) and Watson Parker, *Gold in the Black Hills* (Lincoln: Uni-
versity of Nebraska Press, 1982). An especially useful source, reproduc-
ing newspaper accounts of the Black Hills Expedition, Custer's reports,
and the journals of Colonel Grant and Major Forsyth, is Herbert
Krause and Gary D. Olson, *Prelude to Glory: A Newspaper Accounting of*
Custer's 1874 Expedition to the Black Hills (Sioux Falls, S.Dak.: Brevet
Press, 1974). Lieutenant Calhoun's diary and pertinent official docu-
ments appear in Lawrence A. Frost, ed., *With Custer in '74: James*
Calhoun's Diary of the Black Hills Expedition (Provo, Utah: Brigham
Young University Press, 1979). An enlisted man's view is John M. Car-
roll, ed., *Private Theodore Ewert's Diary of the Black Hills Expedition, 1874*
(Piscataway, N.J.: CRI Books, 1975). Interesting perspectives on Custer
and the Black Hills are in Richard Slotkin, *The Fatal Environment: The*
Myth of the Frontier in the Age of Industrialization, 1800–1890 (New York:
Atheneum, 1985).

For life at Fort Lincoln, see Elizabeth B. Custer, *"Boots and Saddles,"* and

Katherine Gibson Fougera, *With Custer's Cavalry* (Caldwell, Idaho: Caxton Printers, 1940).

Among the mountains of commentary on the Campaign of 1876 and the Battle of the Little Bighorn, by all measures the best synthesis is John S. Gray, *Centennial Campaign: The Sioux War of 1876* (Fort Collins, Colo.: Old Army Press, 1976; Norman: University of Oklahoma Press, 1988). A biased but reasoned account, quoting exchanges of correspondence and telegrams, is Robert P. Hughes, "The Campaign against the Sioux in 1876," *Journal of the Military Service Institution of the United States* 18 (January 1896), reprinted in W. A. Graham, *The Story of the Little Big Horn*, 2d ed. (Harrisburg, Pa.: Military Service Publishing Co., 1945). Much firsthand material is included in W. A. Graham, *The Custer Myth: A Source Book of Custeriana* (Harrisburg, Pa.: Stackpole Co., 1953). Official documents are reprinted in John M. Carroll, ed., *General Custer and the Battle of the Little Big Horn: The Federal View* (Bryan, Tex., and Mattituck, N.J.: J. M. Carroll Co., 1986). A day-by-day recital is James Willert, *Little Big Horn Diary: Chronicle of the 1876 Indian War* (p.p., La Mirada, Calif., 1977). The reconstruction of the Little Bighorn presented in this book draws heavily on two important works: Jerome A. Greene, *Evidence and the Custer Enigma: A Reconstruction of Indian-Military History* (Kansas City, Kans.: Kansas City Posse of the Westerners, 1973) and Richard G. Hardorff, *Markers, Artifacts and Indian Testimony: Preliminary Findings on the Custer Battle* (Short Hills, N.J.: W. Donald Horn, Publisher, 1985). For vital testimony of participants, see *The Reno Court of Inquiry: The Chicago Times Account* (Fort Collins, Colo.: Old Army Press, 1972); and Kenneth Hammer, ed., *Custer in 76: Walter Camp's Notes on the Custer Fight* (Provo, Utah: Brigham Young University Press, 1976).

Index

The Oklahoma Western Biographies

STORIES of heroes and heroines have intrigued generations of listeners and readers. Americans, too, have been captivated by the lives of religious, political, and military leaders and of intrepid explorers, pioneers, and rebels. Although occasionally treated as a stepchild of history, biography continues to marshal armies of devoted readers.

The Oklahoma Western Biographies endeavors to build on this fascination with biography and to link it with another topic of abiding interest to Americans: the frontier and the American West. Volumes in the series provide brief, soundly researched, interpretive biographies of westerners. Individual volumes center on the lives of notable persons, but they also illuminate larger historical experiences of the American West.

Because they are prepared by leading scholars, the biographies will appeal to specialists, but they are intended primarily for general readers and students. Each volume is a lively synthesis based on thorough research in published primary and secondary sources.

Above all, The Oklahoma Western Biographies aims at two goals: to provide thoroughly readable life stories of significant westerners and to show how these lives illuminate a notable topic, an influential movement, or a series of important events in the history and culture of the American West. The series will include volumes on all subregions of the West, its major ethnic groups, and its varied sociocultural, political, and economic experiences.